Inhabitance

Inhabitance

ECOLOGICAL RELIGIOUS EDUCATION

Jennifer R. Ayres

BAYLOR UNIVERSITY PRESS

Cover and book design: Savanah N. Landerholm
Cover image: Tollef Runquist, *Kitchen Window Flowers*, oil on board, 2011

The Library of Congress has cataloged this book under ISBN
978-1-4813-1137-3.

Printed in the United States of America on acid-free paper with a minimum of thirty percent recycled content.

FOR MY DAD, BRUCE

MY FIRST AND BEST TEACHER OF INHABITANCE

Tell me, what is it you plan to do
with your one wild and precious life?

—Mary Oliver, "The Summer Day"

CONTENTS

ACKNOWLEDGMENTS

I write this from a tiny cabin perched on the side of a hill, overlooking an inlet somewhere north of Vancouver, British Columbia. I am still on "East Coast Time," so there is nothing to do but stare out into the dark, the trees and lake below not yet distinguishable from the inky, thick sky. The owner of this cabin has situated the kitchen table against the front windows so I can sit here, writing and warmed by the wood stove, and look for sunrise. Now, the sky becomes deep plum purple, with just a few hints of magenta creeping over the horizon. I can barely make out the outlines of the tall cedar trees against that curtain, and if I fix my gaze just right, I can also see the silver-gray water peeking through below.

This world is a wonder.

Inhabitance, which has been four years in the making and many more years in my heart, is a testimony to that wonder. To the presence of divine love and creativity among us. To the love, beauty, suffering, and future of this planet and all of its inhabitants, including human beings. So this book should first be understood as a love story, a story shared with any human being who has sought to be a good inhabitant. So many people and communities have nurtured this story that I have tried to tell. They have strengthened my understanding of the questions at stake, the profound theological questions motivating my quest for inhabitance, and my own vulnerable, faltering love for this world.

The seed for this book was planted in an essay I wrote for the *Teaching Theology and Religion* journal. I want to express my gratitude to the Wabash Center for their workshop on writing the scholarship of teaching and learning, and to my colleagues Kevin O'Brien and Forrest Clingerman for offering constructive feedback on that essay. In a lovely coincidence, the essay was sent out for blind review to my colleague John Senior, who immediately recognized my stories and identified me as the author. After he'd sent his review to the journal (which, happily, published the much-improved essay), I ran into him at the Dancing Goats café in Decatur. He confessed that he'd been my reviewer and said something like, "It was a pretty good article, but I think its main problem is that the argument you are making is a book." And so a book was born.

John and I continued our conversation, as he was interested in the implications of what I was calling the "cultivation of ecological faith" for religious leadership. With the encouragement of the Louisville Institute, we formed a Collaborative Inquiry Team with two remarkable religious leaders: rev. abby mohaupt and Rev. Laura Beach. At the time abby was a bivocational Presbyterian minister, working in a congregation in the Bay Area and with migrant farmworkers at Puente de la Costa Sur in Pescadero, California. Laura serves Methodist congregations in western North Carolina, where she also works in community development in partnership with the rural poor. This team was more grace than I could have imagined, and through our work together, I encountered practices and commitments that exponentially deepened and complicated what I now understand to be ecological faith.

Thanks to the generosity of the Louisville Institute, our group met for four retreats in which we hiked, paddled, wondered, visited ecological ministries and national parks, ate well, and worked out our definitions of ecological faith. The research grant from the Louisville Institute also supported a consultation of eight religious leaders and theological educators who helped us better conceptualize the work: Veronica Kyle, David Orr, Jeff Hawkins, Ambrose Carroll, Ted Hiebert, Laurel Kearns, Mark Douglas, and Tyler Sit. The consultation raised wonderful questions about the role of theological education in cultivating leaders for the church in this ecological age. The grant also supported team members' visits to fourteen communities engaged in a wide range of ecological practices: Agape Community (Hardwick, Massachusetts), Berea Mennonite Church (Atlanta, Georgia), Church of the Pilgrims (Washington, D.C.), Conetoe Missionary Baptist Church (Conetoe, North Carolina), Elkin Presbyterian Church (Elkin, North Carolina), Farm Church (Durham, North Carolina), The Garden Church (San Pedro, California), McQueen

Chapel United Methodist Church (Lemon Springs, North Carolina), Montclair Presbyterian Church (Oakland, California), Peacehaven Community Farm (Whitsett, North Carolina), San Jose Parish (Beloit, Wisconsin), Sweaty Sheep (Louisville, Kentucky, and Santa Cruz, California), Trinity United Church of Christ (Chicago, Illinois), and Wilderness Way Community (Portland, Oregon). Some of the stories of these communities appear in these pages, and some will appear in writing from other research team members. For major insights that have shaped this book, I especially want to thank Adrienne Wynn, Stuart Taylor, Neddy Astudillo, Richard Joyner, and Ashley Goff. Although many nurturers of inhabitance are described in these pages, the wisdom and commitment of these five persons have profoundly informed how I understand the vocation of inhabitance.

I work in a generous institution that challenges me to do my very best thinking, giving me time, space, resources, and conversation partners to develop and refine this book over the last four years. Candler School of Theology has provided research and sabbatical leave both before and after my tenure review. That time was a gift and was supported by financial support from the Emory University Research Committee. I also spent a year with the Fox Center for Humanistic Inquiry, strengthening the environmental philosophy undergirding this book with interdisciplinary conversation among colleagues from across the university. Walter Melion, Keith Anthony, Colette Barlow, and Amy Erbil have cultivated a quiet and hospitable space to think. I still miss my study there, with its three lovely windows.

Colleagues at Candler and Emory have read portions and responded to this work. Steve Kraftchick and Carol Newsom have done so in great depth. Both of these wonderful colleagues have strengthened what appears in these pages with their sharp minds and compassionate critique. I must confess that it is something of a dream come true to have a mentor like Carol Newsom read and respond to my work so carefully. I have shared other portions of this work with colleagues at Columbia Theological Seminary and the Religious Education Association. Chuck Foster, in particular, has been gracious enough to offer me feedback both in person and in writing. This book also reflects the contributions of two wonderful research assistants: Andrew Toney-Noland, who managed the research team's work and contributed his own ideas and insights to our definition of ecological faith, and Codi Norred, who helped me develop important concepts like ecological play and the ecological self in the manuscript itself. Thanks also to Ulrike Guthrie for her work on the index.

Truthfully, however, I perhaps never would have finished this book if not for the gentle and no-nonsense support and strategic coaching from Allison

Adams and the Center for Faculty Development and Excellence. Each Tuesday and Friday, Allison and colleagues from across the university station themselves in a café on campus or online and write in silence for just one hour. Although I failed more times than I succeeded in making it to these group writing gatherings, I will forever be grateful to Allison and the "Sit Down and Write" group for introducing this practice into my life. Even after returning from sabbatical, I have been able to preserve this quiet time each morning to write and edit this book, partly thanks also to the mutual encouragement of the Slow Seminary group, a community of reflective scholars and friends at Candler who pray together and support each other in setting healthy boundaries and pursuing what matters the most. Thank you, Slow-Mos: Alison, Anthony, Arun, Beth, Ellen, Greg, Joel, Liz, and Susan.

Nor would the book be complete (or as complete as any work of the heart ever is) without the encouragement, pestering, and editorial vision of Carey Newman and the staff of Baylor University Press. Carey has been a wonderful editor, seeing the promise of the book while maintaining a critical lens. When I felt extraordinarily stuck, Carey talked me through it on the phone and once even workshopped the book with me while on a visit with other authors in Atlanta. The book is, of course, better for his insights, and for the careful work of Jenny Hunt, Cade Jarrell, and Savanah Landerholm.

The purple of the Vancouver sunrise has now given way to a heavy blue-gray, and another soul is stirring. Soon the cabin is filled with the sounds and smells of breakfast, prepared by my partner in the work of inhabitance, David Leonard. A serious hiker, guitar picker, and committed father, Dave has kept me grounded and immersed in this world's wonder as I have written this book. He's kept my dog when I needed to focus, he's inspired my courage and endurance on hikes more strenuous than I anticipated, and he's taken me to paddle in a local lake when the writing anxiety became almost too much to manage. And I am grateful for the younger Leonards, Charlie and James, who regularly remind me of the importance of recreation, telling me jokes, challenging me to games of H-O-R-S-E, and testing my (disappointing) knowledge of various Star Wars movies or video games. James, aged nine, also likes to write books, by the way, which he proudly announces are self-published. He is a little disappointed that I have written only three. Thank you, Leonard boys.

This book is dedicated to my first teacher of inhabitance, however: my dad, Bruce Ayres. Thank you, Dad, for the years of camping and canoeing—and for showing me how to love a place, up close and in detail.

INTRODUCTION

To Inhabit the World

My father, Bruce, is the kind of guy who insists on giving driving directions, even when the departing guest waves him off, saying, "It's okay, I have Google Maps." He wants to tell you the landmarks that signify each turn, and his directions inevitably include a "Turn west on Cornatzer Road." "Turn right" is not in his standard lexicon of phrases. "But I'm never lost," he says with pride.

Dad always knows where he is in a specific sense, in detail, and in a relational way. It goes back a long way. When our plane took off from Honolulu after Christmas in 1982, my dad's childhood home, it was the first time I saw him cry. That very morning, he and I had hiked Diamond Head Crater together, leaving Mom and my brother Dee (who was just six years old) back at Aunt Baba's house. As usual, Dad walked ahead of me. Going up the ninety-nine steps, with color exploding all around us, I was for once glad for his habit of taking off and leaving us about twenty paces behind, because I could climb those steps with tears streaming down my face, unnoticed. I was ten years old. And family and places and experiences that were a part of who I was—and am—had revealed themselves to me there. Despite decades spent away from his childhood home, it was easy to see in Hawaii how Dad was so rooted in that place. He knew where he was, thus knowing *who* he was.

It was as the plane took off to bring us all back to North Carolina, with the sea and the islands and the mountains receding in a purple-green cloud, against this backdrop of dusky ambiguity, that I saw my dad's tears beginning

1

to pool in the corners of his eyes. I don't remember what happened, but I felt love. Love between my dad and me, a love that had a place—and love *for* a place.

It was love, profoundly located.

In 1968, Senegalese conservationist and forestry engineer Baba Dioum told the General Assembly of the International Union for the Conservation of Nature and Natural Resources, "In the end we will conserve only what we love."[1] For my little brother and me, Dad's capacity to love and live well in a place, born in Hawaii, also profoundly shaped our childhood in North Carolina. We would spend weekends in some place in the foothills or mountains, the four of us tucked into our Coleman pop-up camper. We learned how to cook over a fire and how to leave no trace. Leave no trace: Dad was a stickler about that—he totally mortified my brother and me by chasing people down with garbage they had tossed out their car windows.

Dad taught my brother and me how to paddle, and we enjoyed lazy and strenuous afternoons on the Yadkin, the Dan, and the ironically named New River, likely one of the five oldest rivers in the world. Winding northward from North Carolina, through Virginia and West Virginia, the New River is 360 miles long and 65 million years old. I loved the time Dad and I spent together in that Coleman canoe. It was for us a space of connection to each other, to the river, and perhaps even to God. We were bound to God's earth in the silence of that holy space. We would see the same beauty, hear the same birds, feel the same cool water splashing against sunburned arms. The wonder and love nurtured by these encounters with the river nurtured within us a shared and fierce urge to protect that place, that holy water. Dad has always known, instinctively, how to live deeply in and love a place. This is essential to his character and to who he is as a human being. He is, in short, a loving and responsible inhabitant.

TO BE INHABITANTS

An inhabitant is a creature who lives well within the context and bounds of its habitat. The word "habitat" may bring to mind the dwelling places of nonhuman creatures—the ecosystems that they affect by their presence and upon which they depend to survive. Marine turtles depend upon reefs, and sand dunes, and sea grass.[2] Pollinator species like bees, butterflies, birds, and bats depend upon nontoxic and diverse plant life.[3] Human beings depend upon plants, animals, fresh water, and clean air. All of these creatures in turn affect the ecosystems in which they dwell, and human beings are no different.

Human beings are inhabitants of God's world. We have a unique way of being inhabitants, however, in that our capacities for moral reflection and anticipation of the future shape our perspectives and, sometimes, behaviors as inhabitants. Humans can be moved to protect ecosystems, cultivating a sense of responsibility and even affection for other members of their habitats: other humans, animals, and other forms of life. A desire to be a loving, conscious, and integrated member of a habitat might even prompt concern and affection for seemingly small and distant members of the ecosystem like soil microbes, corals, and pollinators.

To say that human beings are inhabitants is true in a general, planetary sense in that human beings are creatures in a wondrous, complex, and mysterious world infused with divine creativity and love. Inhabitance is practiced, however, in local habitats, ecosystems, and neighborhoods. One becomes an inhabitant by seeking to know and love a particular place in some detail and honoring its rhythms, limits, and possibilities. It is to embrace one's own vulnerability, the fact that one is a living, suffering, and dying being in a living, suffering, and dying world. And it is to embrace the emotional vulnerability inherent in knowing that fact. In this vulnerability, however, is the promise of truly coming alive.

ELUSIVE INHABITANCE

There is one problem: the way of inhabitance is stubbornly elusive, particularly in the United States.[4] Despite years of effort in ecclesial, educational, and public policy spheres in the United States, we remain, collectively, destructive inhabitants. Consider the evidence: The United States is gripped by an anti-regulatory political movement, undoing decades of environmental policy in agriculture, transportation, public parks, and wildlife protection spheres. The United States is the *only* state refusing to be a party to the Paris Climate Change Accord. This state of affairs in the United States may be surprising, given decades of environmental education in primary, secondary, and higher education. These educational approaches have often fallen short, however, because they assume that good ecological perspectives and practices are yielded by a clear presentation of evidence—that knowing the facts will prompt human repentance and an ecological conversion. This has not proved to be the case.

In part this reflects a failure of education, rooted in a fundamental misunderstanding of how human beings learn. *Especially* when it comes to moral formation, as the development of ecological consciousness assumes, education cannot rely solely on cognitive understanding. Good ecological learning, the kind that nurtures inhabitance, is learning of the head *and* heart. Holding on to the affective aspects of ecological learning is a challenge, however, in the context of social and ecological alienation, itself a consequence of a pathological valorization of individualism, a pattern of unreflective and unrestrained industrialization, and, in recent decades, an uncritical embrace of the efficiencies and networking capacities of technology. Educational systems and philosophies that privilege technical understanding above affective and moral understanding have contributed to these trends.

Another way of describing the social and ecological alienation is this: Human beings in the United States and other places are *lonely*. Human loneliness is a social, economic, and fundamentally *ecological* crisis. When human beings do not understand themselves to be members of a community or members of an ecosystem, they fail to recognize the webs of connection that bind human and nonhuman life together. They mistakenly begin to believe that their happiness, success, and even ecological impact are determined by their individual choices and actions. They no longer understand themselves as members of a community, with all of the pleasures and obligations that attend to that membership. And so, these problems of alienation, loneliness, unchecked industrialization, and environmental degradation are fundamentally theological and ecological problems.

TOWARD A THEOLOGY AND PEDAGOGY OF INHABITANCE

The theological and ecclesial response to these challenges is a recovery, enrichment, and embodiment of *inhabitance*. An inhabitant desires and cultivates the wisdom necessary to live in God's world well. Faith communities that nurture inhabitance as a way of life for Christians tap into the creating, redeeming, and reviving power of God. They understand what it means to be *members* of the Body of Christ on an embodied and relational level. What is more, they understand themselves as members of creation, participants in the divine drama of life and death, joy and suffering, fear and wonder, love and grief. Howard Thurman was known to say about vocation, "Don't ask what the world needs. Ask what makes you come alive, and go and do that. Because God knows the world needs people who have come alive."[5] In short, *inhabitants* are people who have come alive.

Sometimes ecological consciousness is set aside in the interest of what seem to be more pressing ecclesial and moral problems, something like an "add-on" for those who share this niche interest. In the face of persistent and violent social and economic injustice, creation care strikes the ear as a project for the privileged, for persons and communities not preoccupied with basic and immediate survival. In the face of a transforming religious landscape, in which many congregations bury more members than they welcome each year, the stewardship of the planet may seem a luxury, something to worry about in the long term, perhaps after the roof stops caving in. Pushing the cultivation of inhabitance off to the margins or into an undefined future, however, robs faith communities of the deepest source of their power as Christians and as community: profound connection with divine love in the world and with each other as embodiments of that love. A failure to cultivate inhabitance might indeed mean the failure to come alive.

The cultivation of inhabitance, then, cannot be assumed or left to happen "organically." It requires an explicit and intentional pedagogy, a pedagogy of inhabitance that understands the contextual challenges to which it responds, sets a clear purpose for religious leaders and educators, and develops a set of ecclesial and pedagogical practices that form human ecological character. The educational challenge is daunting—it requires a fundamental rethinking of what it means to be human—and thus cannot be reduced to a presentation of new ideas about these matters. It even requires a reexamination of what it means to *know.* The cultivation of inhabitance is thus a process of formation demanding human minds, affections, and embodied experience. Observed in practice, education for inhabitance turns on two orientations toward God's world, our habitat. First, it is profoundly located: it nurtures and springs forth from faith communities who know and love the particular places in which they are situated. Second, it embraces vulnerability: it courageously dwells in the space between life and death, honoring the ways in which, as members of a living and dying world, human bodies and human emotions are exposed to wonder, love, grief, suffering, and, indeed, hope.

CHARTING THE WAY OF INHABITANCE

Clearly, inhabitance is more than a descriptive phrase or even a moral goal. It is a process of becoming, imbued with theological, moral, and ecological significance. In what follows the way of inhabitance unfolds. Chapters 1 and 2 pose inhabitance as the paradigmatic human orientation and vocation, in theological and moral perspective. Theologically, human beings are inhabitants in that they are creatures in a habitat created, sustained, and loved by God. Although this habitat is a wounded and fragile home for divine love and creative power, human beings can hear their identity in the stories of creation and the promises of future flourishing. Humanity's identity as inhabitants thus becomes its vocation, a life's work of learning to become just, loving, and responsible members of a vulnerable and sacred household. Given that the vocation of inhabitance is an ongoing process of becoming,

chapters 3 and 4 consider the educational task of forming and transforming human beings to be loving inhabitants of their ecosystems, proposing
distinct purposes, grounding assumptions, and pedagogical strategies and
practices that respond to ecological challenges and possibilities. Finally, in
chapters 5 and 6, educational practices for inhabitance come into view, as
real communities strive to cultivate love and affection for God's world and
our particular and vulnerable places in it.

1

LONGING FOR HOME

Becoming Members of the Household of God

"LAUDATO SI', mi' Signore"—"Praise be to you, my Lord." In the
words of this beautiful canticle, Saint Francis of Assisi reminds us
that our common home is like a sister with whom we share our life
and a beautiful mother who opens her arms to embrace us.[1]

The Vatican's first occupant heralding from the global south wasted no time
in addressing the deepest ecological questions of our time. The very first
encyclical penned wholly by Pope Francis issues an urgent call to Christians
and, indeed, "all people of good will" to "protect our common home."[2] Pope
Francis is not the first to evoke familial language to describe the planet and
human beings' relationship to it, but his extended reflections on this language
in the encyclical draw readers' poetic and emotional attention. The human
vocation to tend the earth is sacred work that is as intimate as tending one's
own home and family. Home is where human beings learn to be their fullest
selves and where they live into their deepest and most mundane responsibilities. Home is where humans share life together, where they celebrate, are
nourished, grieve, and build futures together. And it is where they learn to
love in the most vulnerable and unguarded way that humans know how
to love. In some homes it is precisely this vulnerability and unguardedness
that make possible deep wounding and harm, broken relationships, and experiences of alienation.

The theological claim that the planet is our "common home" demands a
reimagining of human life and responsibility, the ordering and direction of
human affections, and the very heart of Christian faith itself. From an ecological perspective, calling the planet "our home" and describing human beings
as members of a common household reorients human life and identity. From

a theological perspective, understanding the planet as full of divine creativity, action, and renewal expands how Christians live in relationship to a God of love and mystery. From a social and ethical perspective, a full exploration of the meaning of the image of "common home" must avoid simplistic and romanticized invocations of "home" in a broken and suffering world.

In sum, people of faith and conscience must rediscover how to be human in this world, in all of its complexity and wonder.

Theologians, biblical interpreters, and ethicists concerned about the state of the ecological context have often focused their energies on what humans should *do*, describing human responsibility to tend the land in various places and periods in history. The cultivation of ecological faith requires attention to these matters because they concretely and directly address the challenges of living out the human vocation of tending, stewarding, or serving the earth. But the cultivation of ecological faith also requires attention to *who* humans *are*.

Indeed, human beings at least partly derive their work and identity from their mythic origins in the very soil beneath their feet. By being born of the topsoil, they thus *belong to it*, just as they belong to their families, their communities, and the social groupings that shape them into who they are.[3] Just as they belong to human communities from whom they derive their identities and moral responsibility, so they belong to the "land community," which shapes their identity and gives direction to their moral responsibility.[4] Some of these communities are suffering, and human and nonhuman members of these wounded communities cry out for responses of love and commitment.

In short, to be human is to be an ecological creature. An ecological theological anthropology is not solely an accounting of how humans *act* ecologically but instead is about how humans are, from the start, *ecological beings*. Human beings live and act as members, with varying degrees of consciousness, of an ecological web. Whether they perceive themselves as "members" or not, human living and acting can strengthen the ecological web, tend it, or harm it.[5] In turn, human life is constrained and affected by the health of this ecological web. Pope Francis describes these bonds of interdependence as familial, employing the language of another, earlier Francis to cast the planet as a loving mother and a sister in need of care.[6] This earthly family of which human beings are a part shares a common home. Together, human and nonhuman creatures are members of a household, a site of nurture and a site of obligation.

This anthropological and moral claim, the root of an ecological reconception of Christian faith, must be interrogated and expanded. While ecotheologians, biblical texts, and even environmental scholars alike frequently employ the image of the planet as "home," the metaphor reaches limits when confronted with the state and scope of the planet, the human condition, and the present and future presence of a creating God. The tensions that arise at the limits of the metaphor, however, summon the moral imagination to the work of inhabiting God's world well. The art of responsible and loving inhabitance demands not only human obligation but the whole self, including human affections and dispositions.

ECOLOGICAL FAITH

Human Beings Longing for Home

Sometimes, the terms *ecological* and *environmental* are used rather interchangeably. Describing the work of Christians to rediscover what it means to be human in this world as "ecological faith" is more than a semantic choice, but the semantics are illuminating. Ecology is derived from the Greek term, *oikeo*, which means "to inhabit." An *oikos* is a household, the place inhabited by families. The term, then, literally might be described as "the knowledge (*logos*) of inhabiting."[7] The study of ecosystems, then, is the study of how living beings survive, thrive, adapt, and so on, within their habitats. Immediately apparent is the necessity of studying relationships between living beings.

Importantly, the living beings that make up an ecosystem include human beings in all of their creativity, suffering, and relationality. From the first, any account of ecological faith must acknowledge that some members of an ecosystem suffer more than others. Some members impact the ecosystem more than others. And when it comes to the human members of an ecosystem, these disparities correspond to the ways in which race, class, and gender influence relative social, economic, and political power. Human beings' experiences of their habitats—their capacities to survive, thrive, adapt, and so on—are not monolithic. One of the advantages of ecological thinking with regard to instances of environmental injustice is that it is necessarily relational and systemic. It invites one to think about the connections between elements of the ecosystem, a way of thinking that extends to how we think about human and social systems. Ecological faith looks for patterns, relationships, and effects from the standpoint of an *embedded member* of the habitat.

Contrast this sense with the study of environment, a term derived from the French term *virer* (*viron*), which means to encircle. An *environ* is that which encircles or surrounds. While it is not necessarily the case that considering the environment as "surroundings" leads human beings to distance themselves from it and fail to appreciate the relationship that connects them to it, the etymological difference between environmental and ecological helps to clarify the human relationship to the rest of the ecosystem.[8] Whether human beings understand their habitat as their surroundings or as a system in which they are embedded matters. Hence, the preference for the term "ecological faith": *it is a faith that turns on the capacities necessary to inhabit God's world well. It is a way of life seeking to become loving, just, and responsible members of God's household.*[9] Defining and contextualizing ecological faith thus requires attention to three dynamics: the location and architecture of the ecological household in which humans belong; meaning of human life in this habitat; and the art, disposition, and practice of inhabiting this household. The way of ecological faith is, in short, faithful and responsible *inhabitance*.

The Tension between the Big and the Small

One might conceive of inhabitance in an ecological household in a global or even planetary sense. Human beings understand themselves, in a general sense, as inhabitants of God's whole household, the whole divine creation: earth and heaven together.[10] The process of *becoming* reflective, knowledgeable, and responsible inhabitants, however, unfolds in a local sense. In other words, we become members of a particular household, knowing its other inhabitants, its architecture, and its spirit in the specific. One comes to know and love a particular place, up close and in detail. This tension between the large and the small, the universal and the particular, presents a bit of a quandary.

The admonition to focus attention so narrowly might seem somewhat counterintuitive. After all, who has not been struck at once by the vastness of the universe and the corresponding vulnerability (and yet, disproportionate power) of the human being? The fleeting awareness has the capacity to spark in human consciousness an apprehension that they are connected and indeed incorporated into something larger than themselves.[11] Climbers, surfers, hikers, stargazers, and contemplatives describe similar sensory reactions to being in the presence of nature's most evocative landscapes: panoramic vistas, crashing waves, silent and soft earth, canopies of stars. All of these images connote the vastness of the earth and, even more, the universe. Human beings are reminded by these experiences that they are actually quite small, young, and finite in relationship to this planet on which they find themselves.

Indeed, many a psalmist would also testify to the sheer enormity, complexity, and beauty of the earth:

> O Lord, our Sovereign, how majestic is your name in all the earth!
> You have set your glory above the heavens.
> ... When I look at your heavens, the work of your fingers,
> the moon and the stars that you have established;
> what are human beings that you are mindful of them,
> mortals that you care for them? (Ps 8:1, 3-4, NRSV)[12]

Profoundly, as small as humans are, they are deeply and inextricably woven *into* the earth, as well. Contemplation of the vastness of the universe has the capacity to reorient human conceptions of both the scale of God's household and humanity's place within it. Such awareness is the seed of humility and wonder. And yet, that same preoccupation with the vastness, the majesty, and the long endurance of the earth also, paradoxically, threatens to diffuse human moral vision. Awareness of the planet's breadth and complexity might actually contribute to a sense of rootlessness. In other words, in apprehending the full landscape, one might very well *lose* one's precise place in it. How can human beings grasp both the breadth of the landscape and their precise location within it? This kind of dual awareness requires ongoing and detailed attention to the particular places in which human beings find themselves, as Pope Francis observes:

> The entire material universe speaks of God's love, his boundless affection for us. Soil, water, mountains: everything is, as it were, a caress of God. The history of our friendship with God is always linked to particular places which take on an intensely personal meaning; we all remember places, and revisiting those memories does us much good. Anyone who has grown up in the hills or used to sit by the spring to drink, or played outdoors in the neighbourhood square; going back to these places is a chance to recover something of their true selves.[13]

While the "entire material universe speaks of God's love," humans know that love in the particular: a neighborhood, a spring, a home. When human beings understand a place as a "home" to which they are arriving or returning, they are saying it is a place to which they belong. It is a place in which the promise of recovering one's "true self" beckons human attention and moral energies. Calling a place "home" inspires the desire to know it, as best as possible, with a "loving eye." That is to say, by approaching the earth (and its particular places that are most familiar) with a desire to see, know, and love it, humans encounter it as a living subject with which they might cultivate a relationship.[14] Poignantly, the identity-shaping power of home beckons even when it is far away or inaccessible, when the relationship to it is broken, when one is alienated or displaced from home. Anyone who has visited a homeplace after a long time away, or who has experienced the grief of losing a homeplace, knows what it means to love a place. It is to want to know it in intimate detail rather than in a disengaged abstract sense. Human beings must love in the specific to love the whole. It requires placing their bodies in a particular place, smelling, hearing, feeling, tasting, and, yes, seeing it.

Occasionally theology students bristle at the idea of knowing and loving a *particular* place well. "Should we not love and care for the *whole* earth?" they might ask. Especially among students in theological education (or pastors or young professionals, for that matter!) who understand their current locations to be quite temporary, the admonition to focus intently on where they are just now might smack of provincialism. Ecotheologians and environmental educators alike argue, however, that the reverse is true: human beings cannot truly care for the earth in a global sense until they care for the particular places in which they find themselves in the immediate sense: "It is hard to care for the earth if one has never cared for a piece of it."[15] It is only in attending to the unique contours of a slice of landscape that one can begin to understand oneself to be in a place, to inhabit it, to belong to it.[16] Any other means of locating oneself is theoretical, or perhaps even superficial, in comparison.[17]

BEING HUMAN, BELONGING TO HUMUS

Ecological Theological Anthropology

To be human is to be an ecological creature. The work of human life is to be profoundly located in our ecosystems in ways that are sustaining, loving, and hopeful. Ecotheology is drenched with the image of humans as being "at home" on the planet, and yet this metaphor calls for some caution and critical reflection. Some argue that this claim rarely deals with some of the more vexing theological problems associated with human life on earth.[18] For example, beginning with an assumption of an original perfection, in which human beings are properly situated and in harmony with the rest of the created order, reduces the theological task to primarily tasks of retrieval, a retracing of anthropological steps.[19]

Humans and other creatures, however, live in a dynamic, changing, and interdependent world. That world is being created anew by a God whose creating power is described in origin stories, is active in history, and is luring humans and other creatures in anticipation of a future new heaven and new earth. Humans as ecological beings, therefore, must understand themselves in dynamic relationship to creation through memory, discernment, and hope. Biblical accounts of human origins continue to bear explanatory power insofar as they communicate something about divine and human identity and vocation in history and in the future. These stories, while not the *whole* story, provide a narrative starting point for describing what it means to be an ecological being.

Origin Stories

In the second creation account in Genesis, the writer describes God as having "formed the human from the topsoil of the fertile land and blew life's breath into his nostrils. The human came to life. The Lord God planted a garden in Eden in the east and put there the human he had formed. . . . The Lord God took the human and settled him in the garden of Eden to farm it and to take care of it" (Gen 2:7-8, 15, CEB).[20] The translators for the Common English Bible note that the Hebrew term here translated "human" is *adam*, and the Hebrew word here translated "topsoil of the fertile land" is *adamah*. In this agricultural account, the human being is formed directly from the topsoil, an original connection that is evident in what this creature is called: *adam*, formed from *adamah*. The closest the English language comes to this seemingly genetic connection between person and soil is the idea of a *human* being formed from *humus*.[21]

This soil-creature is placed in the midst of a garden, where its work is set before it: to take care of the land. Indeed, the Hebrew term here is *abad*, which elsewhere is translated "to serve."[22] Without succumbing to the temptation to be naïve about human power in relationship to the rest of the ecosystem, these distinctive linguistic cues in Genesis' second creation story paint a portrait of an archetypal human markedly different from the one readers encounter in the Genesis 1 creation account. At the risk of drawing the distinction too sharply, side by side in these two stories an image of the human being as reigning powerfully over the earth is juxtaposed with an image of the human being as serving the earth as a dependent member of it.[23] These contrasting portraits of the relationship between humans and the land in biblical origin stories stand in tension with one another, but this very contestation demonstrates how essential the work of sorting out the human-land relationship is to understanding human purpose in the world. That the human-land, or human-planet, relationship is an ongoing source of tension, creativity, and challenge in human life is an indication of its centrality in constructions of human identity and purpose.[24] In other words, human vocation necessarily includes attention to how human beings should relate to their ecosystems, to God's world. Genesis 2 presents a call to loving and just inhabitance, living in deep relationship to the ecosystem of which human beings are an interdependent part, while Genesis 1 demands a reckoning with the disproportionate power carried by human beings within that ecosystem.

The Yahwist's creation account urges readers to consider "the land," the earth, the planet as that place to which we most radically belong. Not radical in the sense of extreme or revolutionary, although in a time of technological, economic, and ecological alienation, living as if human beings belong to one another and to the land might very well seem revolutionary. "Radical," however, also has an agricultural sense, meaning "from the root." A radish, for example, is quite literally a root vegetable. Radical belonging, then, means a kind of belonging that gets to the very root of human existence. Whether they live in cities or in the rural countryside; whether they live in an apartment building, a dormitory, a cottage, or a farmhouse; whether they see stars at night or streetlights; whether they are surrounded by rolling green hills, the red and orange hues of the desert, or a built environment in which determined weeds poke their stubborn heads through cracks in the sidewalk, people of faith and conscience belong to the land upon which all of these communities are built. From the first, human beings are born to belonging: "When our dying day comes and the fever of life has passed, we will return to the topsoil that brought us forth, joining in yet another way the great community that birthed us and sustains us. We are born to belonging, and we die into it; our lives are braided into all that is."[25] The origins of human life as recounted in the Genesis stories communicate to readers that fundamentally, they belong.

The challenge to reacquaint themselves with the land community to which they ostensibly "belong" might strike some as unrealistic or atavistic. Particularly in places where "nature" feels quite removed and technologically driven and consumer-oriented cultures make even social belonging (let alone ecological belonging) elusive, a "return to the land" sounds rather parochial or reminiscent of a rural, pastoral ideal long since deconstructed.[26] And yet, sacred texts affirm that human beings are born to belonging. An ecological anthropology for this time thus must take this claim seriously, interrogating its meaning in relationship to a diverse array of social, economic, and cultural challenges. An ecological anthropology for this time must also consider *how* human beings belong to the earth when the earth is in peril.

Inhabiting a Wounded, Broken, and Dynamic Household

Biblical accounts of human origins and creation serve as powerful metaphors that continue to speak to human life and vocation in all kinds of ecological contexts. The affirmation that human beings belong to God's household of creation is a compelling word of resistance in a world of transience. It is a claim to integrity and resilience in the midst of change and threats to human and nonhuman life and community. The path toward belonging, however, is not a simple one of return: human beings are not meant to recover what Jürgen Moltmann called a "paradisal primordial condition."[27] Return is impossible—in scientific, historical, and theological perspective. For one thing, the state of the planet precludes the possibility of its return to a mythical original perfection. That is perhaps obvious. Furthermore, anthropologies that place disproportionate weight on these origin stories are prone—perhaps even guaranteed—to elicit despair because what they implicitly demand is impossible.

But beginning and ending a theological anthropology with the accounts of the world and humanity's origins also fails to account for a number of *theological* problems.[28] Perhaps chief among such problems is the question of human failures and, more theologically speaking, sin. The reformed tradition understands sin as both act and condition. In other words, sin is not limited to particular actions or failures but is a constitutive part of what it means to be human. Human beings are "entangled in the curse," John Calvin believed, and though God is actively working to redeem humanity and the whole creation, humans always are caught in this dynamic of sin and regeneration.[29] They always are prone to sin (individually and together), and they always are being remade and regenerated by God. Reformed understandings of the pervasiveness, stubbornness, and complexity of sin are particularly useful for those who are trying to be attentive and responsible members of this supposed "household." It is to say that a feeling of *longing* for home necessarily implies that human beings are not *yet* flourishing and responsible members of this home.

Christian conceptions of the meaning and purpose of human life remain appropriately grounded in the doctrine of creation, however, particularly as human life is situated in relationship to a God whose creative activity and presence is *ongoing*. To live in response to an active and creative God is to invest one's life in the unfolding of a yet-unknown future. The God of creation is the God of origins, the God of continuous creativity, and the God of a future that is open. The underlying premise is that creation is an unfinished story and God's creative activity continues in the here and now.[30] Creation is an unfinished world in which humans, unfinished creatures, live and move and have their being. Stubborn efforts to "return," then, shortchange divine creativity.[31]

In light of this "unfinishedness" of the household of divine creation, Christian ecological anthropology must also be *eschatological*. This claim worries some ecotheologians, who fear that eschatological images might lure Christians to forsake this world for the next. Such fears are not baseless. Indeed, one well-known megachurch pastor, a couple of years ago, boasted, "Save the environment? I know who made the environment. He's coming back, and he's going to burn it all up. So yes, I drive an SUV."[32] In light of God's ongoing creative work, however, eschatological claims are meaningful *because* they rest in God's promises, which are given meaning in the context of God's revelatory activity in history.[33] If a creating God is a God of origins, history, and future, then the present habitat is rife with meaning and divine presence, not something to be tossed aside in either the folly of returning to mythical origins or the premature seeking of a new and better future creation.[34] For example, when the Johannine community is trying to make sense of the coming kingdom of God (a process of meaning-making recorded in the book of Revelation), they imagine that God will dwell among mortals, making of this earth a new creation (Rev 21:1-6). This image stands in contrast with other eschatological images in which humans are whisked away from the earth, leaving behind this partial, broken, and unfinished place. As God is making a dwelling place on earth, God is working to redeem, not abandon creation (Rom 8:19-23). History is infused with both redemption and promise, for humans and for the planet.

Certainly, the promise of an alternative flourishing future that rests in God's promise stands in tension with the experience of living in a suffering, exploited, and alienating planet. This tension results from what often is described as an "already but not yet" reality. The God who creates and sees that the creation is good is the same God who is beckoning a now broken and vulnerable creation to its home. The primary problem with theological conceptions of earth as home is that it is simply not that. At least, *not yet*. In the meantime, human life might be said to be marked by *longing* as much as it is marked by *belonging*.[35] Human beings might dwell in God's household, but that household is not yet determined by the relationships of love, compassion, and justice that make a household a home. Or perhaps the household, as it exists, is a space of brokenness and woundedness, waiting for healing. The work of ecological faith, then, is embracing the divine remaking of human life so that it is ever more "at home" on earth. That work is about learning inhabitance.

ECOLOGICAL HOMECOMING

THE ART OF INHABITANCE

Inhabitance is an art. Learning inhabitance summons human beings' deepest resources of moral wisdom, affection, and creativity. While human beings might possess usable knowledge *about* their surroundings, this does not imply inhabitance. To get to know a place in which they find themselves temporarily or even permanently, people often first seek to know it in a general and utilitarian sense. They know the borders, the train lines, the major streets and landmarks. They might know something about the culture of the place: its art, its religious identity, its political tensions, its history. This knowledge is at somewhat of a distance, however; it is a factual or technical way of knowing a place. Nothing about it is necessarily false or mistaken, but technical knowledge holds the thing to be known at an objective distance, so that the knower can *use* the knowledge gained in some way. Seeking this kind of instrumental knowledge does not impress upon the human being any moral obligation or emotional relationship to the thing known.[36] It is to be a spectator of sorts. This way of seeing and knowing the world through the lens of the "arrogant eye" assumes that one knows all that is necessary to know about the other.[37] Even when living in a place for a longer term, one might still take this instrumental and technical approach to knowing it, a way of living in a place that might be described as "residence" rather than "inhabitance."

As noted above, however, the very word *ecology* implies a more relational and committed way of knowing. The origins of the term derive from the Greek terms *oikeo* and *logos*, meaning "the knowledge of inhabiting." Inhabitance thus summons and relies upon a distinctive way of knowing or *epistemological framework*.[38] Ecological knowing requires a desire and intention to *know* another, a way of knowing markedly distinct from knowing all the facts *about* another.[39] One can manage to get by—indeed to succeed, by most standards of achievement—with this kind of factual knowledge. Indeed, armed with this kind of knowledge (sometimes described as rationalist, distanced, and instrumentalist), one can technically and efficiently live in a place without being a member and tender of it—encouraging what Wendell Berry describes as "itinerant professional vandals."[40] In contrast, being an *inhabitant* requires a kind of intentionality and relationality not required of the casual resident, a desire and capacity to live well in a place as an interdependent member of it.[41]

From a theological perspective, inhabitance as a way of life requires that human beings orient themselves as members, as inhabitants, of God's ecological household. To inhabit a place with the desire to belong to it is an intentional choice, and yet this seeming choice strikes at the deepest core of human identity. Cultivating this capacity for inhabitance, cultivating ecological faith, thus requires personal and social transformation at a level far deeper than that of figuring out "greener solutions." It requires a reorientation of human identity and life so that human beings remember who they are. Perhaps it is not unlike the story of the young man sometimes called the prodigal son, who had traveled far and wide, living extravagantly and wastefully—perhaps, as an itinerant vandal.[42] A resident. When he returns home, however, his father welcomes him home with a loving embrace, exclaiming that his son "was dead and has come back to life! He was lost and is found!" (Luke 15:24, CEB). His return is a kind of resurrection, traversing the space from death to life.

Being awakened to ecological life is just this kind of transformation, a resurrection of sorts. While one might be tempted to think about ecological challenges as problems for which the scientists, engineers, and technological developers must identify "solutions," these approaches fall short of personal and social transformation. As such, they rob people of faith and conscience of the possibility of resurrection, the discovery of new life in connection with the earth: "Rather than a problem to be solved, the world is a joyful mystery to be contemplated with gladness and praise."[43] The way of inhabitance is an immersion into this mystery, this unfinished world, with courage and curiosity. Serendipitously, some ecological educators are coming to the same conclusion: "Rather than technological breakthroughs, what we need, I think, is more like a homecoming."[44] Being transformed as inhabitants is perhaps the paradigmatic ecological vocation, cultivating human identity at a level far deeper than problem-solving.

The idea of vocation sometimes is confined to the work of discerning what sorts of jobs one should do or, better, where one's passions meet the world's need.[45] Divine summons, however, are not so neatly defined and compartmentalized. The art of faithful inhabitance imparts to every sector of human life—familial and social relationships, natural and built environments, civic society and local communities, work, commerce and financial commitments, and religious communities—sacred and strenuous tasks.[46] In every sphere of life, God is calling people of faith to particular ways of living in relationship to God's earth, human communities, and God's own divine presence in the world. In this sense John Calvin understood the earth to be the *theatrum gloriae*, the theater of God's glory.[47] The earth, as the theater for God's creative work in the world, demands a response. If all of creation is a testimony to God's creativity and power, human beings must discern the appropriate posture to assume. Everywhere God is creating, redeeming, and, importantly, inviting human beings into that work.

2

BECOMING INHABITANTS

The Ethics of Ecological Faith

DIRTY VIRTUE

THE FORMATION OF CHRISTIAN ECOLOGICAL CHARACTER

If the sacred stories of human origins and eschatological visions remind human beings who they are—creatures of the earth, lovingly shaped from the soil and placed in the midst of it as its caretakers—then inhabitance, as an outworking of this identity, repeatedly summons them to reorient themselves as faithful inhabitants of God's earth and anticipators of God's future. It is an ongoing, unfinished process of discovery, an unfolding of human character and identity. Such ecological faith perpetually beckons human beings toward the soil, the ground, the place of their birth, and the future of God's dwelling. As such, ecological faith is dirty faith![1]   *humous*

"Dirty faith" may sound illogical or even sacrilegious. Christian conceptions of the good have been conflated with conceptions of purity such that an appeal to the dirty might strike the ear as transgressive in some way. Many theologians have evoked the polarities of clean and unclean, spotless and stained, to contrast good and evil. When describing the human condition of sin, John Calvin, for example, often used particularly evocative language: "The heart is so steeped in the poison of sin, that it can breathe out nothing but a loathsome stench."[2] Socially speaking, as enlightenment philosophy and industrialization placed more and more distance between the human

19

being and the toil of the earth, being "dirty" seemed more an indictment of
human failure than an affirmation of human identity.

But dirt is good.

Ask anyone who has placed her hands in the soil, whether it be in an
apartment window box, a river bed, a compost heap, or a row of plants: she
will say that dirt is good. Its smell is healing, its color inspiring, its mois-
ture life-giving.[3] What is needed is a kind of ecological consciousness: a
capacity to recognize soil (and all the components of a habitat) as good, and
the will and skill to preserve it. Practices and dispositions of inhabitance
together root a process of ecological character formation, cultivate this kind
of ecological consciousness. Human beings are necessarily ecological beings.
Ecological religious education helps shape them into *inhabitants.*

Ecological religious education takes as its fundamental purpose the shaping of Christian ecological character. This is an altogether different endeavor
than providing the appropriate environmental content and eliciting the correct
environmental answers. It is not even, in the end, about developing the most
environmentally sound actions, policy initiatives, or consumer practices,
although these are good outcomes. To develop an educational theory underlying the process of ecological character formation, one must start with *whom*
ecological faith calls human beings to be, rather than *what* ecological faith
calls them to believe or do. One must begin with a full portrait of *inhabitance.*

Faithful and responsible inhabitance is a way of life seeking to become
loving, just, and responsible members of God's household. To define it according to a set of capacities and a way of life is to say that inhabitance comprises
a set of dispositions or virtues that attune Christian consciousness to its
ecological context, its ecological roots, and its ecological responsibility.
Nurturing inhabitance requires the cultivation of theologically grounded
ecological character, or virtues. Attending to the cultivation of virtues shifts
the environmental question from what Christians should do to how Christians should *be.*[4] The virtue ethics tradition is thus particularly well-suited
as an approach to cultivating ecological faith, embodied in the development
of "ecovirtue," evidenced in persons who actively and resiliently seek the
well-being of the earth and all its inhabitants.[5] An ecovirtuous person in our
time should embody a set of ecologically oriented characteristics, although
delineating ecovirtues is not a simple task.

Certainly, traditional theological and philosophical catalogues of virtues
including justice, courage, and temperance bring with them implications for
the cultivation of ecological virtue and wisdom: arguments about agricultural
restraint, for example, most certainly demand capacities for temperance.

Perhaps an ecological age demands an expansion of the virtue catalogue, developing distinctively ecological virtues, such as sustainability or resilience.[6] A typological focus on the catalog of virtues, however, obscures a bit the breadth and depth of the ecological faith proposed here. Particularly if virtues are cast in a narrow, moralistic sense, one might confuse virtues with a sense of obligation.[7] Virtue ethics, however, concerns itself with the cultivation of dispositions, which include ways of seeing the world, emotional responses to it, and habits of interacting with the world. And these dispositions and virtues contribute to a good life.

Those who have spent time with farmers, particularly farmers who remain very close to the ground and practice organic or biodynamic agriculture, can attest to the wisdom that they embody. While they may very well carry theoretical wisdom from what they read and encounter, they also embody a practical wisdom that guides their day-to-day decisions.[8] This wisdom is born of careful observation, measured responses, ongoing engagement and evaluation, and planning for the future.[9] In theological language, the kind of wisdom thereby cultivated, which Aristotle described as *phronesis*, is deeply grounded in both everyday life and divine mystery and love: "And it seems then to belong to someone with practical judgment [*phronesis*] to be able to deliberate beautifully about . . . the sort of things that are conducive to living well as a whole."[10] This kind of wisdom is demonstrated in the capacity to move seemingly effortlessly, as if it is second nature, between contemplation of God's creativity and power and the work of deliberating how to live and act morally in one's particular place.[11] *Phronesis* dwells in the space between abstract and concrete, between big ideas and pragmatic choices, holding these together in an organic unity.[12] It is the wisdom discovered in the midst of practice that contributes both new expertise in the practice and new understandings that shape and reenvision broader theoretical and theological claims.

The cultivation of ecological faith is deeply reliant on *phronetic* wisdom. *Phronetic* wisdom is already an ecological way of thinking in that it "involves skill in making distinctions and seeing connections [which implies] an obligation to act."[13] It requires perpetual engagement in ecological practices, engagement that yields the kind of wisdom that emerges between everyday experience and more abstract knowledge and belief. *Phronetic* wisdom is born in the creative tension between what people of faith believe about God's world and what they do within it. As *phronetic* wisdom develops, it also does the slow and steady work of shaping and directing human dispositions so that even human affections (in addition to their thoughts and actions) are attuned to God's presence and persuasion in the world.[14] This is the center of inhabitance. Ecological faith does more than inform cognitive beliefs about God's world or encourage moral ecological action. It cultivates the deepest roots of human character, "both inwardly and outwardly, [drawing from] traditions rooted in patterns of death and renewal, birth and rebirth."[15] It demands a reorientation of human character, of inward and outward life, attuning the human heart to the beating, creating, loving heart of a living God.

Virtues Need Affections

The inward and outward formation of ecological character eludes simple description, in part because it is so fundamentally comprehensive. Indeed, many texts and teachers have set out to trace the outlines of this expanded, "earth-honoring" faith. A more pointed focus on the "how" of ecological faith and consciousness, however, introduces some convicting questions.

- Why, in religious traditions that have been engaging the environmental crisis for decades (and the ecological context for far longer), does ecotheology remain a "niche" interest?
- Why, despite an increasing focus on environmental science in public schools and the increasing popularity of university major and minor courses of study in the environment and sustainability, does society still seem to struggle to find adequate knowledge and moral will to make thoroughgoing changes in the use of resources, the creation and management of waste, and human political commitment to preserving the environment?
- Why, when the subject of the environment arises, do otherwise genial people shift in their chairs and sigh with (assumed) resignation, or worse, irritation?

In short, why do human beings not yet live in an "ecological age"?[16] Here is one possible answer: at the risk of putting too fine a point on it, human beings simply do not adequately *care*.

Immediately, however, one must qualify and contextualize this assessment. To say human beings do not adequately care is not to say they are necessarily indifferent, or irresponsible, or even "careless," though these charges are sometimes apt. Instead, to say that human beings do not *care* points to a deeper problem in human consciousness and commitment: Efforts in environmental education, religious and otherwise, have failed to cultivate the *affective dimensions* of ecological identity. Consequently, many human beings—individually and collectively—lack the *capacity* to care adequately.

This failure to nurture such capacities is primarily one of education and formation, insofar as educational practice has sometimes assumed that learning *about* the environment and the threats to it will motivate and obligate learners to act morally and ecologically. By holding the ecosystem at arm's length in objective study, learners risk objectifying it, and consequently flattening, simplifying, and striving to control it.[17] By valuing transcendent, detached knowledge over particular, specific knowledge, human beings pretend that they can see "everything from nowhere," a posture that Donna Haraway calls the "god trick."[18] While understanding that privileges "objective knowledge" *might* yield responsible action, a different relationship is necessary to transform humans' affective relationships to their ecosystems.

When the emotions are piqued in the process of learning, however, human beings have learned to distrust or ignore them. Children might ashamedly wipe away tears of grief when they see habitats destroyed, animals suffering, woodlands mowed down. Adult learners might feel embarrassed by the visceral response of wonder and joy upon placing their bare feet in the dirt or holding a vulnerable creature in their hands. A culturally reinforced sense of shame about emotional vulnerability has contributed to a pervasive mistrust of emotion as a catalyst for learning.[19] Dismissing the affective dimensions of learning, however, and situating ecological consciousness too fixedly in the sciences, risks failing to cultivate a transformative ecological faith. It risks not cultivating ecological love: Pope Francis poignantly compares ecological transformation to the experience of falling in love. Ecological faith is rooted not in "intellectual appreciation or economic calculus . . . [but in] bonds of affection":

> If we approach nature and the environment without this openness to awe and wonder, if we no longer speak the language of fraternity and beauty in our relationship with the world, our attitude will be that of masters, consumers, ruthless exploiters, unable to set limits on their immediate needs. By contrast, if we feel intimately united with all that exists, then sobriety and care will well up spontaneously.[20]

If human capacities for wonder, or grief, or even love do not have a role to play in the educational task of cultivating ecological faith, then it is no surprise that people of faith and conscience have despaired, opted out of, and abandoned their ecological identity and responsibility.[21] Human beings have been educating themselves into alienation rather than inhabitance. To turn it around, human beings must bring their fullest selves—rejoicing, loving, weeping, healing—to bear in the work of seeking and tending their ecological home.[22]

ON THE ECOLOGICAL DISPOSITIONS

To live and indeed to thrive in our ecological context, then, this work of inhabitance must be grounded in human affection as surely as it is responsibly engaging the science, thereby drawing on the deepest sources of human commitments: "It is not half so important to know as to feel. If facts are the seeds that later produce knowledge and wisdom, then the emotions and the impressions of the senses are the fertile soil in which the seeds must grow."[23] The great revivalist preacher Jonathan Edwards understood the affections as the sole "springs" for human action and knew that true religious awakening would require a "fervent, vigorous engagement of the heart."[24] To speak of the formation of Christian ecological character or of an ecological conversion thus requires attention to the affections.

And so it is in the cultivation of ecological faith. Inhabitants must look for opportunities that the work offers to expand their affections, inviting them to recognize that the earth, their home, also is an appropriate object toward which they might direct their emotional energies of wonder, love, grief, and hope. The ecological and theological homecoming described above depends upon the cultivation of ecological virtues in the broad and practical sense, but also the cultivation of ecological dispositions—the cultivation of a heart that is open to wondering at, loving, grieving, and hoping for the world.

Awe and Wonder

When counselors at Camp Teva carefully shepherd a blindfolded group of ten- to twelve-year-olds to the very edge of a mountain they have just climbed, they carefully sit each child down, instructing them to leave their blindfolds in place until they are instructed to remove them. Then camp director Nili Simhai calmly instructs them to remove their blindfolds and to say whatever the first word is that comes to mind. As the children remove the blindfolds, a chorus of "WHOAAAAH!" ripples across the mountainside, with a very clear and exuberant interjection of, "Oh, my God!" Rabbi Fred Scherlinder-Dobb says this about such spontaneous expressions: "That 'Whoa!' is the beginning of prayer."[25]

That "Whoa!" is also the visceral and unedited verbalization of *wonder*. Indeed, wonder is perhaps humanity's first and best hope for rediscovering themselves as joyful, grateful, and responsible inhabitants of God's world. For those wearied by floods of news reports and seemingly impenetrable climate science, wonder can serve as an "antidote" to boredom, numbness, despair, and even alienation from the world.[26] Transgressing the line between joy and fear, wonder is often evoked by a destabilizing event that then compels the attention and a desire to know more. This desire to know more is an indication of wonder's "affiliative, luring side" that draws one in, calling forth sometimes speechlessness and sometimes extraverbal responses, like "whoa."[27] While adults might feel self-conscious about such spontaneous expressions of wonder, children are not similarly embarrassed by their exuberant responses. Certainly, Rachel Carson's perception of the natural world was transformed by exploring it with her toddler nephew, Roger. In this children are the teachers of wonder: "A child's world is fresh and new and beautiful, full of wonder and excitement." Adults who accompany children may thus "rediscover with [them] the joy, excitement and mystery of the world we live in."[28]

The elements of joy, excitement, and mystery are wonder's animating forces. Wonder is thus a dynamic disposition, always active and moving the one "struck in wonder" to draw ever nearer to the source of this experience. It is this luring aspect of wonder that pushes the wonderer to want to know more, in both the technical and the emotional sense. The child who wonders wants to put her face as close as possible to see the intricacies of lichens and to smell the honeysuckle nectar.[29] Wonder evokes a desire for a visceral way of knowing. Indeed, it is so visceral that it feels very much like (and, indeed, incorporates) fear.[30] While wonder moves toward curiosity and desire, it begins with awe and even fear—borne in the recognition that human beings are vulnerable creatures when confronted by a larger animal, shaking ground, swirling waters, labyrinthine woods, geysers that shake the earth with a roar, or even other human beings with violent intent. Indeed, one must not dismiss responses of fear in pursuit of the more pleasurable aspects of wonder. Fear is as central to wonder as desire.

Wilderness, for example, is a frightening place for many. African American history testifies to the ways in which wilderness, while poignantly a path to freedom, was also a threatening place. Enslaved persons fleeing toward freedom through the woods might be captured there, violently apprehended, tortured, or even killed if not returned to the horrors inflicted by slaveowners. For a long time, woods would continue to be a site for lynchings. Even now, the woods are a hidden place, where human vulnerability can be exploited as easily as it can be honored. So to name wilderness superficially as the site for wonder and personal transformation fails to account for the very painful history associated with nature for vulnerable communities.[31]

While the woods were host to many threats for African Americans, they also offered a peculiar kind of refuge, whether for a momentary escape from the violence of enslavement, or as a temporary passage from enslavement to freedom. Take, for example, the "hush harbors" where slaves met, often in the woods, their secret gathering protected by the outstretched branches of old trees. These meetings were spaces for them to worship freely and remember and practice traditions from their homeplaces.[32] Paradoxically, then, it is perhaps precisely this vulnerability that opens the way for wonder. In wonder's vulnerability, immediacy, and shock is planted a seed of longing to know more fully this source of joy, excitement, mystery, and even fear. Surprise leads into longing, and thus ecological wonder lures and compels human beings to know, to feel *more*.

Love and Desire

"We will not fight to save what we do not love."[33] This stark conclusion, drawn by evolutionary biologist Stephen Gould, echoes Rachel Carson's conviction that emotions (perhaps more so than facts) are the fertile soil in which the seeds of ecological wisdom are planted and nurtured. Indeed, he goes a little further, insisting that human beings must more specifically *love* their ecological context. Such an admonition may strike the ear as metaphorical or even hyperbolic: Is love not something that is exchanged in tender moments between humans? Between lovers, friends, or parents and children?

The language of love might be unexpected from environmental scientists. Biologist E. O. Wilson, however, has argued that human beings can, in fact, experience and express a kind of love toward other creatures and life forms. Indeed, this affinity for other life forms is inscribed into human biology and consciousness. He calls it "*biophilia*," which means, literally, "love of life." Wilson uses the term to describe the (largely innate) "urge to *affiliate* with other forms of life."[34] Ecotheologians would connect this biological urge to affiliate with a keen sense of the interdependence of creation. Despite *biophilia*'s "innateness," however, humans sometimes struggle to cultivate a sense of affiliation—and certainly, love, in any sense that one usually means that word—in a scientific and intellectual culture that emphasizes differentiation. Stated more starkly, human beings tend to practice a kind of "apartheid at the species level," whereby they allow *anthropophilia* (love and concern for humans) to supersede instinctual inclinations toward *biophilia*.[35]

When love is anthropocentric, thus directed toward and expressed between human beings, caring relationships toward nonhuman life primarily serve human ends. The rest of nature is a "storehouse of resources" for human use, thereby summoning human efforts to preserve and conserve those resources *in the interest of human need*.[36] Because humans love other humans, they take care of this shared planet so that present and future human generations might have the resources necessary for a good life. Some have argued that this approach to environmental concern, which enters the conversation via human concerns such as environmental health, is "shallow ecology," a utilitarian view that fails to comprehend the intrinsic value of "the well-being of both human and nonhuman life."[37] Importantly, however, concerns for human life—particularly human lives made disproportionately vulnerable by racial, economic, or gendered oppression—should not be so quickly discarded as "shallow." After all, human life is embedded in—a part of—the habitat ecological faith means to tend. Ecological concern that *ends* with human health, however, does prove short-sighted and fails to apprehend human embeddedness in the ecosystem. In this case the charge of "shallow" ecology is apt. Although even shallow ecological care is preferred to no ecological care at all, this utilitarian perspective continues to carry deep within it Francis Bacon's view of nature as an object to be "bound into service" for human gain.[38]

If human beings, as inhabitants, are to extend the boundaries of human love so that they are transformed as loving members of their habitat, what is the shape of that love? There are many ways of loving and many ways of conceiving the beloved. Philosophers, ethicists, and theologians have wrestled to name the true meaning and action of love. Without rehearsing these taxonomies in too much detail, some discussion of *how* humans love God's earth is in order.[39] Perhaps the broadest category, already encountered in the brief description of *biophilia*, is *philia*. Philia undergirds the innate connectedness that might inspire human beings to affiliate with other living beings, because it implies loyalty and the particular responsibility to care for those closest to them, especially relatives.[40] It is a relational love, and so the affiliative (note the root word) bonds connecting humans with other living things are appropriately defined as *biophilia*. Would that human beings could rediscover loving affiliation with nonhuman life; perhaps they would be better lovers of the cities, rivers, forests, ponds, prairies, gardens, and oceans in which they build their lives on a daily basis. Humans would be better lovers of their places.

If love is limited to those with whom one has established a relationship, however, it constrains the sphere of ecological responsibility and care. Affiliative love does not necessarily account for human responsibility for the life that appears at the deepest depths of the sea or teems invisibly in the soil beneath their feet. However, inhabitants must also love the creatures who live in places not habitable by humans and thus not related to them in a palpable way. In this case perhaps a less self-interested, less clannish love is in order. *Agape* is the term most frequently used to describe pure, unselfish love.[41] Thomas

Aquinas described *agape*, which he interpreted as *caritas* (charity), as the capacity to "will the good of another."[42] It is embodied in sacrificial giving to the beloved, with little or no regard for the lover's own life or well-being.[43] Theologically, *agape* is predicated on the self-giving, condescending love of God toward creation, a divine love embodied in the person of Jesus Christ in the Christian tradition. God's love for human sinners is utterly unmerited.[44] Humans participate in and communicate *agapic* love for neighbor as a manifestation of God's love.[45]

Certainly, the planet needs humans capable of *agapic* love: absent some degree of self-forgetting and unmotivated concern, it is hard to imagine how humans might love the microscopic organisms in the soil.[46] *Agape* is an essential framework for conceiving generous and unselfish practices toward nature. As a benevolent form of love, one free of self-interest, it does not necessarily entail reciprocity and mutuality. In fact, the self-giving kind of love that is embodied in *agape* expressly deconstructs the expectation that the lover receives something in the process of loving.[47] This deconstruction of expectations is important because it is how human beings love those whom they might otherwise find "unlovable." Christians love not because the beloved has value but because they are divinely and abundantly loved and thus have the capacity to be *loving*.

In contrast with *agape*'s sacrificial giving from a posture of abundance, the third form of love, *eros*, connotes desire and longing.[48] In its embodied and sensual grasping and longing, erotic love shocks the senses of more intellectually or ascetically oriented Christian theologians and biblical scholars, who have sometimes tended toward taming and spiritualizing love.[49] Perhaps the embodied knowledge that inheres in *eros* is too difficult to manage, measure, or categorize, much like the raw vulnerability exposed by dispositions of awe and wonder.[50] Popular Christian biblical interpretations have sometimes traveled quite an interpretive distance to insist that the erotic poetry in Song of Songs was an allegory of Christ's love for the church or God's love for the faithful, stripping it of its embodied longing. Matthew Henry's interpretation and warning serves as a good example:

> It must be confessed . . . that with the help of the many faithful guides we have for the understanding of this book it appears to be a very bright and powerful ray of heavenly light, admirably fitted to excite pious and devout affections in holy souls, to draw out their desires towards God, to increase their delight in him, and improve their acquaintance and communion with him. It is an allegory, the letter of which kills those who rest in that and look no further, but the spirit of which gives life.[51]

In other words, the Song of Songs is beneficial for Christians so long as readers do not linger too long in the erotic and sensual language. Lingering there, in the space of the flesh, the immediate, and the earthly, is spiritually danger-ous. Perhaps this book needs a parental advisory label: "Warning: *Eros* kills!"

The poetic, aesthetic, and kinesthetic dimensions of *eros* in the Song of Songs present philosophical challenges for its readers, who might wonder what to do with such raw speech that recounts the presumed writers' quite unmediated embodied experience. And so it is with nature, is it not? The visceral connection between a human and an animal's gaze, the wonder at a fiddlehead fern's complexity, the awe at the precipice of a yawning valley or crashing wave—these embodied and primal exchanges need the language of *eros*. When searching for a language of love that nurtures humans as fully rela-tional and ecological beings, Christians need the language of both *agape* and *eros*. Between them dwells a tensive relationship, a tension that has historically effectively silenced serious theological reflection upon love as *eros*, even divine *Eros*, "the Eros that is the divine desire for the creation, for the creature."[52]

Agape entails losing one's own life for the sake of the other, giving one's self away.[53] *Agape* works, in part, because it turns on obligation. Many ecotheologians are nonplussed by the idea of obligation as it relates to caring for God's earth. Certainly, the divine commission in Genesis 2 to tend or serve the earth turns on this very obligation. *Agape* reaches limits as a way of thinking about ecological love, however, if loving God's earth is *solely* about obligation and self-giving. Without the creative power of embodied, full-hearted desire, such self-giving love toward creation risks depleting the moral self in an ever-accumulating mount of ecological obligation. Inhabi-tants thereby might lose sight of their own desire and yearning for ecological rootedness. They risk losing the affective power that inheres in being lovers.

Even when human beings are fiercely *trying* to love and protect nature, if they understand that love as primarily self-giving, obligatory, and with-out regard for their own fulfillment or mutual affection, they remain prone to utilitarian, instrumentalist, and rationalist perspectives. As they seek to conserve resources, human beings might continue to think of this work as primarily human-oriented and technical in character. This way of practicing concern for nature restrains emotions and values distance and respect, all in the interest of "discarding . . . the merely personal and, by implication, the merely selfish."[54] The implication is that universal principles of reason, justice, and even *agapic* love will yield solutions that will make the earth inhabitable, predictable, and less vulnerable.

Less likely to *die*.

But on its own, this is no way to love. It is no more a way to love God's earth, inhabitants' longed-for home, than it is a way to love another human being. It risks being reduced to the antiseptic and calculated. It denies the inexhaustible mystery of the beloved. And it robs the lover of the wonder of joy, fear, discovery, and vulnerability that comes with the perpetual work of learning and loving another. So how shall we love?

Conceptions of ecological love, absent the power of *eros*, are impoverished, excluding the possibility that God is also *Eros*, the divine, creative, "fathomless excess," inviting humans to participate in creativity and newness.[55] In contrast with *revealed* love in *agape*, *eros* turns on the lure of mystery, newness, and *unknown-ness* in erotic desire.[56] In erotic encounter humans are afforded "the feeling of wonder, surprise, and astonishment."[57] Erotic love is an unquenchable "thirst for otherness," a desire to transcend the self by connecting with another, approaching the "elusive mystery" inherent in relating to another being.[58] To love God's world erotically is to be seduced by it, in a way: to be beckoned by its images, its sounds, its smells, its taste, its touch through which inhabitants are invited into a new, unknown, and mysterious place, seeking union and transcendence. Erotic engagement with God's earth allows the human being to engage the world with physical touch and intimacy rather than solely detached observation. In contrast with objectifying knowledge presumed to be acquired through an omniscient gaze, the subject encountered erotically retains a veil of mystery. The lover is invited into intimacy by the beloved, without an accompanying assumption of knowing all there is to know. It preserves the integrity of the other in the same moment that a yearning to merge with the other is born. It lures a person to want to know more, and more, and more of the other, a horizon of knowing that is ultimately never reached.[59]

Being drawn into creative, elusive mystery demands direct and sensual bodily encounters with the material world. It is in drawing closer to the world and more deeply into embodied experience that humans encounter divine love and creativity. Erotic love is the longing for union with another, the desire to take down as many boundaries as possible in order to unite the self fully with the life of another. In erotic love every sense is employed to know as much as possible about the beloved. One must get close to love another in the sense of *eros*. Indeed, one must touch the other—and be affected by the other. Humans in *eros* enter into the mystery of another, making themselves vulnerable to heartbreak and grief. By risking this kind of vulnerability, however, humans also approach a holy embodied connection to another. In this case the "other" is the planet and all of the particular places humans inhabit therein.

Eros calls human beings to inhabit a place lovingly and longingly even as they do not fully understand it and, even less, control or manage it.

Certainly, Christian environmental ethics needs a love of earth grounded in *agape*. If human love for the planet were to turn only on their union with it and their yearnings toward it, essential ecosystems would be ignored. A Christian theology and ethics of inhabitance, however, asks what must be nurtured within human beings to make them *better* members and caretakers of God's creation. Pedagogically speaking, then, inhabitance requires *eros*, which activates human desires, motivations, and vulnerabilities.[60] To love this way is to love a wounded, suffering, and dying world.

Grief, Lamentation, and Repentance

At the root of the powerful affective dispositions of wonder and love lies a fundamental tension of human life: soaring joy and deep, raw vulnerability. To live at "full stretch" in God's world requires accepting that with the thrilling joy at the heart of wonder and love comes, always, the possibility of suffering, disappointment, and even deep grief. Human beings know, instinctively, this tension: it is the source of the unmistakable lump in the throat or the quickened heartbeat. One need not dig very far to find the root of that vulnerability: death.

At the summit of Mount Washington in the White Mountains of New Hampshire is a quite lovely observatory. One can drive to the summit (admittedly, a somewhat harrowing drive with very little between the passenger's door and a vast expanse of valley far, far below the road), park comfortably, and brave the frigid wind and walk around the summit. The views are stark and stunning. Despite standing on solid rock, one feels vulnerable and small, like the next gust of wind just might be the one that lifts a 150-pound body right off the top of that mountain. It is magnificent and awesome in the truest sense of that word.

Others, however, arrive to the summit by another means. Thru hikers making their way across the "Presidentials" have hiked across a thin swath of rocks above the treeline, exposed to hazardous weather conditions many seasons of the year. The route is twenty-three miles long, but hikers gain a total of nine thousand feet in elevation. It is not a kind hike. More than 150 people have died on this hike, many of them freezing to death. Multitudes more have abandoned their adventure in this severe place. A face-to-face ecological encounter—or, more profoundly, a body-to-body encounter—with nature in places like this might very well prove a life-and-death experience. Death's proximity is part of the range's beauty, however. A deep respect and awe settles in the heart, and with trembling knees and dizzied vision, even experienced and careful hikers might viscerally apprehend the permeable line between life and death. Inhabitance requires an appreciation of this vulnerable space. Death is real, and it is everywhere.

The International Union for the Conservation of Nature's "Love. Not Loss" campaign is premised on the persuasive argument that human efforts to inspire environmental responsibility that are based in fear-inducing, dire predictions of ecological disaster—loss or, more precisely, death— are not actually effective. Ominous warning cries might sound to hearers a bit like Chicken Little's "The sky is falling! The sky is falling!"[61] The anthropomorphized animals featured in the campaign videos are frustrated and perplexed by how easily they are ignored despite the urgency of their concerns. The campaign proposes that, instead of guilt and fear, most human beings are motivated to act by love and commitment. Indeed, this is true, and certainly long-term responsible action needs a source of positive energy to be sustained over a lifetime. Is it true, however, that one can choose between love and loss? Certainly, the tactic of scaring or guilting learners into tending their habitats is pedagogically and morally suspect. Ecological education premised on superficial or casual affection for a romanticized place is, however, just as impoverished as ecological education premised on fear and foreboding. When human beings really love something, they deeply fear and eventually grieve losing it. But to love without remainder necessarily implies grief, "the price we pay for love, the cost of commitment."[62] To choose love, especially the visceral, embodied love of *eros*, necessarily entangles human beings in the reality of loss because "to love is to love a dying thing."[63] To love another human, an animal, a place, is to lower one's defenses to a degree that real loss is possible.

In loving, humans willingly make themselves vulnerable to the experience of grief, even when the "beloved" is a nonhuman creature, a landscape, a species, an ecosystem, a way of life, a future. Ecological grief wells up when these are lost or when one anticipates their loss in the future.[64] Until rather recently, grief among ecologists and nature-lovers has been an underappreciated phenomenon. Aldo Leopold long ago conceded that "one of the penalties of an ecological education is that one lives alone in a world of wounds."[65] Almost fifty years passed, however, before Phyllis Windle, ecologist and chaplain, forcefully argued that grief is a necessary component of ecological consciousness and commitment, capacities at risk "if we fail to grieve (alone and with each other) for the magnificent trees, the lovely animals, and the beautiful places that we are losing."[66] Honoring the space to grieve ecological losses, whether they be losses of species, homeplaces, or a way of life, serves as a recognition that human beings are profoundly connected to nonhuman life.[67]

Perhaps even more poignantly, in loving a suffering, wounded, and dying world, human beings make themselves vulnerable to the recognition of their own complicity in ecological death and suffering.[68] From a reformed theological perspective, one cannot lament ecological losses and fail to acknowledge the role that human sin plays in the unfolding drama. On one hand, the imprint of human sin in ecological degradation might be clear: violent images of mountaintop removal inflicted in the interest of propping up an unsustainable system of energy production and usage; the accumulation and toxic burning of e-waste in the poorest human communities in the global south; the continued use of toxic herbicides and pesticides to maintain aesthetically pleasing produce and lawns, despite mounting evidence of damage caused to animals and ecosystems. In many of these cases, ecologically minded Christians might readily agree that human sin is to blame, and they might even be eager to identify the primary culprits: they are the ones who are getting rich from these practices at the expense of future generations, on the backs of the poor and the voiceless. Ecological sin, however, also evades everyday attention: human homes are warmed by cheap energy powered by coal, tar sands, or hydraulic fracking. The effort to take a not–really–old laptop computer to an electronic recycling facility does not guarantee that the machine's components will not be shipped to another less-regulated country, where a laborer—perhaps even a child—will inhale the toxic fumes as she tends a pyre of old motherboards for a few cents' pay. And on a paycheck stagnant since the recession, the only produce some families can afford is grown cheaply and efficiently with the help of Roundup and a whole host of destructive agricultural practices.

Although the moral choices are limited by constrained options, partial knowledge, and economic factors, human beings *participate* in the practices that routinely and lethally harm creation. They are thus "entangled in the curse."[69] Sin is both act and condition. The theological category of sin includes those things that humans do and fail to do, but it also describes a constitutive aspect of human nature. Conceiving sin as a condition of human nature requires acknowledgment that always, within themselves, human beings bear this seed, so that even their best efforts are affected in some way by their proclivity toward pride, or self-abnegation, or unfaithfulness. Conceiving sin as condition bears another implication, however. It means that sin is present in the social circumstances in which one lives and makes moral decisions. Certainly, this is true in the case of the examples above. While one might be morally and individually culpable for a *particular* ecological decision, all participation in broken social, economic, and cultural systems is *conditioned* and *constrained* by those broken structures within which humans act.

A theological conception of sin as condition offers an account for human complicity (no matter how unwitting) in patterns and practices that issue in ecological harm. Even more, it offers a corrective to any simplistic division between the often-corporate "bad guys" and the organic-gardening, bicycle-riding "good guys." Some ecotheologians clearly and compellingly argue that ecological sin is rooted in individual and corporate unwillingness to live within the boundaries set by human finitude.[70] An important distinction should be made here: finite power, temporality, and understanding are not themselves indications of human failure. Finitude is not the same as sin. Even testing the boundaries of human finitude should not be so immediately and categorically castigated as sin. In testing those boundaries, human beings exercise capacities for transcendence, expanding their vision and accessing a broader, more systemic view of creation, thereby better understanding who they are. Indeed, the desire to transcend the self and join with some force outside the self is the core motivation in erotic longing. The human capacity for transcendence, Reinhold Niebuhr argued, allows one to see and recognize not only a "beyond" but also the finitude of human consciousness and moral activity.[71] Human beings thus apprehend how they are woven together with the rest of the ecosystem and the corresponding great and disproportionate power that they wield in this ecosystem.[72] This tension between embeddedness and power is the tension at the heart of the two origin stories recounted in Genesis: human as member of creation, and human as ruler of creation.

This power humans have used for the preservation of the planet—but also in service of its destruction. Every human being who eats, uses technology, and travels (just to name a few basic actions) is embedded in this system and complicit in its brokenness. Whether complicity in this system of harm is explicit or implicit, intentional or by necessity, humans must contend with the recognition that human life, societies, technologies, and institutions contribute daily to the suffering and devastation of the planet. There is no way around it.

Moral paralysis threatens people of faith and conscience when they are confronted by this seemingly intractable truth. As a result, inhabitance must become for Christians a way of life that grieves, repents, and ultimately thrives even in the midst of ecological death. In some way it is reinhabitance, a kind of sanctification, whereby human beings learn how to live in a place that humans have injured or exploited.[73] That way of life is situated within a whole creation that awaits redemption. The God who creates and sustains the world also redeems it, as Paul writes to the Romans:

> For the creation waits with eager longing for the revealing of the children of God; for the creation was subjected to futility, not of its own will but by the will of the one who subjected it, in hope that the creation itself will be set free from its bondage to decay and will obtain the freedom of the glory of the children of God. We know that the whole creation has been groaning in labour pains until now; and not only the creation, but we ourselves, who have the first fruits of the Spirit, groan inwardly while we wait for adoption, the redemption of our bodies. For in hope we were saved. (Rom 8:19-24a, NRSV)

When confronted with the suffering of the planet and human culpability in it, grief, lamentation, and repentance are necessary. Indeed, the persistence of ecological sin and structural harm ought to continue to trouble idealistic or romanticized ecotheological frames of being "at home on earth." The idyllic image of a home as a space of organic harmony, sufficiency, mutuality, and shared flourishing belies the actual dysfunction in the ecological household: imbalances in ecological suffering, responsibility, and relationships to natural resources are evident in our habitat. These imbalances affect human life even as they affect all corners of the ecosystem. Together with the rest of creation, however, humans anticipate liberation and redemption from the creating God.

Hope and Resilience

Even if it is the case that human beings cannot *yet* claim the earth as a healthy home in which all members are flourishing, the image of "home" serves as a future hope and moral guidance. Human beings are *longing* for home. And, with courage, trust, and love, humanity might become a prodigal— squanderers of life, all but dead—now resurrected. In short, inhabitance must be built on a theology of hope. This hope, however, is accountable to and takes shape in this broken and suffering world.

Hope is about resurrection, a new life, rather than a return or work of memory. A simplistic idea that human beings should return to what Jürgen Moltmann calls a "paradisal primordial condition" is appropriately discarded because it is not only unrealistic but theologically inadequate.[74] An ecological Christian anthropology built on the premise of a *return* to the origin

stories in Genesis truncates the active and creative presence of God working in history and luring us toward a future with hope. A full accounting of
human life in relationship to the creating God sees history and the world as
"unfinished." Goodness yet awaits, perhaps more than human beings might
imagine. Humans live within an unfolding history of creation and live toward
a "new creation." Human identity must thus be located in memory, in history,
and in an eschatological future. We live in the in-between.

Living in the in-between, however, is a challenge. It is such a challenge,
in fact, that some Christians are inclined to forsake this world for the next,
the "new creation." Such dualistic thinking, however, constrains theological
imagination by eliminating the creative tensions between present realities
and God's renewing work of making a divine dwelling place *on earth*. An
ecological Christian anthropology that lives into this creative tension thus
"walks the fault line between a hopeful orientation toward the future and a
humble cherishing of the good green earth."[75] To hope for a good future while
loving the present is central to inhabitance.

This disposition of hope necessitates a willingness to live courageously
and creatively in and for this unfinished world. This willingness—and all of the
hoping, striving, and disappointment it implies—is perhaps best described by
Moltmann as the "unquiet heart": "In this hope the soul does not soar above
our vale of tears to some imagined heavenly bliss, nor does it sever itself from
the earth. . . . It does not calm the unquiet heart, but is itself this unquiet heart
in us."[76] Living in the tension between present realities and future fulfillment
puts inhabitants in a state of unrest. It generates within an "unquiet heart," a
deep yearning for future flourishing that Christians are challenged to seek in
the present. A faith that honors the unquiet heart is one that can live creatively
toward the future, imagining possibilities just out of reach in the present. This
dispositional shift nurtures a resilient and nimble ecological faith.

Recently, environmental science and the environmental movement have
crafted a subtle but reorienting shift in language. For many years environmentalists identified "sustainability" as their goal, in recent years broadening
the concept to include economic sustainability and equity, so that human
communities could live with the community of the land in a way that would
be sustainable for all in the long term. This language and integrated set of
concerns made its way into ecotheology, too. A sustainable community, this
position holds, is one that can insure a healthy natural environment, a just
distribution of resources, and just treatment for all humans. This is what makes
for a livable world, and it is the root of Christian hope in an ecological age.[77]

"Sustainability," however, no longer adequately represents the future for which environmentalists are striving. For one thing, the language has become so powerful that mega corporations like Monsanto have coopted the word, applying it to practices and resource use that many environmentalists would hardly recognize as ecologically sustainable. Perhaps more compellingly, however, is the realization that in globalized economic and political networks, the earth's human civilizations have now passed a "point of no return," and the hope to establish systems and practices that are economically and environmentally sustainable is no longer realistic.[78] In light of this, the concept of *resilience* has emerged as an alternative.

An admission like this sounds fatalistic. And yet people of faith and conscience have not given up hope for a good future entirely. Instead, they are exploring language that both acknowledges the impossibility of the restoration of a mythical original state and finds hope in an unknown future with unknown outcomes: resilience. In a world now persistently "out of balance," ecological resilience assumes uncertainty, unpredictability, and change in the ecosystem: "Where sustainability aims to put the world back into balance, resilience looks for ways to manage in an imbalanced world."[79] Ecological faith is also a resilient faith. Inhabiting God's world well—a changing world that is always being created and redeemed by a dynamic God—requires resilience. Resilient hope depends on commitments and practices that cultivate the capacities to live with creativity and courage in the midst of struggle and in anticipation of an unfinished future.

RENEWING ECOLOGICAL FAITH

When construed in explicit relationship to inhabitance, these dispositions—wonder, love, grief, and hope—establish new and deep roots in Christian life. Indeed, in this sense ecological faith renews Christian faith itself. Just as in intimate and familial relationships, the work of cultivating the affections—attuning them toward the living, breathing, hurting, dying world—cannot be reduced to command and response. Even the best sermons cannot on their own force dispositional transformations. Human beings do not feel wonder, love, grief, and hope just because they are told that these are good things to feel. No, cultivating inhabitance and its attendant dispositions is a lifelong process and happens as much by the things human beings do and the communities and contexts in which they find themselves as it does by getting the right ideas. Having described the *telos* of ecological faith—inhabiting God's world well, with wonder, love, grief, and hope—the question of "how" now presents itself. A pedagogy of inhabitance is in order.

3

RELIGIOUS EDUCATION FOR INHABITANCE

To be human is to be an ecological being. From an ecological perspective, in some ways this assertion is simply fact. Humans, like other creatures, are embedded and implicated in an ecosystem. From a social and psychological perspective, this assertion raises meaningful questions about how human beings understand themselves to belong to a community as well as an ecosystem. It also suggests that humans as ecological beings can be affected by and relate emotionally to their ecosystem. Finally, from a theological and ethical perspective, the assertion that humans are ecological beings presents a teleological challenge and divine hope: that by participating in God's work of transforming and renewing the world, humans might become *good* ecological beings—good inhabitants.

This work requires a transformation of Christian faith and theology. As Pope Francis put it, Christians are in need of an ecological conversion, yielding a thoroughly and profoundly ecological faith that turns on the capacities to inhabit God's world well.[1] Ecological faith invites Christians into a way of life seeking to become loving, just, and responsible members of God's household. This way of life, inhabitance, is the paradigmatic human vocation, a vocation that lays claim to every corner of human life, from work to recreation, from commerce to spirituality. Having provisionally outlined the theological contours of ecological faith and the vocation of inhabitance, an educational question now insists itself: How?

The question might very well be paralyzing. The challenge to teach toward no less than ecological conversion—toward a transformation in worldview, in theological knowing, and in daily practice—is daunting in the face of busy-ness and malaise. Cultivating hope strikes the ear as fanciful prose in the face of unspeakable environmental degradation. These are daunting challenges, and yet they are the challenges that demand an ecological transformation of religious education. And though these questions are about how humans become loving and just *ecological* beings, they also are about how humans become, well, more *human*. One might wonder whether ecological religious education is a niche conversation just for the green-hearts among us. In so far as ecological thinking points Christians toward a theological and moral framework of interconnectedness, relatedness, and an understanding of how we inhabit a place, however, it bears implications beyond the well-being of trees, glaciers, and snow leopards (although these are important!). To embrace wonder, to risk full-hearted love, to grieve and repent harm, to find hope in struggle—all of these dispositions are as fundamental to human life and meaning as they are to the planet's ecological challenges. Religious education that cultivates these dispositions among people of faith and within faith communities is process of formation and transformation for a "good life." This kind of religious education prepares, challenges, and nurtures learners in becoming more human before God. Perhaps even more fundamentally, they are central to the Christian life, enriching Christian spirituality by inviting human beings to live "at full stretch before God," to borrow Don Saliers' evocative phrase.[2] In other words, an ecological reimagining of religious education has the potential to transform and deepen Christians' self-understandings, their capacities to live well in communities, and their relationships to a creative and loving God. It contributes to human capacities to live a good life, integrating emotional, intellectual, moral, contemplative, and embodied knowledge and experience. Certainly, a vibrant and resilient ecological faith—*a faith that turns on the capacities necessary to inhabit God's world well; a way of life seeking to become loving, just, and responsible members of God's household*—is a primary indicator of the good life.

The challenge that religious education has faced, when it comes to cultivating ecological faith, is the gap that spans the distance between ecotheology and environmental ethics, on the one hand, and educational theory, on the other. Ecotheologians and environmental ethicists have described with evocative language and moral force the shape of ecologically attuned Christian faith. When an ecological faith has taken root in human hearts and communities, we see the fruits in their practices, language, and moral commitments. In moments both sacred and mundane, their dispositions of wonder, love, grief, and hope are embodied, considered, and visible. The human vocation of inhabiting God's world well is evidenced in their lives and their commitments. The ecological beings—the inhabitants—who practice and are shaped by just such an ecological faith have cultivated the "loving eye" toward the rest of nature and know themselves to be an integral thread in the tapestry of creation, even as they understand themselves to be "mysterious and stumbling creatures."[3] This posture of love, humility, and hope opens human hearts to God's unbounded creativity and love.[4]

Theological and ethical conceptions of inhabitance need, then, practical theological approaches to *how* Christians might go about cultivating the dispositions that support and nurture this transformation in consciousness and practice. More pointedly, ecological faith needs an ecological theory and practice of religious education that elucidates the *how* of ecological faith: religious leaders who wish to nurture faithful inhabitance within their communities need to understand how human ecological consciousness is formed; how moral commitments to the earth are born and sustained in the face of resistance and incremental progress; and the particularities of how children, adolescents, and adults learn, including attention to what roots that learning so that it shapes dispositions and character.

It is perhaps already apparent that this kind of ecological transformation requires something more than a good lesson plan on endangered species or a sermon series on land stewardship. While these efforts fit into the scope of ecological religious education, they must be an integrated part of a deliberate process of formation for the whole person—indeed, for whole communities. Cultivating inhabitance is a process of religious and moral formation that resonates with modes of education ancient and new. Ecological religious education seeks to form and transform persons so that they might inhabit God's earth well, nurturing the capacities and dispositions integral to good inhabitance. As a model of character education and virtue formation, it stands in a long and contested tradition that holds that the cultivation of virtue is an educational process and that some educational frameworks and practices are better suited than others to do this work.[5] Approaches to religious education informed by these perspectives already contribute something to the cultivation of ecological faith.

What has been largely missing, however, is a comprehensive theory of *ecological* religious education.[6] What about the grounding assumptions and pedagogical principles of religious education toward inhabitance are themselves ecological? When limited to the status of an outcome of religious education, the cultivation of ecological faith remains a narrow goal. If, however, the deeper work of forming ecological character reframes the entire project of religious education, faith communities just might find themselves surprised by the possibilities for transformation in educational ministry and in Christian faith.

Indeed, some environmental education scholars, like nature writers, already are reaching for spiritual and explicitly religious language to buttress some of the intangible, numinous aspects of environmental education. As the field has developed, scholars and practitioners increasingly recognize the need for expanded conceptions of what constitutes ecological understanding and the roles that emotion and imagination play in that process.[7] In an effort to conceptualize these supracognitive capacities, these scholars have in some cases explicitly invoked theological categories. Scholars in ecotheology, environmental philosophy, and environmental education alike default to the evocative language of wonder, mystery, reverence, and even prayer to describe the ecologically conscious person.[8] Environmental education, then, should cultivate these dispositions, and this work poses an urgent call to practical theologians and, in particular, religious education to excavate their religious traditions for the sources that might cultivate the emotional and imaginative capacities necessary for an ecologically conscious public. Even those for whom theology is an unfamiliar discourse recognize the persistent educational challenge and mystery of how emotions, dispositions, and souls are formed and transformed.

Drawing on the work of both religious and environmental education, this chapter introduces the purpose, context, and grounding assumptions that orient a theory of ecological religious education. One particular tradition in educational theory and practice—*paideia*, or moral formation for participation in a community—sets for religious educators particular purposes, practices, and even tensions for developing a distinctively ecological approach to religious education. The discussion will critically trace some of the philosophical, historical, and pedagogical roots of education as *paideia*. Assuming some retrieval and reforming of some basic claims of *paideia* in an ecological key, the following chapter takes up the implications for pedagogical approaches and ecclesial practices.

A THEORY OF RELIGIOUS EDUCATION IN BRIEF

For seminarians each course can feel like a revelation. From core courses in biblical interpretation, systematic theology, ethics, and history to more specialized courses in theology and sexuality, human development, death and dying, feminist theology, and, yes, ecotheology, some students struggle to contain their enthusiasm for the seemingly daily worldview and life-changing insights. They can hardly wait to get into congregational settings to transmit what they have learned to all the adult learners who would be just as transfixed as they have been.

Tucked into this theological and ecclesial exuberance is an implicit operative educational theory: once the right fact, or idea, or insight has been transmitted, lives will be changed. A correlate theoretical approach goes this way: once the right experience or learning activity has been facilitated, lives will be changed. Learning, however, is about far more than transmission of content. Likewise, it is about more than a powerful experience.[9] It is a dynamic and relational process, full of nuance and mystery. Thus, it requires a careful consideration of and theorizing about *how* learning happens. A full and sound theory of learning must attend to a wide range of factors, including context, purpose, foundations, and practices. One convenient summary of the components of a simple theory of religious education is this: "Given our situation, here is what religious education should help us do or understand, here is why, and here are the means by which we will proceed."[10]

A theory of *ecological* religious education in the broad Christian tradition might thus be summarized: As ecosystems and social structures are in a season of rapid and disruptive change, ecological religious education should nurture in Christians the desire, capacities, and commitment to be just and loving inhabitants of God's earth. Grounded in an understanding of God as creator and redeemer of the world, an understanding of ecosystems as extensions of community, and an affective and relational way of knowing the world, ecological religious education cultivates inhabitance through a set of embodied, affective, and reflective practices. In what follows the major claims of this theory will be expanded and placed in conversation with literature from philosophy, history, virtue ethics, and educational theory.

THE SITUATION

WHAT IS GOING ON?

ECOSYSTEMS AND ECCLESIAL STRUCTURES IN A SEASON OF CHANGE

Responsible and efficacious education begins with a careful analysis of the context to be addressed. "Context" is a necessarily ambiguous term and might be drawn as locally as the youth group in a particular congregation or as universally as the planet. In most cases educators have in mind a particular set of learners, even if they also have in mind those learners' larger contexts. What must religious leaders and educators understand about these learners and their social, ecclesial, political, ecological contexts? In the case of ecological religious education, four contextual tensions come to the fore.

Human Beings Affect Ecosystems

First, and perhaps most obviously, human ways of being in the world have dramatically changed and now threaten the health of ecosystems. In this, what has been described as the *anthropocene* era, scientists argue that there is little room for debate about the significant impact human activity is having on climate patterns, biodiversity, and pollution.[11] Human activities such as automobile driving, power usage, and agriculture are the dominant causes of the unambiguous rise in global temperatures, creating "the warmest period in the history of civilization."[12] Some scientists have argued that the planet is entering the "sixth mass extinction," with species dying out at a rate one hundred times faster than what would be considered a "natural" rate of extinction, absent human intervention.[13] And the rates of human consumption and waste production continue to create severe pollution problems in the planet's atmosphere and water supply, despite efforts to recycle everything from paper to laptop computers.[14] Daily, human beings are confronted in every mainstream media outlet with the fact of our environmental crisis. This is the context for ecological religious education in its broadest sense: the planet, the household in which humans live, cries out for the attention of ecologically conscious people of faith and conscience.

Environmental Education Has Not Solved the Problem

The apparent absence of an ecologically conscious public capable of responding to crises in climate, biodiversity, and waste, however, is another crucial aspect of the context of ecological religious education. In the general public and in religious communities, ecological illiteracy proves a stubborn foe for education efforts. Approaches to education themselves, environmental or otherwise, may very well be partly to blame. Treating education as the mastery of knowledge, for example, presumes that processing data or other information is how "ignorance" is solved and that better inhabitance would necessarily follow.[15] Accompanying the assumption that ignorance is a solvable problem is the expectation that with enough technology, human beings can "manage planet earth." These two assumptions clearly and immediately reveal one approach to environmental education in which ecological challenges are treated as technical ones, awaiting the right accumulation of knowledge to develop the right solution.

More generally, education often is framed primarily as a means for individual upward mobility and success. And while this assumption might at first blush seem to have precious little to do with the purposes and practices of environmental education, in effect, "all education is environmental education."[16] To say that all education is environmental education is not, of course, to imply that explicitly environmental questions are addressed in all contexts and practices of education. Instead, education in the United States perhaps teaches quite a bit about how much human beings should consider the environment in relationship to politics, economics, business, medicine, and, indeed, religion: that is, not at all. What students learn about the environment in these diverse fields is that it matters only peripherally to an individual's personal and professional success. The ecological context is considered a specialized interest in some settings and makes no appearance at all in many educational settings. In many educational institutions, "the environment" is confined to the field of biological science, a disciplinary segregation that implies that the field of environmental studies is primarily a conversation for *specialists* with very particular technical knowledge. Concurrently, this disciplinary segregation is augmented by a profound *silence* on the environmental context in other corners of educational systems. Other disciplines are "off the hook," so to speak, leaving environmental issues to the experts and the fanatics. The absence of environmental concerns from fields like economics, medicine, political science, and, indeed, *theology* constitutes what might be described as a "null curriculum." A null curriculum is simply what is *not* taught and learned in an educational setting. What is *not* included in a curriculum has important consequences for the learner.[17] In other words, the failure of medical professionals, business leaders, and clergy to consider the environmental dimensions of their work is the consequence of the absence of environmental perspectives in many disciplines and their coursework. If all education is environmental education, what students are learning in classrooms of higher and theological education is that the environment is of peripheral concern.

Of course, public schools and religious communities have introduced instruction in climate science, environmental ethics, and ecotheology, and yet these efforts have not produced a public capable of making the kind of systemic changes necessary to address crises of the scale described above. Individuals might recycle, drive fuel-efficient cars, and take shorter showers, but these efforts of personal choice do not add up to a society that is ecologically literate. Ecological literacy is "that quality of mind that seeks out connections.... The ecologically literate person has the knowledge necessary to comprehend interrelatedness and an attitude of care or stewardship."[18] Such literacy gives rise to more than atomistic individual choices and compels persons in a society to see their lives intertwined with one another and, importantly, with the life of the planet. Ecological literacy certainly includes an understanding of climate science and even personal practices like household waste reduction, but it stretches far deeper than that: it transforms both worldview and the human affections. That environmental education efforts have often prioritized climate science and personal decision-making has resulted in a public that is something less than fully ecologically conscious.

In an educational context in which environmental questions are reserved for science class and the specialists, ecological literacy is a challenge. Students learn the science but may struggle to integrate it into their lives. Consider, for example, a 2014 Pew Survey on perceptions of climate change: while sixty-one percent of Americans believe that evidence demonstrates that the planet has been warming in recent decades (and most of them believe this is human-caused), only about twenty-eight percent of participants agreed that this issue should be a top political priority for the presidential and congressional agendas.[19] The profound segregation between environmental education and most disciplines in elementary and secondary schools, as well as institutions of higher education, is mirrored in the segregation between economic, political, and environmental concerns in the public sphere. Educated persons may very well know *about* environmental challenges, but this knowledge does not necessarily issue in corresponding political or economic commitments.

The assumption that education is for the purpose of personal mobility and success, coupled with a structure of specialization that leaves environmental questions—construed as technical questions to be solved—to the experts and absent from classroom discussions of economics, politics, and culture, results in a public profoundly unprepared critically and creatively to live in and respond to its ecological context.[20] Cast in pedagogical terms, this is a failure to cultivate ecological literacy and ecological consciousness. Cast in theological terms, it is a failure to cultivate Christian ecological imagination. This is the educational context of the learners who will be engaged in an ecological religious education.

A World of Wonder and Creativity

This critique of educational efforts in both school and religious settings is a source of a peculiar kind of hope, however, because if ecological religious education can engage persons on a deeper level, at the level of human affections, its transformative potential remains as yet untapped. Herein lies a third contextual factor, regrettably overlooked in many environmental education efforts. Despite environmental challenges, human beings live in a world of wonder and creativity, a world with the power to evoke human awe, bemusement, joy, curiosity, grief, love, imagination, and longing. This is as true for the delicate architecture of an orchid as it is for the teeming and steaming pile of compost in the school garden. This alluring power of the planet and all of its life provides strong educational motivation, if recognized as such.

Indeed, it is likely a better educational motivator than fear, which sometimes seems to be a primary curricular currency when it comes to the environment. The use and abuse of ecological fear as a moral incentive led one science writer to resort to the kind of coarse language reserved for drastic situations: "The problem is, if you're trying to motivate people, scaring the shit out of them is a really bad strategy."[21] To resist the doomsday approach is not to reject the science, of course, which is frightening. What this writer rejects is the assumption that human beings can or should be scared into being better ecological citizens. Especially for those who read science news, who understand the severity of the challenges the planet faces, what is needed is a reminder of the goodness of God's world. The mystery of the world and all the life found in it has an alluring quality. To love God's world is to be seduced by it, to be compelled by God's creative, loving, redemptive, and transformative activity in the world.[22] To encounter the world with wonder is to embrace the paradox of fear and desire, overcoming fear in order to draw close to the beauty and creativity divinely woven into a complex world. In so doing, human beings might enter into relationship with the world in a way that is not forced or manipulative but a response to inexhaustible persuasion. Even while confronted by serious ecological threats, this wondrous, mysterious, persuasive, and, indeed, seductive world is also the ecological context for ecological religious education.

Social Loneliness and Alienation

Finally, in a context of individualism and alienation, human beings struggle to find and connect with communities of meaning and commitment. To relate to a beckoning world of wonder and creativity is an enticing vision. That humans struggle, individually and together, to relate so fully to the world and all that live in it is a summons to consider the fourth and final set of contextual factors to which ecological religious education responds. Together, these factors might be described as "networked individualism."[23]

Although virtually "connected" via social media to friends, family, colleagues, acquaintances, and even pubic figures around the world, with the capacity to reach out for conversation any time day or night, research suggests that Americans in the United States are suffering from a "loneliness epidemic."[24] Both the causes and consequences of loneliness are capturing the attention of therapists, social critics, public health experts, and religious leaders.[25] Loneliness is "the subjective feeling of having inadequate social connections," an experience reported across age and socioeconomic difference.[26] One might expect that older adults would struggle with loneliness as they live alone or in unfamiliar retirement homes, and as they lose partners, siblings, and friends. However, a recent study in the United Kingdom found that participants aged eighteen to thirty-four were more likely to say that they often or sometimes felt lonely or depressed as a result of loneliness.[27] Social scientists have observed the trend, too, lamenting the breakdown of community, the decline of social and religious institutions, and the rise of social media use as a proxy for authentic human engagement.[28] Absent formal and informal spaces of belonging and social interaction, human beings risk understanding ourselves as isolated units in a network.[29]

In short, people struggle to connect.

And if loneliness is the perception of "inadequate ... connections," then loneliness is an *ecological* problem as much as it is a social one. If the ecological mind seeks out connections, then nurturing ecological consciousness is as much an antidote to the personal and social experience of loneliness as it is to environmental challenges. A sense of inhabitance fortifies the bonds between members of a human community even as it fortifies the bonds between those human communities and the ecological communities in which they live. In the seeking and practicing of inhabitance, Christians might better understand themselves as once and future members of an ecological and social household: the household of God.

PURPOSE

WHAT SHALL RELIGIOUS EDUCATION SEEK TO BRING ABOUT?

THE CULTIVATION OF INHABITANCE AS HUMAN VOCATION

Given the environmental, pedagogical, theological, and social contexts just described—ecological crises, educational failures in cultivating ecological consciousness, a world of wonder and creativity, and a culture of loneliness and networked individualism—religious education must now discover its ecological purpose. Although naming an ecological purpose for religious education responds to such pressures, it also opens a way for a new kind of hope embodied in individual and community wisdom at work in the world.

If education is *not* for accumulation of knowledge in the interest of developing green solutions or, worse, personal upward mobility and success, educators are faced with the challenge of determining a clear purpose for ecological education. Certainly, vague calls for education with an eye toward "planetary well-being" have hardly issued in the kind of ecological learning that "sticks."[30] But sticky learning is what is needed to establish the kinds of informed, sensitive, and committed persons that will be good caretakers of the earth, our "common home."[31] Ecological education, particularly religious ecological education, cultivates persons and communities whose deepest affections and moral commitments are bound up in the health of the planet and all of its communities. It works against the singular obsession with personal success, prizing instead full-hearted love and commitment: "The plain fact is that the planet does not need more successful people. But it does desperately need more peacemakers, healers, restorers, storytellers, and lovers of every kind. It needs people who live well in their places. It needs people of moral courage willing to join the fight to make the world habitable and humane."[32]

The peacemakers, lovers, and healers of moral courage necessary for this ecological time are persons with ingrained, embodied ecological sensibilities who can lead us into a new ecological age.[33] They are *inhabitants*. An inhabitant is a creature who lives well within the context and bounds of its habitat. Human beings have a unique way of being inhabitants, however, in that they can be moved to protect their ecosystems and the human communities, even those seemingly unlike their own, who share their ecosystem. In so doing, they become faithful inhabitants of God's world, tending and serving the land.[34]

As the paradigmatic human vocation, *inhabitance*—seeking to live well in a place and in God's world—is a lifelong journey of discovery, formation, repentance, and striving. Rather than claiming that God's world is *already* home (in the romantic sense) and that human work is mainly recognition of and response to this fact, an ecological journey of inhabitance proposes that Christians seeking to become good inhabitants always are being formed and transformed in this identity and for this work. Inhabitance is both who human beings are becoming and what they do. And it is the purpose of ecological religious education.

Religious education that nurtures the desire and capacities to be just and loving inhabitants of God's earth is both grounded in the wide sweep of Christian texts and practices, as well as the particular challenges as described in the contextual factors above. In other words, ecological religious education that nurtures inhabitance both embodies core truths and commitments in Christian traditions and is particularly suited for today's context. Inhabitance requires ecological consciousness, ecological imagination, and ecological faith.

Ecological Consciousness

On the most basic level, ecological sensibilities are built upon an *ecological understanding*. A person with ecological understanding thinks relationally, locating things in a proper context and understanding how they relate to each other.[35] Inhabitants understand their ecosystems. Ecological understanding, however, must be coupled with a consideration of how these concepts *matter* in an inhabitant's life, or how an inhabitant is morally motivated by this understanding. *Ecological consciousness* stretches the concept of ecological learning beyond cognitive understanding to attend to the affective and moral aspects of *inhabitance*: it is not "just a comprehension of how the world works, but, in light of that knowledge, a life lived accordingly."[36] Ecological consciousness infuses the whole life: perceptual, affective, and thus moral.

Learners who have developed ecological consciousness not only understand the world and their ecosystems as interrelated, but they also understand themselves *as beings embedded within this interrelated ecosystem*, as inhabitants.[37] An inhabitant is intimately aware of her relatedness with all points of the ecosystem. This profound sense of connection is the core of knowing, feeling, and doing for the ecologically conscious person.[38] It is inspired by not only the desire for knowledge but "the sense of wonder, the sheer delight in being alive in a beautiful, mysterious, bountiful world."[39] An inhabitant's embeddedness in the world means that one can be affected by its beauty, its power, and its suffering. An ever-deepening understanding of the self as embedded in an ecosystem contributes to a sense of *belonging*.[40] These forms of knowing implicate the emotions.[41]

If inhabitants understand their "being" as intimately related, even belonging, to the soil, plants, animals, humans, water, and air around them, their "doing" in that ecosystem takes on the character of commitment and responsibility. Just as human beings might understand themselves to be responsible for the well-being of other persons and human communities because they are tied together in an interdependent web of life, so, too, they are obligated to all forms of life with which their lives are woven.

Aldo Leopold made this argument forcefully half a century ago. As technological and industrial advances began rapidly to alter the relationship between human beings and the land, Leopold set out to reframe the land as an extension of human "community," which thusly demands moral attention:

> All ethics so far evolved rest upon a single premise: that the individual is a member of a community of interdependent parts. His instincts prompt him to compete for his place in that community, but his ethics prompt him also to co-operate. . . . The land ethic simply enlarges the boundaries of the community to include soils, waters, plants, and animals, or collectively: the land.[42]

Indeed, to be conscious of oneself as a member of the land community is to be a "biotic citizen," deeply aware of one's dependence upon and responsibility for even the smallest forms of life, the microbes in the very soil upon which all life—including human—depend.[43]

Although educators use diverse terms to describe purposes of ecological education—understanding, literacy, and consciousness—many who describe their approach to education as "ecological" instead of "environmental" share a basic commitment that weaves together thinking, feeling, and acting. This agreement—even with the tensions inherent in sorting out the priorities and relationships among the capacities for thinking, feeling, and acting—makes all the more perplexing the conclusions that some scholars are drawing about ecological education, described above: it is not working.

Despite educators' best efforts for the past thirty years or so, there persists a "generation of ecological yahoos."[44] The perennial problem of an ecologically *un*conscious public confirms an emerging pedagogical consensus that teaching and learning *about* the environment is fundamentally insufficient; that learning must be experientially and emotionally based; and that cross-disciplinary, project-based learning better evokes the kinds of motivating questions and commitments that characterize ecological consciousness. However, even where these pedagogical assumptions have been incorporated into approaches to ecological education, they have met still limited success, according to some.[45] This critique raises another category for consideration: in addition to ecological consciousness, with all of its attendant emotional and moral considerations, ecological education must also nurture the ecological imagination, the source of ecological creativity and future vision.

Ecological Imagination

Whereas ecological consciousness links thinking, feeling, and doing, imagination adds a dimension of creativity and vision and the capacity to consider possibilities beyond present realities.[46] The imagination, as a human faculty, requires both cognitive perception and puzzle-solving capacities as well as emotional connection and hope for the future. It lures learners to conceive of possibilities beyond that which seems immediately and strategically possible. In the case of nurturing inhabitance, this capacity is essential, particularly in the face of an onslaught of bad environmental news. Imagination makes possible the disruption of habitual perspectives and practices and, more, anticipates transcending of current circumstances.[47] Imagination is a kind of "wide awakeness," a state in which otherwise inconceivable possibilities present themselves, prompting human desire and longing.[48] Imagination thus has a disclosive quality—revealing to the imaginer something otherwise "unseen, unheard, or unexpected."[49] Theologically speaking, imagination is the capacity required for Christian hope.

As with Christian hope, however, an inhabitant's imagination is not oriented toward an entirely novel possibility or future without reference to present realities. Instead, what is disclosed by the imagination is the relationship between perhaps seemingly disparate elements. Through imagination human beings apprehend the interconnected web in which they live—their *habitat*—aiding them in contextualizing experiences, entities, and possibilities in a coherent system. Seeking out the connections and unity in complex systems, *like ecosystems*, requires an active, awake, and creative imagination. And when human beings begin to see these connections everywhere, the moral demand becomes clear. Indeed, imagination is what births empathy.[50]

If imagination is the very capacity that makes it possible to perceive, envision, and respond compassionately to these essential connections, then few approaches to education would seem better equipped to nurture and leverage the imagination than ecological education.[51] Indeed, in an informal survey, it was the environmental science professor who defined imagination as "finding relationships others have overlooked."[52] And once human beings understand themselves to be woven into those relationships, then their empathy might be awakened not only to other human beings but to all living beings. Perhaps because imagination is in essence something that dwells in the realm of invisibility, future, and creativity, however, ecological educators find it difficult to describe adequately or theorize.[53] In this way, too, it is not unlike Christian hope. Indeed, a theology of inhabitance is uniquely situated to engage imagination's numinous and unpredictable character. In relationship to a creative (and creat*ing*) God, ecological faith invites human creativity, trust, and courage in an unfinished world.

Ecological Faith

A theological framing of ecological consciousness and imagination brings the purpose of ecological religious education into full view. Ecological education that nurtures inhabitance capaciously embodies core truths and commitments in Christian traditions and is particularly suited for the ecological and social context today. Even Christianity's sacramental life, its core practices, can be imagined anew in light of ecological, educational, and social contexts. The waters of baptism might draw one into membership in the body of Christ *and* into the local watershed. And the wine and bread of the Eucharist might draw one closer to Christ *and* the topsoil that yields these earthly elements.

On Baptism of the Lord Sunday each January, for example, many congregations observe a "reaffirmation of baptism," whereby they remember that in the sacrament of baptism, Christians are joined to the body of Christ. Elkin Presbyterian Church is no different. When Stuart Taylor was called as pastor of that congregation, however, he was taken with the sight of the Yadkin River coursing through the center of town. He undertook a personal study of the local watershed, bringing along the congregation as he learned more about its history and the challenges posed to it. "Our watershed is our ecological address," he said in a 2015 sermon on the baptism of the Lord. "It is the location of the life community that we are a part of, that is sustained by the water." As the congregation launched into a collaborative program of "watershed discipleship" with other community organizations, Taylor invited the congregation to let the reaffirmation of baptism ignite their imaginations about their relationship to the Yadkin River:

> There is an interesting little detail about the story of Jesus' baptism that I have never noticed until now. The original Greek doesn't say that Jesus was baptized in the Jordan River. The original Greek says this: Jesus was baptized "into" the river Jordan. Jesus was baptized not in the river Jordan but into the river Jordan. Is this preposition an insignificant detail or a world of difference? What is the difference between being baptized in the river and being baptized into the river? What would be the difference for us? Could we be re-baptized "into" our river? Could we learn to re-inhabit our watershed?[54]

A gospel story often spiritualized, eclipsed by its supernatural details such as a rending of the heavens, a descending dove, or a divine voice, is here retold by a pastor with an eye for the mundane, the material: for the habitat. He juxtaposes the baptism of Jesus "into" the Jordan River next to the liturgical practice of recalling a community's baptism, placing that memory along the banks of their own river, thereby inviting them to inhabit it anew. In so doing, Taylor invites hearers to reconstruct imaginatively and ecologically their self-understandings as members of their watershed.

If the waters of baptism can be ecologically located, so can the basic elements of the Eucharist. The sanctuary of the Church of the Pilgrims on Dupont Circle in Washington, D.C., retains its traditional pulpit and elevated chancel. On an average Sunday morning, however, nothing happens there. It is dim, as if it were an empty theater, and though it is in full view of the gathered congregation, it feels as if it is "off to the side." The action, liturgically speaking, is closer to what might be described as the center of the people gathered. The communion table is there, and it is not uncommon for the people gathered to stand in a circle around that table to receive the sacrament of the Lord's Supper. It is an intensely connectional practice with each participant able to look other participants in the eye. The community is being formed and fortified each time they stand around that table. At Pilgrims (as many members call it), however, there also are occasionally other symbols and material evidence of the interconnections that ground their community. Most notably, compost. Worshippers have been greeted with compost spilling out of the baptismal font, compost filling a column supporting the font, and even a giant pile of compost serving as a communion table. Sharing the sacred meal lovingly prepared and placed atop a pile of rich, pungent, and even wormy earth, worshippers are reminded not only that they belong to one another but also that they belong to the earth.[55] The presence of that very earth in the center of a community's worshipping life is a poignant representation of their connectedness with each other, with the planet, and with God.

These sacramental practices of inhabitance—of living well within an ecosystem—embody the particular commitments of Christian life. But they also playfully and imaginatively respond to the contextual challenges posed above. They bring into the center of Christians' shared life the fragility of the planet, its waters and its soil, thus serving as a reminder that human life flourishes and suffers in tandem with nonhuman life. By inviting direct and embodied encounters with such elements, they might disrupt ecological illiteracy at a level deeper than cognitive understanding. Worshippers know the temperature of the Yadkin river in May, and they know how compost smells at the end of August. They begin to know and care about a place in particular, not just know *about* it from a distance. These practices reveal in intimate detail a world of wonder and creativity by inviting participants into a playful and imaginative relationship with ordinary elements and sacramental action. And finally, these practices invite worshippers to bring their memory, their emotions, and their bodies together, honoring the earthly (and watery) core of their community and their very being. If alienation and isolation are threats to human flourishing and community, these kinds of practices serve to reconnect Christians in love and mutual care.

The purpose of ecological religious education that nurtures inhabitance is threefold: it cultivates the imaginative and affective dispositions that attune human beings to notice, appreciate, and honor the relationships that bind them to God's world; it strengthens human will and felt responsibility to protect and delight in the ecosystem, particularly those places that are closest; and through participation in intentional and social practices, it builds up diverse human capacities to act lovingly, reflectively, knowledgeably, and justly in the world. This purpose and its three dimensions are most fully expressed with the resources of theological, sociological, and philosophical language.

GROUNDING ASSUMPTIONS
WHAT COMMITMENTS COMPEL AND SHAPE RELIGIOUS EDUCATION?

THEOLOGICAL, SOCIAL, AND PHILOSOPHICAL GROUNDING FOR ECOLOGICAL RELIGIOUS EDUCATION

Underneath the ideas and practices that give shape to an educational initiative or program, powerful operative assumptions shape how educators read their contexts; how they imagine an educated person or community looks, thinks, or acts; and the practices and content they employ in service of those analyses and visions. In many cases these assumptions remain rather implicit or perhaps even subconscious. However, a critically reflective educator must pause to examine grounding assumptions, perhaps making them explicit, and perhaps imagining new or revised commitments that might give new life and direction to religious education in a given time and place.[56] The theory of ecological religious education here proposed is most powerfully shaped by a set of theological, sociological, and philosophical assumptions: an understanding of God as creator and redeemer of the world, an understanding of ecosystems as extensions of community, and an affective and relational way of knowing the world.

Theological Grounding
Humans Relating to God as Creator and Redeemer of the World

Ecological religious education's most basic purpose is deeply theological: to cultivate among learners a desire and the capacities to inhabit God's world well.

Discussed at length above, the theological assumption grounding ecological religious education is an *ecological theological anthropology*. In other words, humans are ecological beings, inhabitants in a household created, loved, and being redeemed by God. Because of human sin, this household should be understood not in a romantic sense of "home" but in a real and conflicted sense as a site of shared identity, shared wounds, and shared responsibility. There is not a perfect home to which humans are being called by God to return. Indeed, such a return is not only impossible because of acts, structures, and the condition of sin; a preoccupation with returning would represent a failure to recognize God's ongoing creative activity in the world, God's redemption of a broken and suffering world, and God's infinite and effective love evidenced in the making of a new creation here on earth. This is not to say that origin stories—accounts in Genesis that demonstrate the shared mythic beginnings of humans and other living things—do not matter. Held in creative tension with an awareness of God's ongoing creative, loving, and redeeming work in the world, these origin stories situate human identity as members of God's unfinished household with all the joys, pains, and responsibilities associated with that self-understanding. Ecological religious education invites and accompanies persons into the discovery and work of inhabitance, a vocation practiced and embodied in social and ecological community.

Sociological Grounding

Ecological Community as Site of Formation and Transformation

If the theological grounding of ecological religious education resides in a reimagining of who God is and who human beings are in relationship to God, its sociological grounding resides in the insistence that human beings come to know these things in the context of a community of faith and practice. In an ecological key, that community of love and accountability is expanded to include nonhuman life.

First, ecological faith and identity is formed in community. Although there may be explicit modes and moments of religious education in which a pastor, educator, or teacher is responsible for designing and facilitating learning experiences, on a deeper level it is the whole community who educates. Everything a community *does* is formative for each member of that community, whether it be explicit preaching and teaching, patterns of relationships within and beyond the community, or practices of worship, service, and justice-seeking. The educative power of the faith community has been a strong theme both in historical examples of religious education and in religious education theory in the last half century.

After a strong and successful Sunday school movement in the eighteenth and nineteenth centuries, religious education had in many circles become synonymous with what might be described as formal religious instruction, a set-aside time and space for learning biblical and theological texts and traditions. In the late twentieth century, religious educators critiqued the assumption that these spaces of formal instruction, often reserved for children and adolescents, were the only contexts in the life of a community of faith in which religious education was or should be happening.[57] In other words, everything the community of faith does, teaches. By participating in Christian practices in the context of communities of faith, Christians are formed in a way of life abundant that responds to some of the world's deepest needs.[58] Communities of faith (particularly congregations) are where Christians learn to be vulnerable, hopeful, and reflective human beings, largely by participating in these practices together with wise and knowledgeable companions. Practices themselves, even ones in which persons seemingly act alone (such as contemplative prayer), are necessarily "socially established" in that they have been developed, critiqued, and refined through communities of faith across time and place.[59] When human beings participate in these practices, then, they participate in a tradition, an ongoing conversation about what constitutes the good life.[60] This mode of education, emphasizing community, character, and tradition, is reminiscent of the Greek concept of *paideia*, discussed below.

The invocation of community in both moral and educational discourse is now well established. The community is both where religious education happens as well as its purpose: through shared practices, good religious education forms a community of people that hold each other in mutual regard and act in the world with love, forgiveness, integrity, courage, and delight. In this alone one might find ample support for an ecological religious education. Participating together with other human beings in ecological practices— whether those practices are tending a garden, hiking, or a reaffirmation of baptism with special attention to the local watershed—invites and nurtures ecological consciousness. What if communities of faith, however, also understood their *ecosystem* to be their community, as Aldo Leopold urged, and not just the backdrop against which their human community acts? Such self-understanding is the root of ecological consciousness. Leopold noted the prevalence of the language of community in social ethics discourse and wondered whether the concept of community might be expanded to include nonhuman members of the local ecology.[61] Expanding human conceptions of community in this ecological vein might fundamentally change how Christians think about ecological contexts, questions, and challenges. Instead of thinking about an ecological question from the assumed perspective of an objective and benevolent observer, ecological consciousness leads one to perceive oneself as a *member* of an ecological *community*, a self-understanding that demands more of the relational self. Developing this ecological consciousness is thus a goal for ecological religious education that requires some philosophical reflection.

Philosophical Grounding

Knowing Ecologically and Education of the Whole Person

Educational philosophy asks, "What does it mean to 'know'?" This seemingly abstract question is at the heart of every educational endeavor. In the field of philosophical discourse, theories of knowledge are called *epistemology*. In ecological religious education, the question takes on new significance, as ecological knowing has often been strongly associated with the scientific method. Ecological knowing in this sense assumes that the most reliable knowledge is best acquired through dispassionate inquiry, through reason rather than emotion. The scientific method seeks to eliminate bias wherever possible and assumes that objective distance between the knower and the known is the best means of ensuring unbiased analysis. But are distance, presumed objectivity, and reason freed of human emotion the best means of knowing someone or something? Knowing *about* a person is not the same as *knowing* a person.[62] Thus, to form an ecologically engaged public, the old adage "those who know better, do better" is not robust enough an educational theory to accomplish these goals.

A different kind of knowing is needed for inhabitance. Insights long excluded from epistemological consideration—including embodied, emotional, and relational awareness—are essential components for the formation of ecological consciousness and commitment. In its awareness of the self as an ecological being, embedded in relationships with the natural world, ecological consciousness stands in stark contrast to instrumental consciousness, whereby human beings might understand the relationship between themselves and the world around them in terms of productivity and efficiency.[63] Instrumental consciousness, the extreme outworking of dispassionate inquiry at the expense of relational knowing, holds that which is being perceived at a distance, as if dispassionate observation renders a more accurate understanding than embedded awareness.[64] It risks perceiving nonhuman life solely as resources provided for human needs. When applied in an ecological context, even among those who would seek to preserve it, instrumental consciousness results in a detached and potentially harmful relationship to other forms of life.

To know ecologically requires the recruitment of the heart and body alongside the mind. It is a profoundly relational knowledge, founded upon the "joyous, creative energy of shared connections between self and other."[65] This kind of learning requires a pedagogy of engagement and attention to embodied experience through participation in complex and meaningful earth-honoring practices within a community of commitment. For example, before physician and evangelical Christian Matthew Sleeth accompanied a group of Christians in a helicopter tour of mining sites in eastern Kentucky, he and the rest of the group had learned a little bit about the practice often described as "mountaintop removal." Just reading about the practice and the myriad disruptions it introduces into the ecosystem is enough to give one pause. However, on the tour Sleeth and the other participants gasped as they saw with their eyes the devastation wrought at the top of the mountains that are sacred to so many in Appalachia. Sleeth described what he saw in the most violent and exploitive language he knew as a medical doctor: rape. Another participant described the practice as an "assault on the mountain."[66] This image, imprinted in the memories of the tour participants, would be accompanied by conversations with local families who described fears of drinking or even bathing their children in the water. Here were people that could be the group's neighbors, afraid to bathe their children in tap water. In their encounters with abused land and people, the group grieved the wounds suffered by the bodies and spirits of the members of this entire ecosystem.

There are other means by which one might learn *about* mountaintop removal. One might very well read analysis of the damage caused by such extreme mining practices. Upon reading such analysis, one might even be moved to resist these practices. But this kind of knowledge does not have the same educative power as placing one's body on "half a mountain": seeing with one's own eyes bare, wounded, and assaulted sacred mountains; or sitting across the table from fellow Kentuckians who are poignantly describing the health crises they are experiencing as a result of this way of mining. The educative power of practices—embodied and relational actions accompanied by reflection—resides in their capacity to nurture precisely these embodied, emotional, and relational modes of knowledge. Intentional and reflective practices are important modes of education because they open to the practitioner levels of awareness, *ways of knowing*, that "outside of these practices are beyond our ken."[67] Through their bodies, their relationships, their emotions, and their minds, practices open up to human beings knowledge that cannot be grasped on a solely cognitive level. In short, human identity and moral consciousness is shaped as much by the things people do as by the things they cognitively know or believe.[68] By attending to the emotions, the body, and relationships, practices are a key component in an education of the whole person, an approach to formation described by the ancient Greeks as *paideia*. *Paideia* is a framework of grounding assumptions that incorporates theological, sociological, and philosophical insights, so it serves us well to pause here and consider this framework—its contributions and its limitations—with some specificity.

PAIDEIA AND THE FORMATION OF ECOLOGICAL BEINGS

In the simplest of terms, *paideia*, though not neatly translated into other languages, describes the whole process by which ideals are shaped and cultivated in a culture and by which persons are formed for participating in a society.[69] *Paideia* stands in contrast with more technical or more theoretical forms of education, whereby the acquisition of skills or ideas is an educational end in and of itself. Those skills or ideas might very well be of use in a career, in a community, or in a society, but the process of technical or theoretical education stops somewhere short of character formation. While technical approaches to education might sound reasonable, an education that forms and transforms persons for active, meaningful, and responsible life requires more than an exchange of information. Such education must also inculcate in learners certain virtues and modes of character so that they are adequately prepared to be good and noble participants in democracy and the political sphere.

Paideia *in Historical Perspective*

The ancient Greeks might have asked it this way: What kind of education nurtures nobility and leadership among members of a society?[70] In ancient Greece *paideia* was the process by which learners' "whole personality" and character were formed and deliberately guided in order to prepare them for service in society.[71] In so doing, learners attain virtues (*arête*) that are politically efficacious, inspiring noble leaders to seek and achieve greatness. This educational path is marked by discipline and the deliberate formation of character in the context of community. Wisdom is thus passed through generations, via traditions, models, and the general environment in which virtue formation is taking place.[72] Ostensibly, all persons who desire that their minds and character be formed in service of the larger community may pursue this trajectory in a deliberate process of education.[73] Early Christian thinkers would adopt *paideia* as a means both to instruct Christian communities and to engage biblical texts, serving as a protective force and ordering principle in the life of the Christian, binding the body of Christ together in the spirit of God.[74] Christian formation was precisely this enculturation into a way of life, embracing the contributions of a sharp mind, an active imagination, and a unifying spirit. Aristotle argued that virtue and wisdom are nurtured through the cultivation of "habits" and what Alasdair MacIntyre would later describe as "practices." Engagement in these practices over time shape human character such that learners develop reliable "ways of being" in the world. Thus, a society made up of ordinary persons educated in the interest of cultivating virtue and wisdom is one in which flourishing is within reach for all.[75]

Critiques and Contributions

Would that education so ably yield a society full of persons of strong character, wisdom, and the freedom to flourish! Before uncritically embracing a comprehensive process of formation like *paideia*, however, important questions and critiques must be raised: Historically speaking, social hierarchies often determined which students were judged capable of being educated in this way. Even when expanded to a larger population, the goal of identifying, preserving, and educating for a *universal cultural ideal* might easily ignore and repress the diversity of human intelligence, creativity, and cultures. Finally, a comprehensive framework of character education such as *paideia*, precisely *because* it educates the heart and soul alongside the mind, risks reinscribing unjust social structures, preserving hierarchical class structures, and encouraging less-privileged learners to become "good" participants in structures that may cause them harm.[76]

Given these critiques, a reader might rightly wonder why the concept of *paideia* is afforded so much consideration here. *Paideia's* worthy emphasis on the cultivation of virtue and wisdom in service of shared flourishing might be wrested from the cultural baggage of its development and critically reimagined for a time such as this. Where *paideia* is retheorized as an educational framework applicable to all persons, responsive to particular cultural contexts, it holds transformative potential for the theory and practice of ecological religious education. Some of the basic commitments of *paideia* worth retaining for the cultivation of inhabitance include:

1   *Education is a process of formation and transformation.* Far more than
    transmittal of content or data for cognitive comprehension, educa-
    tion both nurtures and changes learners in realms beyond the cogni-
    tive, including somatic, emotional, and moral understanding. These
    capacities are necessary for knowledgeable and loving inhabitance in
    God's world.

2   *Human beings are formed in communities.* This kind of education is best
    and most fully expressed in the context of communities where learners
    build relationships of trust, love, respect, and responsibility. Those
    communities might be explicitly educational settings, but they also
    include families, neighborhoods, friend groups, and religious commu-
    nities. They include the ecological community, as well.

3   *Human beings are formed as much by those things that they do as they
    are by those things that they read, or hear, or believe.* The formation of
    character—such as inhabitance—happens through engagement in
    practices, meaningful actions in which learners participate together in
    communities. These practices include liturgical action, service, fellow-
    ship, instruction, advocacy, and recreation and other embodied encoun-
    ters with particular places.

4   *Educated persons understand themselves to be responsible members of a
    larger community. Paideia* privileges the role of the community as the
    site of formation and the thriving of the community as the *outcome* of
    education. Education for ecological inhabitance cultivates in learners
    a sense of membership, connection, and responsibility to contribute to
    the larger community, including the ecological community. It cultivates
    love and commitment toward the community.

5   Having been formed as responsible members of a community, educated
    persons individually and together are obligated to *critique structures,
    ideas, and practices that consciously or unconsciously harm* members of
    that community. Complemented by the principles of liberative and
    critical pedagogy, a revisioned ecological *paideia* should incorporate
    critical literacy as a constitutive component of inhabitance. Character
    formation for ecological and social responsibility must include the
    essential capacities to critique and transform social structures—and
    even the very values and modes of education itself.[77]

Theories of religious education for participation in a society, community, or
ecosystem often appeal to the principles of *paideia* as a means of describing
and seeking the goal of individual and social flourishing.[78] Similarly, theories

of ecological education have appealed to *paideia* to reimagine education as character formation, in contrast with attempts to "stuff all kinds of facts, techniques, methods, and information into the student's mind."[79]

Religious education for inhabitance is a kind of *paideia*. It is a process of formation and, sometimes, transformation in the context of community. The faith community—indeed, the whole ecological community—both shapes human identity and calls forth humanity's best efforts to strengthen that community so that all of its members flourish together. Human beings learn who they are as ecological beings in ecological community by participating in a set of practices that both shape them and empower them to engage critically the theological and moral traditions in which they are situated. To those concrete pedagogical approaches and ecclesial practices we now turn.

4

EDUCATIONAL PRACTICES FOR INHABITANCE

Embodied, Affective, and Reflective Pedagogy

As I write this book, the city of Flint, Michigan, has not had safe drinking water for four years. Four years. Since the state switched the city's water supply from Lake Huron to the Flint River as a cost-cutting measure, bacteria, chlorine, and lead have poisoned the city's water system. The city suffered an outbreak of Legionnaire's disease. City and state public officials have concealed the risks while children and other vulnerable persons have been exposed to dangerous levels of lead in their drinking water.[1] An independent panel found that the city's residents, more than half of whom are African American and forty-two percent of whom live in poverty, were subjected to environmental injustice: "Flint residents, who are majority black or African-American and among the most impoverished of any metropolitan area in the United States, did not enjoy the same degree of protection from environmental and health hazards as that provided to other communities."[2] The situation in Flint is an environmental, economic, and public health crisis. And it cries out for a rapid response.

Also, in April 2018, researchers found a juvenile sperm whale that had washed ashore in Spain, having died from a ruptured digestive system, likely attributable to the sixty-four pounds of plastic garbage the mammal had ingested as it floated on the surface of the water in between deep dives for its prey. This was not the first such incident, and researchers believe that plastic accumulating in the planet's oceans could kill more animals than climate change.[3] Here, another crisis cries out for rapid response.

These are just two ecological crises that demand our immediate and comprehensive attention. In the face of urgent crises alongside those relating to the global food system, air quality, waste, human health, animal suffering, and land access and use, the compulsion to react, to do *something*, is very strong. And, indeed, some responses can be quickly discerned and implemented. The deliberate and long-term educational work of cultivating inhabitance, however, takes time, even when time seems short. Practical theology and Christian religious education theory, however, require the reflective mode developed by deliberate attention to the "whys" that give rise to practice.

The theory of ecological religious education here described has devoted a good bit of real estate to the exploration of its grounding theological, sociological, and pedagogical assumptions because the pedagogical temptation is strong to move directly from an analysis of the context to reactive practices— or, similarly, from a statement of purpose to prescribed practices. In contrast, this proposal for religious education for inhabitance has taken the long route, because moving directly from crisis (no matter how urgent) to action risks lingering in an unreflective, reactionary mode. Similarly, moving directly from an educational goal (no matter how laudable) to action risks failing to establish roots appropriate to a particular context and approach to learning. In the interest of ecological learning that is steadfast enough for the lifelong work of inhabitance, serious attention must be paid to the theological roots of this human vocation. Similarly, the virtues and dispositions of an inhabitant must be imagined and explored in some detail. A clear picture of who the inhabitant is—in relationship to God and embedded in a community in both the social and the ecological sense—helps to clarify the educational tasks ahead. In light of this commitment to understand ecological religious education at a level deeper than reaction or prescription, this theory has first been grounded in theological, moral, sociological, and philosophical perspective.

Finally, however, the more strategic "how" of ecological religious education comes into view. A grounded theory of religious education issues in a set of pedagogical considerations and practices in service of identified purposes. These practices arise out of the interplay between a theory's educational context and the grounding assumptions. Appropriate practices emerge only after carefully asking and answering the prior questions: What is going on? What shall religious education bring about? And what commitments shape and compel religious education?

To repeat the summary of the theory of ecological religious education articulated in the previous chapter: As ecosystems and social structures are in a season of rapid and disruptive change, ecological religious education should nurture in us the desire and capacities to be just and loving inhabitants of God's earth. Grounded in an understanding of God as creator and redeemer of the world, an understanding of ecosystems as extensions of community, and an affective and relational way of knowing the world, ecological religious education cultivates inhabitance through a set of embodied, affective, and reflective practices. Having studied the landscape, identified the deep purpose, and excavated the grounding assumptions of religious education for inhabitance, it is now time to turn to the "how": the frameworks, strategies, and practices that cultivate ecological faith. Effective and responsible pedagogical and ecclesial practices that cultivate inhabitance and its ecological dispositions are grounded in a clear understanding of how human beings best learn in a general sense and, more particularly, in holistic approaches to education that incorporate the body, the emotions, and human capacities for relationships.

PEDAGOGICAL DESIGN

How Do We Learn?

Many educators in ecclesial and other pedagogical settings now feel keenly the urgency of nurturing ecological consciousness among individual learners and communities. They may even have ideas of what an ecologically loving person or community looks like or how they might interact within their ecosystems. Absent a clear understanding of how people learn and what *kind* of learning ecological learning is, however, ecological religious education risks developing proposals that are unreflectively reactive or idealistically prescriptive. This is the hard part: thinking strategically and concretely about how ecological religious education should go about fulfilling its purpose of cultivating the dispositions, commitments, and practices of good inhabitance.

All who teach are vulnerable to making two pedagogical mistakes: assuming that the primary teaching objective is either the full and accurate transmission of content ("covering" a topic) or the implementation and facilitation of an experience that is presumed to be educative.[4] Such mistakes focus on what the *teacher* knows and will do, sometimes without reference to what the learners will understand or be able to do. These objectives begin with what the teacher knows, thinks is important, and knows how to do. These are worthy considerations, of course, in any educational theory and practice. If ecological religious education's core purpose, however, is the cultivation of good inhabitants of God's world, a theory and practice appropriate to this purpose must begin at the end, considering what good inhabitants of God's world understand, what they are able to do, and how they act in the world. Beginning at the end requires a "backwards curriculum design," in which the educator imagines a learned person—a wise person—who has experienced the kind of education envisioned and thus exemplifies the capacities and know-how that might demonstrate or serve as evidence that the desired learning has happened.[5] Backwards curriculum design begins with the question, "What should learners be able to *do* or understand?" then determines the evidence by which learning is measured, and only then considers what content, practices, or approaches will serve these named learning outcomes.[6]

With its emphasis on learners' understanding and capacities, backwards educational design is well suited for an educational purpose as holistically oriented as the cultivation of inhabitance. Pedagogies that prioritize capacities (rather than a singular focus on content) respond to the shift in what it means to "know." Beyond mastery of data or text, ecological knowing or epistemology incorporates relational knowing that sometimes is eschewed in more orthodox epistemologies. As exemplified in the scientific method, presumed objectivity is prized at the expense of intimate, familiar, subjective knowledge. This knowing at arm's length, however precise, does not necessarily elicit commitment or love from the learner. And inhabitance turns on just such capacities. If inhabitance requires a reorientation of what is considered to be salutary knowledge, or wisdom, then it requires a reorientation of the pedagogical means by which teachers and learners together seek that knowledge. Introducing learners to texts and data, particularly as a starting point for ecological religious education, is simply not robust enough a pedagogical approach for the depth of learning ecologically conscious educators most hope will happen. A pedagogical approach that privileges the development of capacities and dispositions is in order and requires attention to both the starting point and the process of learning.

Many a teacher has been saved in her class planning by Benjamin Bloom and his taxonomy, developed in the mid-twentieth century. Bloom understood learning to be a scaffolded process with each increasingly complex cognitive function building upon what came before. Learning builds upon itself. Educators sometimes mistakenly ask students to perform complex tasks before they are prepared to do such things. For example, participants in a bible study might be asked to compare one gospel's account of the feeding of the five thousand to that in another gospel. Absent familiarity with the other gospel account, or perhaps even a working understanding of the diversity in the synoptic gospels, the participants are not prepared to analyze the text in this way. When asked to perform a complex intellectual task without the necessary foundation upon which to stand, learners are likely to be confused and even discouraged.

For learners to complete successfully the most complicated assignments, they must be prepared for those complex tasks by first accomplishing more foundational tasks, which then serve as the "scaffold" upon which higher-order thinking is accomplished. Conversely, if learners are to grow in understanding, they must be challenged to move beyond the most basic cognitive tasks, using what they are learning in their own writing or project design. Learners must first be able to recall and understand basic facts and ideas, and then they are able to use and draw connections between those ideas, themes, and concepts. In the most complex tasks, learners are then equipped to evaluate or defend learned ideas and even create new work, inspired by what they have learned.[7]

Bloom's Taxonomy

create — Produce new or original work: Design, assemble, construct, conjecture, develop, formulate, author, investigate

evaluate — Justify a stand or decision: Appraise, argue, defend, judge, select, support, value, critique, weigh

analyze — Draw connections among ideas: Differentiate, organize, relate, compare, contrast, distinguish, examine, experiment, question, test

apply — Use information in new situations: Execute, implement, solve, use, demonstrate, interpret, operate, schedule, sketch

understand — Explain ideas or concepts: classify, describe, discuss, explain, identify, locate, recognize, report, select, translate

remember — Recall facts and basic concepts: Define, duplicate, list, memorize, repeat, state

Figure based on a diagram by Vanderbilt University's Center for Teaching

Students designing learning experiences in basic religious education courses might receive handouts with a buffet of verbs associated with each kind of learning in Bloom's taxonomy for their use in designing learning events. These verbs remind educators that there is more to learning than recalling or even explaining the significance of facts and concepts; and they remind them that more complex tasks like "compare" or "evaluate" require some prior understanding. Educators can draw on Bloom's taxonomy to design learning experiences that prepare learners to be active participants in society, generating new knowledge and critically engaging traditions and unexamined assumptions. Bloom's taxonomy is extraordinarily helpful in pedagogical planning for the cognitive aspects of learning.

At Candler School of Theology, the core course in religious education is called "Religious Education as Formation and Transformation." When education is cast as a process of formation or even a process of transformation, Bloom's neat and helpful taxonomy begins to feel nonetheless insufficient. Perhaps most immediately obvious is the fact that the taxonomy begins with what one "knows" or can recall. While childhood exercises of reciting bible verses, recalling the books of the bible, or memorizing catechisms are important means of engaging the resources of Christian traditions, assuming such exercises to be the definitive starting point of religious learning overlooks an essential moment for most learners: engagement.

In other words, why does the catechism matter? What life experience or fundamental question does it address? For many learners, especially adolescent and adult learners, education that does not begin with these questions may never engage the learners in the first place. As helpful as Bloom's taxonomy is in understanding the process of cognitive learning, it does not necessarily help educators understand the emotional and motivational foundations for learning.[8] For education to be exciting, engaging, and enduring, it must begin where the learners are: addressing questions that learners already bring to the subject, interpreting learners' experiences, and presenting compelling questions that learners might not yet have considered. A moment of engagement is the first moment of learning. In defense of this claim, Lee Shulman proposes a "new table of learning," which begins with engagement and then proceeds through (though perhaps not in a hierarchical order) other modes of learning that sound somewhat familiar:

- Engagement and Motivation
- Knowledge and Understanding
- Performance and Action
- Reflection and Critique
- Judgment and Design
- Commitment and Identity[9]

Notably, however, Shulman's taxonomy ends not with creating (or, in his language, "design") but with commitment. He argues that an educated person is a committed person, which then yields new opportunities for engagement, thereby making all of us perpetual learners: "In commitment, we become capable of professing our understandings and our values, our faith and our love, our skepticism and our doubts, internalizing those attributes and making them integral to our identities. . . . Commitment is both moving inward *and* connecting outward; it is the highest attainment an educated person can achieve."[10] Commitment is far more than cognitive mastery of a subject—it is a way of living informed by understanding, capacities, skills, and moral responsibility. So construed, education is for the purposes of nurturing and preparing persons for lives of commitment. Religious education for inhabitance, at its most formative and transformative potential, does exactly this. What is inhabitance, if not a life of commitment? And that kind of education cannot be rushed.

GOOD ECOLOGICAL EDUCATION TAKES TIME

Ecological imagination, ecological faith, and the way of inhabitance are not the sort of educational outcomes that can be quantified by standard rubrics or on objective tests. Certainly, such measures might offer some insight to the patterns and practices that contribute *toward* the cultivation of these capacities. Literacy (in the full sense that ecological education intends), consciousness, and imagination are not measured so precisely or efficiently, however. Religious education for inhabitance values and aspires to the formation of wisdom and character, a process of learning necessarily inefficient and difficult to measure.

In part this is a challenge of time. As educational reforms have multiplied and quantified the expectations of what learners should "achieve" in classrooms in public schools, in colleges and universities, and even in our religious communities, educators find less and less time for the necessarily slow pace of ecological learning. Ecological learning is a lifelong process with outcomes that might often be difficult to measure. As such, in an educational system fixated on personal success, allotting time to this kind of leisurely learning might feel like a luxury and a risk too great to take.

So instead, ecologically minded educators try to fit something, anything, into the curriculum that might nurture some kind of ecological learning—a short article, a video, an experiment. They try to cover the content *now* with a vague hope that the content introduced will develop roots and grow in the future. And while these constrained efforts might yield some development of ecological capacities in learners, they reflect a privileging of what might be described as "fast knowledge." Fast knowledge is increasingly homogenous and "acquired and used more rapidly and on a larger scale than ever before."[11] Driven by rapid technological change (consider how technology is used in classrooms now, contrasted with schooling as recently as twenty years ago) and the global economy (hence the dogged focus on education as a means of personal success and mobility), the quest for fast knowledge has deep implications for education in a wide range of settings. The assumptions at the root of the pedagogy of fast knowledge include many of the characteristics of rationalist or instrumentalist theories of knowledge: "Only that which can be measured is true knowledge; . . . there are no significant distinctions between information and knowledge; wisdom is indefinable, hence unimportant; . . . there are no limits to our ability to assimilate growing mountains of information."[12] These themes reflect a "progressivist" understanding of human and social development, assuming that with increased knowledge comes better living and more just practices. And yet this approach to the cultivation of knowledge overlooks risks and long-term consequences. More importantly, "for all the hype about the information age and the speed at which humans are purported to learn, the facts say that our collective learning rate is about what it has always been: rather slow."[13]

In contrast with fast knowledge, slow knowledge is careful, deliberate, and profoundly shaped by and for a particular context.[14] It is nurtured when we learn within a community motivated by affection and commitment and assumes that "wisdom, not cleverness, is the proper aim of all true learning; . . . [and that] human ignorance is not an entirely solvable problem; it is, rather, an inescapable part of the human condition."[15] By emphasizing wisdom over mastery, and honoring the limits of human understanding, slow knowledge resists the temptation to find the "quick fix" and perhaps makes room for sacred wondering and mystery. In this way it echoes Pope Francis' appeal to embrace mystery in the *Laudato Si'*: "Rather than a problem to be solved, the world is a joyful mystery to be contemplated with gladness and praise."[16]

In its insistence on the development of wisdom (*phronesis*), communities of learning, perceptions of connectedness, and appropriate humility, slow knowledge is the kind of knowledge necessary for an ecologically conscious person or community. It is cultivated together and shared, is deeply related to the context in which it is nurtured, and acknowledges—indeed, embraces— human limitations. And most importantly, it demands human patience and attentiveness. It will not be rushed. In the not rushing, in the attentiveness, wisdom is cultivated and inoculates human consciousness against the seductions of technological progress and the quick fix. Slow knowledge requires ongoing and unhurried encounters with a diverse array of forms of life and requires space to be "absorbed in the moment."[17] Furthermore, learners must not only *have* these encounters but be afforded opportunities to *pause* for reflection during and after these encounters. Slow learning couples embodied and emotionally engaged experiences with time and space for pondering the meaning and significance of those experiences.

This is not to say that spontaneous ecological encounters, moments that shock the mind and heart with wonder, awe, or grief, are not to be valued in religious ecological education. Indeed, educators must recognize the transformative power of experiences like a children's hike to a panoramic vista that elicits shouts of "whoa," or a group of evangelicals' view from a helicopter of the broken bodies of mountains, wounds inflicted by violent means of coal extraction. The sudden and dramatic insights sometimes evoked by embodied and sensory experiences, especially if accompanied by the time to take in and comprehend the experience, can inspire spiritual and ecological transformation. These divine interruptions into what learners thought they knew or understood, when recognized as such, constitute an ecological conversion of the sort Pope Francis describes, wherein divine encounter transforms human beings' relationship with the world. Education construed as a process of formation and transformation recognizes the power of transformative experiences. Their power, however, is intelligible in relationship to the ongoing, slow cultivation of ecological faith.

Can religious education afford the time required for the cultivation of "slow knowledge"? In formal educational settings, the push toward more content coverage and measurable success makes the proposal of slowing down, reading less, and reflecting more somewhat of a pedagogical and institutional risk.[18] In religious communities, "slow learning" meets other institutional pressures: in a season of anxiety about declining religious affiliations and lackluster participation in education programs, religious and educational leaders might be seduced by slick curriculum packets that promise effortless preparation *and* meaningful engagement with learners. The principle of slow knowledge, however, would suggest that efficiency and meaning are sometimes at cross-purposes. Meaning takes time.[19]

Religious education that nurtures ecological faith is in the path of slow learning. It honors what the body, what the emotions, and what the imagination "know." It is relational and spiritual. It is holistic and intersectional. It is oriented toward wisdom. The best ecological religious educational and ecclesial practices are built upon these values. Educational approaches that summon learners' bodies, emotions, and creativity in cultivating ecological commitment and imagination are required to move ecological education from cognitive understanding to the nurturing of a fundamentally ecologically oriented life. It is a way of learning that begins by engaging all the modes of ecological knowing in service of ecological commitment.

ENGAGING ECOLOGICAL EDUCATION

Without rethinking what it means to know or to learn, one might assume that embodied experience, emotional engagement, and the arts are ingredients— seasoning, if you will—to be layered atop the content-driven approach to environmental science that already appears in many school settings. However, research in educational psychology over the last fifty years suggests that human beings learn and cultivate intelligence by varied means. Educational systems that privilege reading, writing, math, and logic sometimes nurture these capacities to the exclusion of other kinds of "intelligence," including kinesthetic, interpersonal, intrapersonal, musical, and spatial intelligence. Each of these intelligences is a means of observing, interpreting, and understanding the world.[20] They require the active and intentional participation of the body, the emotions, and human creativity. In its fullest sense, engagement of the body, emotions, and creativity in ecological learning requires a great deal of intentionality and reflection. Rethinking ecological education with such care might very well challenge assumptions of how all manner of things are learned.

Engaging the Body

Perhaps primary among the questions posed by ecological educators is the role of the body in education. Theorists who advocate for a more "embodied" ecological education have noticed that the body (and its senses and movement) has been conspicuously absent in many attempts at ecological education. For example, environmental science classes and lessons do not necessarily require the students to leave their classrooms. This context for learning reinforces (perhaps as an implicit curriculum) the assumption that learning is an "indoor activity."[21] When so construed, the environment becomes something learners can study at a distance while seated at desks in a classroom or in folding chairs in the church fellowship hall. While there is undoubtedly a place for this kind of technical knowledge, ecological literacy is not limited to such "indoor skills," competencies that can be acquired primarily through reading books, seeing films, understanding graphs and diagrams, or even dissecting cadavers: "Indoor classes create the illusion that learning only occurs inside four walls, isolated from what students call, without apparent irony, the 'real world.' Dissecting frogs in biology classes teaches lessons about nature that no one in polite company would profess."[22] In this approach to education, the "real world"—a living, suffering, and dying world—remains a future and distant place in which environmental education might later be "applied."

Educational efforts that privilege "indoor skills" are not robust enough to cultivate the care and orientation of stewardship that are constitutive of inhabitance. This work requires direct encounters with nature and place alongside intentional reflection upon the meaning of those encounters.[23] The integrated involvement of the body's senses, emotions, and mind alongside is important: on its own, activity's mere movement of the body does not necessarily contribute to learning. That is to say, simply incorporating bodily movement or experience, absent opportunities to engage the experience fully, does not constitute experiential learning: "Simply because students are actively walking in the forest or are digging soil in a garden does not mean that they are necessarily somatically engaged in a way that can . . . support closeness with nature."[24] Learners need opportunities to savor the experience and to reflect upon it.

Sometimes religious educators struggle with this distinction. So liberated are they by the invitation to set aside content-delivery methods of teaching and learning, that the temptation to throw all manner of experiences at learners in faith communities is almost irresistible.[25] They then trust that experience itself is the teacher, forgetting the responsibility that a learning community (including teachers) has to interpret, integrate, and evaluate the experience. John Dewey's theory of experiential learning is thus misremembered, and we have exchanged a truncated focus on content for a truncated focus on experience. Dewey expressed his concern about exactly this potentiality.[26]

The body, its sensory capacities, the emotions, and the mind work together in the cultivation of ecological consciousness through embodied experience. One need only to look to the biographies of some of the great ecologists and naturalists to see how this works on an organic level. The most ecologically attuned writers and thinkers share certain experiences, the first of which is meaningful encounters with nature at a young age. These encounters are often shared and interpreted with wise adults who help make sense of the experience, a crucially important reflective aspect of embodied learning. Some ecologically conscious persons also are profoundly influenced by reading great works that make sense of experiences in nature. Together, experience, reflection, and reading contribute to the cultivation of a spirit of inhabitance. The body's *experience* of nature, however, is primary—and perhaps most at risk of being underappreciated: "Ecological literacy is becoming more difficult, . . . not because there are fewer books about nature, but because there is less opportunity for the direct experience of it."[27] In short, engaging the body experientially in ecological education is a necessary and primary pedagogical approach but is not in itself sufficient for the work of nurturing ecological character. While educators must be careful to incorporate opportunities for reflection, simple pauses for learners to attune their senses to their surroundings, and resources to understand the biological and geological systems underneath these experiences, the more likely scenario is that learners are not afforded the opportunities to be outdoors in the first place. When learners are invited outside the four-walled classroom, however, their sensory experience of nature, particularly when paired with caring mentors who can accompany the learners as they make sense of their experience, can be transformative. As such, this kind of learning necessarily engages learners' emotions alongside their bodies.

Engaging the Emotions

When recounting the Camp Teva mountaintop experience—when the children exclaim with abandon, "WHOAAH!"—Rabbi Fred Scherlinder-Dobb describes this delightful and poignant scene in theological terms. "That 'whoa,'" he observes, "is the beginning of prayer."[28] From an educational perspective, one might also call it the beginning of learning, a moment of bodily and emotional *engagement*. For education to be about the whole person, as *paideia* aims to be, it must work beyond, below, and around cognitive understandings and engage the affective dimensions of being human.

Given the pace of environmental science and discovery, parents and educators might feel ill-equipped in their scientific knowledge to teach children about nature. These insecurities, however, are no reason to abdicate responsibility for ecological education, because ecological education begins in sensory and emotional experience. As she observed her toddler nephew interacting with the wilds of the coast of Maine, Rachel Carson noted his emotional engagement—primarily, wonder—in all that he touched, saw, and experienced. To cultivate persons who can live attentively and indeed thrive in their ecological contexts, education must be grounded in human affection, drawing on the deepest sources of human commitments: "It is not half so important to know as to feel. If facts are the seeds that later produce knowledge and wisdom, then the emotions and the impressions of the senses are the fertile soil in which the seeds must grow."[29] Educators must look for opportunities that this work offers to expand human affections, inviting recognition that the earth, the home for all living beings, also is an appropriate object toward which people of faith and conscience might direct their emotional energies of wonder, love, grief, and hope—the dispositions of inhabitance. Cultivating inhabitance requires nurturing ecological virtues in the broad and practical sense but also requires focused attention on the ecological *affections*—the education of a heart that is open to wondering at, loving, grieving, and hoping for the world.[30]

These affections, to which others could rightly be added, each have their own contours, but they all are rooted in a desire for connection and transcendence, an erotic way of understanding the world.[31] Audre Lorde understood the power of the erotic to be the source of human beings' deepest knowledge and what connects the personal with the political (and perhaps the ecological): "for the bridge which connects them is formed by the erotic—the sensual—those physical, emotional, and psychic expressions of what is deepest and strongest and richest within each of us, being shared: the passions of love, in its deepest meanings."[32] That deep, affective knowledge is thus profoundly relational. The erotic necessarily depends on a relationship with the other, the beloved, the one remaining partially and tantalizingly unknown. It is to understand oneself to be dependent upon and responsible to other humans, communities, and, indeed, the planet. Educational and ecclesial practices that recognize and explore emotional engagement with other humans and with our ecosystems tap into deep sources of human power and wisdom.

Insofar as it engages the human body and human emotion, ecological education rests on the assumption that understanding and knowledge is cultivated through the senses and through the feelings. Learning requires the engagement of the whole self. The body and the emotions help learners more deeply and with greater complexity comprehend and appreciate the relational world in which we live. By mobilizing the body and the emotions, ecological education helps us better understand and live responsibly and lovingly with our wounded ecological context as it *is*. Ecological religious education, however, should also inculcate in learners a yearning and imagination for what could be, for the possibilities of good inhabitance in which human and nonhuman life encounter divine love and creativity in the world. To do this, education for inhabitance must summon human creativity.

Engaging Creativity

If cultivating ecological imagination is in part what ecological religious education is meant to do, it must serve to nurture the human faculties (or intelligences) necessary for that work. It invites learners beyond the perception of the real to conceive, dream, and implement other possibilities. Certainly, a theology of hope demands precisely this. In order to imagine possibilities not yet born, ecological religious education must also nurture and engage human creativity through play and the arts. The arts "have a unique power to release imagination."[33] In the creative spaces of the arts and play, the emotions and bodies are mobilized in a way that engages creative tensions and possibilities.

Theologically speaking, play and other spaces for creativity hold numinous potential not afforded to learners by other, more traditional means. Play is, in short, revelatory, and pedagogical approaches that invite learners to engage play with creativity and imagination prepare them to recognize and participate in divine creativity in the world.[34] In its imaginative capacities, play can disrupt—disorient, even—human awareness, opening space for an encounter with divine mystery and the possibilities of participating in that mystery.[35] In so doing, it is the site of wonder. Human beings at play, furthermore, not only encounter divine creativity but learn new and creative ways of relating to other human beings and, one might argue, the world.[36]

Space for play is sometimes undervalued in educational settings in the United States. In public schools one site of emerging tension is the purpose and place of recess. Like arts curricula, the traditionally unstructured, unprogrammed daily time for children to be outdoors has been sacrificed in recent years to make more time for those subjects in which standardized testing looms: math, English, science, and social studies. Cities like Atlanta and Chicago have cut out recess time entirely.[37] As research increasingly raises critical questions about efficacy and reliability of standardized testing, parents and educational policy analysts are asking, "What have we lost by cutting programs in arts and time for recess?"[38]

In unstructured recess programs, children are responsible for determining how to spend the time, finding and choosing available resources to use, organizing themselves into groups based on shared preference for activities, resolving conflicts, and ensuring fair play.[39] Activities might include traditional games like kickball or pickup basketball, but when the option is presented to them, many children choose to play in the woods or other natural areas near the school.[40] Woods, creeks, forests, and other natural areas offer children boundless ideas and materials for creative play. As one child put it, when in the woods, "I can just be my own self . . . just create anything I want to. I can just go down there, be wild."[41] This eleven-year-old child names clearly how unstructured time outdoors cultivates creativity.

One practice that some teachers are implementing is issuing to the students a loose commission to build "fairy houses" in wild areas on school grounds. A fairy house is exactly what it sounds like, a simple (or sometimes elaborate) abode for a tiny fairy or other woodland creature, constructed of materials found in the woods. When invited to create these structures in the woods, children prove remarkably resourceful, strategic, collaborative, and visionary in building the fairy houses (in some cases, fairy villages, complete with commerce and public services!).

Actual assent to the existence of fairies aside, the task of creating a home in which a fairy might live and thrive invites children to consider a variety of factors in what makes for a good place to live. They learn what kinds of leaves, stones, and feathers are available in those woods. They learn empathy as they try to make life more comfortable for their imagined inhabitants. As one plan works and another does not, children learn to cooperate, learn from each other, and improvise.[42] For these ideas to emerge, however, children need ample time in nature and enough freedom to imagine together. The character of the fairy offers children an opportunity to imagine a good life for another being, to see the world from another perspective.

Somatic, emotional, and creative understandings are essential capacities for ecological consciousness. Without attending to the ways in which learners know through their bodies, their feelings, and their imaginations, ecological education will be truncated, confined to the mastery of facts and solutions. And, as ecological education theorists have argued, a so-truncated ecological education runs the risk of perpetuating technical responses to our environmental challenges. Ecological learning limited to the acquisition of facts and development of solutions does not fundamentally shape the human person in virtue and affections. No, inhabitants need their bodies, feelings, and imaginations for that work. This education of the whole person—body, mind, emotions, and creativity—is a kind of *paideia* reimagined in an ecological frame. It yields a reoriented identity and sense of commitment. And this concern for the formation of ecological character of Christian life is the heart beating at the center of ecological religious education.[43]

ECOLOGICAL RELIGIOUS EDUCATION

To review: As ecosystems and social structures are in a season of rapid and disruptive change, ecological religious education should nurture in Christians the desire, capacities, and commitment to be just and loving inhabitants of God's earth. Grounded in an understanding of God as creator and redeemer of the world, an understanding of ecosystems as extensions of community, and an affective and relational way of knowing the world, ecological religious education cultivates inhabitance through a set of embodied, affective, and reflective practices. It is thus a peculiar kind of *paideia* by which human character and community commitments are formed. The kind of commitment under consideration here is ecological commitment or, in a theological frame, *ecological faith*, a faith that turns on the capacities necessary to inhabit God's world well. It is a way of life seeking to become loving, just, and responsible members of God's household, the way of *inhabitance*. Ecological faith comprises a set of dispositions or virtues that attune Christian consciousness to its ecological context, its ecological roots, and its ecological responsibility. These affections and virtues are cultivated in response to a God who creates, sustains, and renews the world, drawing the inhabitant closer to God and to the world infused with divine love.

In sum, then, *ecological religious education is the ongoing nurture of inhabitance—ecological faith and commitment—through a set of practices and reflection that engage human bodies, emotions, and creativity.* First, it implies the *ongoing nurture of inhabitance.* In other words, ecological religious education is an incremental, lifelong process. Learners never quite "arrive" at ecological faith. It is *incremental* in the way that slow knowledge is cultivated: bit by bit, with time to process and reflect, and at a pace that allows people of faith and conscience to fully engage and internalize each new insight and summons. It is *lifelong* in that it is something not intended for children (although research in the field convicts us that childhood experiences in nature are essential to ecological learning) but for learners in the unique seasons of adolescence, emerging adulthood, career and family establishment, midlife, and old age.[44] New awareness, new commitment, new experiences of wonder, love, grief, and hope are ever-present potentialities, even for the wisest of inhabitants. Religious education, then, must continually nurture the dispositions of ecological faith in a variety of settings and among a variety of learners.

By attending to inhabitance, ecological religious education nurtures not only ecological *faith* but also ecological *commitment.* Indeed, commitment is a core component of ecological faith (in its attuning of Christian consciousness to its ecological responsibility) and warrants special mention here. The cultivation of commitment is a constitutive part of *paideia* education, and without attention to the ways in which ecological religious education contributes to the formation of moral consciousness and responsibility, it treads very close to romanticizing, spiritualizing, and even exploiting the ecological context. In other words, absent a concerted effort to connect ecological affections with ecological virtue and responsibility, ecological religious education risks superficiality and short-changes its moral power.

Through a *set of practices and reflection,* ecological religious education does this work. It is clear that practices that *engage body, emotion, and creativity* are necessary to inspire and encourage inhabitance. As ecological education scholars, religious education scholars, and virtue ethicists alike have noted, it is through practices—complex sets of activities and beliefs that contain within them some sort of benefit or salutary effect for the practitioners and their communities—that identity, character, and commitment are formed.[45] The practical wisdom necessary to be inhabitants "can only be derived from the experience of doing."[46] Practices are the means by which virtues (including ecological virtues) are cultivated, nurturing "people capable of acting with wisdom, foresight, and love."[47] Education that attends carefully to practice marshals all kinds of human knowing and intelligence (bodily, emotional, creative) in service of ecological faith. Practices must include or be coupled with *reflection*, an opportunity to place embodied, affective experience into the realm of consciousness and ideas. In so doing, inhabitants gain new insights, identify new questions, and establish new trajectories for the deepening of ecological faith and commitment.

PRACTICES OF INHABITANCE

Many and diverse Christian communities have been doing ecological religious education for a long time, often without describing it as such. However, members of these communities have learned through tradition, practice, and reflection how to live well in a place. They have learned how to be open to God's creative presence in their local communities, in their bioregions, and in their world. They see the interrelatedness of some of the most pressing moral questions of our time: climate crises, economic injustice, public health, the breakdown of community. Each religious community has a unique "starting point" when it comes to cultivating inhabitance. For some, the ecological aspects of Christian faith and ministry come into focus out of necessity, as an extension of economic justice concerns or public health concerns. For others, ecological faith is born out of a congregation's mission, a commitment inspired by theological and ecological ideas that speak to that community's sense of purpose and identity. Finally, ecological faith sometimes comes into focus for a community because of the place in which it finds itself: rivers, cities and neighborhoods, beaches, wildernesses, and rural farmlands all issue invitations to the religious communities within their ecosystems to relate to the particularities of that place in a particular way.

When surveying communities engaged in ecological faith practices, a set of shared themes emerge that serve to mark the distinctiveness of a particular community's approach to ecological faith as well as offer a shared set of principles, practices, or perspectives that constitute ecological faith. This list of themes is not by any stretch exhaustive but points to some of the resonances and tensions between ecological faith as described above and the living, breathing, faltering communities that seek to live well in their places.

Inhabitance Is Attentive to Place

Communities often choose ecological practices that emerge from and respond directly to their communities and ecosystems. Rural communities engage agricultural questions; urban communities engage questions of food access, environmental health, and green space; seaside and riverside communities engage questions of marine life and watershed protections. In some cases, however, transience is as much a community identity-marker as is place. Some congregations are home for migrant communities, living far from the places most deeply significant to them. Other communities are made up of persons who are homeless or housing insecure. Their relationship to place precludes simplistic or romantic odes to pastoral tableaus. Even in its absence, however, the role of place in forming ecological faith is worthy of exploration.

Often, place figures prominently in the worship life of a community. Some pastors and other religious leaders reimagine the liturgical life with an eye toward the place in which worship is happening. Some congregations bring explicitly ecological and agrarian material and symbols into traditional liturgical forms and spaces, while other communities press the boundaries of what constitutes liturgy, making planting or hiking acts of worship.

Inhabitance Embraces Vulnerability

Inhabitance is embedded in the poignant dance between death and life. As a colleague once told me, when he welcomed his infant son, he looked at the vulnerable creature in his arms and was struck that this being would one day die. "To love anyone is to love a dying thing," he said.[48] Certainly, this is true of the life of inhabitance and the real possibilities for suffering and grief that it introduces. Ecological practices touch every point in the life cycle: seed germination, birth, illness, injury, decline, and death. Participants engage these dynamics in the natural world even as they engage them in their human lives.

In that it attends to the ambiguities, joys, and sufferings of human life, inhabitance is also necessarily holistic and intersectional. Holistic ecological faith comprehends the ways in which human beings are inhabitants of communities both human and nonhuman. Certainly, "ecological faith" connotes for some a romanticized, white-privileged concern, one that only communities who do not face more basic and immediate threats to their well-being (such as poverty, racism, violence, and health disparities) have the luxury to address. However, many communities of faith are engaged in practices that might be described as ecological in its most holistic sense, attending to questions of economic resilience, gender, human health, and spirituality. Inhabitance always has in view the flourishing of human life alongside the flourishing of nonhuman life. Indeed, their well-being is mutually dependent.

As it embraces the real possibilities of suffering and harm in the world, inhabitance also embraces delight and wonder. As a fundamentally embodied way of life, it honors recreation as an essential practice of Christian and ecological life. Many communities host opportunities for members and persons in the larger community to participate in recreational practices that place their bodies in direct relationship to nature: cooking out, floating down a river, fishing, and hiking. Sometimes these embodied practices are explicitly tied to theological or liturgical ideas, while sometimes they are a means for a religious community to play together. This is not to say that play is without theological implications, but quite the contrary: that the recreation *itself* is saturated with theological meaning known to human bodies, inviting them into creativity and joy, apart from any formal connection to more ideational theological claims.

Inhabitance Cultivates Community

Even as they connect persons of faith and conscience to particular places, practices of inhabitance also contribute to the establishment and maintenance of human community. In some cases ecological practices serve the more specific goal of nurturing human communities and the affective, economic, and social bonds therein. In other cases ecological practices serve to nurture human relationships to the ecosystem, and this relationship is an end in and of itself, an extension of community to include nonhuman life. In both cases the human relationships built in the living out of inhabitance grow in both complexity and in depth.

The life of inhabitance is aided, for example, by the nurture of intergenerational relationships. Children often are endowed with capacities for ecological wonder that is sometimes difficult for adults to experience. And yet, they need the mentoring of wise adults who can help them to interpret their experiences with nature. For these reasons, ecological practices that invite the unguarded emotional engagement of children and the accumulated wisdom of adults have the potential to educate persons and communities on a deeper level.

Furthermore, the bonds of community nurtured in ecological practices extend beyond the congregation or immediate social group. Inhabitance is a collaborative way of life and thus is necessarily institutionally porous. Some congregations begin ecological practices and ministries on their own steam.[49] However, many more do so by collaborating with other organizations in the community, both religious and secular. They form partnerships with environmental organizations, local community service organizations, farmers, collaboratives, and so on. They may participate in the local economy.[50] In so doing, they strengthen community relationships and expand their expertise and the boundaries of what is possible for one religious community to do. Indeed, some of these religious organizations are so institutionally porous and nimble that they stretch the boundaries of what constitutes a faith community.

Place. Vulnerability. Community. These aspects of ecological practices invite Christians to deeper understanding of God, self, community, and the world. Christians who have embraced and committed themselves to the way of inhabitance learn new ways of relating to themselves, to their communities, and to the places in which they live. The practices that invite people of faith and conscience to attend carefully to the ways in which place has figured in their story and in their way of life, and to embrace the vulnerability of being embodied and emotionally responsive members of a habitat, bear implications for the construction and maintenance of human community. Inhabitance affords a way of life that is profoundly present, seeking always the possibility for deeper engagement and relationship. It is to recognize and find the courage and creativity to respond to the mystery of God's loving and acting in the world.

5

LOCATED, DISLOCATED, RELOCATED

Religious Education and the Power of Place

> I doubt that we can ever come to love the planet as some claim to do,
> but I know that we can learn to love particular places...[1]

Rev. Stuart Taylor is a religious leader deeply invested in the work of inhabitance. When he arrived at Elkin Presbyterian Church, he immediately set about learning his new place, having arrived from the arid, open, and dramatic landscape of the southwestern United States. Even in his first year of preaching sermons at Elkin Presbyterian, Taylor demonstrated a remarkable commitment to read and understand the contours of the ecosystem in the Yadkin Valley. In one of his very first sermons, for example, he describes praying and walking alongside Basin Creek, a walk he must have taken within a few days of arriving, and after which he knew enough to speak knowledgeably about the place. Taylor's personal and professional life has been invested in the work of ecological faith—inhabiting God's world well—and that work has been intimately and *profoundly located*. He understands that ecological faith is formed and expressed in the particular rather than in the abstract. He knows and loves the particulars of a place, a relationship that then makes possible his more expansive knowledge of and love for humanity, creation, and God. And he understands that a human life is given meaning and a story by the places we inhabit. In a sermon preached not long after his arrival, he observed about Francis of Assisi and about human beings:

> As a youth Francis would be gone for days, wandering about in the forests or over the hillsides. There is no doubt in my mind that the geography of that place shaped and formed his soul. What was true for Francis is probably true for many of us—that the place on the earth where we grew

up or live now will have a formative impact on the geography of our own souls. How does living in the foothills of the Blue Ridge Mountains give shape to your own soul and mine? Hiking recently near the Blue Ridge parkway I had the joyful sense that we live in the Garden of Eden and that I was walking through paradise. What is your special place of beauty? Where have you been deeply touched by the natural world? Remember that and you know how Francis felt toward all the earth and how we might ourselves feel toward all of God's good creation.[2]

"If you don't know where you are . . . you don't know *who* you are," Wallace Stegner begins his essay "The Sense of Place."[3] An observation convicting in its simplicity, it is a powerful commentary on the relationship between place-consciousness and human identity. This trenchant insight, which he attributes to Wendell Berry, rightly identifies the relationship between place and how human beings understand themselves. In fact, the quote likely originates with Ralph Ellison's *The Invisible Man*, in an exchange between the narrator, who lives underground in an urban setting, and a man in need of directions.[4] The origins of the aphorism are significant to the cultivation of inhabitance because although Wendell Berry writes beautifully about rural landscapes and the sense of place, Ellison's *Invisible Man* invokes the same capacities to know a place in an urban environment. In other words, capacities to know and love a place are not particular to a rural, pastoral ideal. In whatever place a person or community finds themselves, that place shapes who they are and cries out for their love and their commitment.

Religious education for inhabitance is deeply embedded in and responsive to particular places. In cities, in suburbs, in small towns and rural crossroads, ecological faith is *in profound and contested ways located*. Whether human beings' habitats are dotted by fields or sidewalks, forests or window boxes, stars or streetlights, ecological religious education prepares them to be attentive, loving, and responsible inhabitants of those places. This chapter explores what it means to be related to particular places and describes ecclesial and pedagogical practices that contribute to this capacity.

THE POWER OF PLACE IN HUMAN LIFE

Black feminist scholar bell hooks is a person profoundly located. With a brilliant mind, ambitious scholarly agenda, and passion for teaching, hooks earned appointments at prestigious universities and colleges in urban centers like Yale and Southern California, places that one might assume would be more hospitable to scholars of color than the rural southern community in

which she grew up. She discovered that racism was not solely a rural or southern problem, experiencing racism in urban environments and elite intellectual
communities. On a level so deep that it surprised even her, however, she also
missed her Kentucky Appalachian roots. She longed for the freedom to run
through the hills of the backcountry, and the complicated social networks
of Appalachia. While her friends were surprised by her decision to return to
the rural south, hooks felt strongly that she was meant to relocate herself in
the midst of the ecosystem of her childhood, with all of its joys, relationships,
freedoms, histories, and wounds: "Coming home to live in Kentucky was for
me a journey back to a place where I felt I belonged. But it was also returning
to a place that I felt needed me and my resources, a place where I as a citizen
could be in community with other folk seeking to revive and renew our local
environment, seeking to have fidelity to a place."[5]

hooks shares her love for and commitment to rural Kentucky with agrarian writer Wendell Berry. As a writer, Berry enjoyed early success, finding
himself traveling the world as a Guggenheim Fellow and landing a coveted
faculty appointment at New York University.[6] He stayed there only two years,
however, finding the pull of his Kentucky home to be an irresistible force:
"I knew that I had not escaped Kentucky, and had never really wanted to. I
was still writing about it, and had recognized that I would probably need to
write about it for the rest of my life. Kentucky was my fate—not an altogether
pleasant fate, though it had much that was pleasing in it, but one that I could
not leave behind simply by going to another place."[7]

Although both hooks and Berry might rightly be cast as "success stories"
in the U.S. educational system, as exemplars of upward mobility who have
left behind the cultural and economic constraints of rural southern life, their
vocational trajectories challenge that narrative of education.[8] Instead of
education being the path out of a place, it was for each of them the path back
into a place. When they vocalized their desires to return to Kentucky, both
were greeted with consternation by academic mentors and colleagues.[9] Berry
and hooks, however, experience themselves as claimed by a place—indeed,
the same place, Kentucky—without romanticizing that place. They understand who they are, in part, in relationship to the place that shaped them and
as moral agents with a responsibility to that place in the present and future.

In contemporary educational theory and practice, "pedagogies of place"
are popping up everywhere. To understand the role of place-based pedagogy
in the ecological religious education's cultivation of inhabitance, one must first
understand what is meant by the category "place." Place-consciousness, or a
sense of place, is "the competent and knowledgeable affection for a specific

locality."[10] Thus it involves understanding, human affections, and a relationship with a particular place. It requires attention to the "immediate and the mundane."[11] As discussed above, although people of faith and conscience may sense some urgency in addressing larger planetary crises of water access, climate change, and waste, environmentalists, educators, and ecotheologians agree: it is in knowing and loving a particular place that human beings know and love the planet.[12] Describing one of the seasons in which he found himself away from his homeplace, Wendell Berry writes: "I had come to be aware of it as one is aware of one's body; it was present to me whether I thought of it or not. When I have thought of the welfare of the earth, the problems of its health and preservation, the care of its life, I have had this place before me, the part representing the whole more vividly and accurately, making clearer and more pressing demands, than any *idea* of the whole."[13] This poignant observation parallels the tension between noticing the intimate details of the small and apprehending a limitless universe, between loving a particular place and loving the planet. If one cannot love the world in part, what is nearest—as near as one's own body—there remains little chance of loving the whole in any real way. Ecological faith is profoundly located. Indeed, larger ecological crises may very well be rooted in an epidemic crisis of human beings failing to love their particular places.[14]

The idea of a "place" is geographical, cultural, narrative, sociological, and political. It is more than the topographical facts of a site or a region, though it certainly includes that. A location becomes a *place* when it is imbued with meaning, with histories, and with contestations. Indeed, a shorthand for what is meant by the category "place" is "space plus character," attending to the relationship between geographical location and the human soul.[15] Place is constructed both individually and socially, so it comes alive between geography, story, and relationships. A place derives its formative power from history—from the experiences human beings have had there and the narratives that persons and communities have constructed about it.[16] So, when bell hooks and Wendell Berry choose to return home to Kentucky, they each are demonstrating and articulating the ways in which the Appalachian hills make deep sense as "place."

The lure of such homeplaces is strong. The cultivation of place-consciousness, however, is not confined to the literal return to a homeplace, a foregone conclusion of the outworking of history, biography, and geography. The work of place-consciousness is the perpetual work to *become* native to this place, as Wes Jackson has put it. In other words, place-consciousness is also oriented toward the future, evidence of a desire to become inhabitants even in new places. Education for inhabitance, in contrast with education for upward mobility, should "validate and educate those who want to be homecomers— not necessarily to go home but to go someplace and dig in and begin the long search and experiment to become native."[17]

Certainly, Rev. Stuart Taylor is a "homecomer" in this sense. Although he grew up in the southeastern United States, he returned to a new place in North Carolina after a vocational trajectory that took him to seminary in Princeton, New Jersey; to Central America and Washington, D.C., as a peace activist; and to Arizona as a Presbyterian minister. In each setting, he developed his capacities to "dig in" and learn the place. As career mobility makes it easier to live as a casual resident in a number of places in one's lifetime, committing to know and love a place is a countercultural way of being. This is as true for religious leaders as it is for accountants, academics, and technology entrepreneurs. The theological framing of vocation often turns on a pattern of being called or sent—responding to and following a divine summons.[18] A religious community with such place-conscious leaders, however, can provide an alternative theological view of vocation and work, thus becoming precisely the educational setting needed to nurture this countercultural way of being. To become inhabitants, Christians need leaders who inhabit their neighborhoods, their communities, and their bioregions well, and who understand this work as central to human vocation.[19]

Ecological educational practices might be inspired by a wide range of relationships to the places in which they emerge. Sometimes ecological practices emerge with a sense of urgency to respond to an environmental crisis in a community. Some ecological practices respond to the complex challenges and opportunities presented by the economic, environmental, and cultural histories of a community. In yet other cases, ecological practices are rooted in a desire to preserve sacred and beloved aspects of a landscape: a forest, an ocean, a prairie, a desert, a river. Each of these approaches to religious education and ecological consciousness relate specifically and reflectively to the particular places in which they are located.

"A RIVER FLOWS THROUGH US"

ELKIN PRESBYTERIAN CHURCH

Stuart Taylor's congregation, Elkin Presbyterian Church, sits across the street from the Elkin City Park and just about a mile north of where the Big Elkin Creek joins up with the Yadkin River. Founded in 1892, the congregation nearly closed its doors during the Depression but today is home to 150

members. In 2013, the congregation called Taylor to be their pastor, and he
came with a deep desire to know and understand this place in which he would
be living. And he wanted to invite the congregation into a deeper relationship with their place. That place is the town of Elkin, North Carolina, in the
region of the Appalachian foothills known as Yadkin Valley. Yadkin Valley
is a wine-making region with as many as thirty-five wineries and designated
as North Carolina's "first federally-recognized American Viticulture Area."[20]

Elkin, proclaiming itself "the best little town in North Carolina," is a
town of five thousand situated in the foothills of the northwestern corner of
the state, halfway between Winston-Salem and the Appalachian Mountains.
Elkin is one of a handful of small towns dotting the Yadkin Valley, among
them the town of Mount Airy, where Andy Griffith was born and upon which
the fictional town of Mayberry was based. Politically speaking, Elkin itself is
politically moderate to conservative, although it is situated across two of the
most politically conservative counties in the state (Wilkes and Surry).[21] Love
and affection for a particular place, though, transcends political and cultural
ideology. In a political season in which ideas like environmentalism, what's
"green," and regulations and protections draw more resistance than agreement
in this region, the human experience of affection for a place is significant.
Home to trails, rivers, and rolling hills, the greater Yadkin Valley is bordered
by the Blue Ridge Parkway to the west, the Yadkin River to the south, and the
Virginia state line to the north. It might be described as a bioregion, defined by
its landscape rather than by legislative decree. A primary means of determining what constitutes a bioregion is identifying its watershed. A watershed is an
area of land that drains to one stream, lake, or river. Every human being lives
in a watershed, as all land is part of a watershed. In other words, all activity
that happens on the land eventually, through systems of drainage, makes its
effects known in the water supply.[22] Certainly, the histories of indigenous
tribes testify to the power of the watershed. As many as twelve thousand
years before Elkin was established as a town, the Yadkin River basin was a
center for human life, culture, and commerce among indigenous tribes and
nations, including, first, smaller tribes from the Sioux linguistic groups and,
later, larger communities from the Cherokee nation.[23]

As a bioregion Elkin is distinctly marked by its big tree-lined watershed
and by the awareness that "a river flows through us."[24] Indeed, verdant images
of the creeks and rivers that meet in the town of Elkin grace the covers of
tourist brochures and website homepages.[25] The communities of the Yadkin
Valley are proud of their watershed, and for some of them that pride translates to a deep desire to protect it. The Yadkin Riverkeeper, one of fourteen

Waterkeeper Alliance organizations in North Carolina, sponsors regular education, clean-up, arts, and advocacy programs.[26] These programs serve the organization's mission "to respect, protect and improve the Yadkin Pee Dee River Basin through education, advocacy and action."[27]

Thus, when Stuart Taylor arrived in 2013, he found several eager companions in his desire to understand and love his new habitat, the Yadkin Valley bioregion, and, more particularly, the Yadkin Pee Dee watershed. He wasted no time. Four months into Taylor's pastorate, in September 2013, the elders of the congregation approved a two-year emphasis on the Stewardship of Creation. Over the course of that first year, the congregation had undertaken a bible study engaging creation themes, called "The Green Bible"; members of the congregation attended a Moravian conference on environmental issues, which featured watershed stewardship as a major theme; the congregation hosted a presentation on the watershed and coal ash spills by the Yadkin Riverkeeper; and Taylor participated in a conference on watershed discipleship with theologian and activist Ched Myers.[28] During the summer, the congregation put together a flotilla and paddled in the Tour de Yadkin. Elkin Presbyterian partnered with other interested congregations to bring a performance artist who explores ecospiritual themes, to plan a creation-themed sermon series, and to conduct energy audits. The congregation produced an exhaustive list of forty-seven "Environmental Action Steps for Elkin Presbyterian." In short, the theme of creation care infused every aspect of the congregation's ministry: worship, fellowship, formal and informal education settings, mission and outreach, even facilities management.

During this same time period, Taylor preached around twenty sermons on ecological themes. In a sermon shortly following the session's endorsement of the creation-care emphasis, Taylor shared some of his dreams with the congregation:

> I am very excited about this mission focus because it builds on the history of this congregation that has been so active on the environmental front. And I am excited about this mission focus on stewardship of creation because it allows us to be tremendously creative. What if Elkin Presbyterian Church as part of an environmental mission focus were to lead an ecumenical effort to write a pastoral letter on another great American River—the Yadkin?[29] What if as a congregation we did a river trip for ourselves floating down the Yadkin, appreciating its beauty, learning about its wonders, and its challenges, preparing ourselves to become better stewards of this great river? I am very hopeful that the church can play a critical role in protecting the environment and becoming river-keepers who understand the sacredness of all God's rivers.[30]

Indeed, watershed discipleship *would* emerge as the central theme of that emphasis. Watershed discipleship identifies the watershed as the context in which discipleship is lived out; reimagines the human being as a student (disciple) *of* the watershed; and articulates our current challenges as a "watershed moment," an opportunity and challenge to Christian frameworks for understanding and living in ecological context.[31] The connection emerged organically because several members of the congregation had long worked with the Yadkin Riverkeeper. During the first year of the Stewardship of Creation emphasis, furthermore, both the pastor and members of the congregation had learned about the theology and practice of watershed discipleship and now stood ready to commit themselves to a series of practices—recreation, conservation, and advocacy—that would draw them closer to these rivers that have so fundamentally shaped their town and bioregion.

By November 2014, Elkin Presbyterian had cohosted an organizing meeting for WatershedNOW, a regional collaborative that has brought together religious communities, local government, public schools, the local arts council, the hospital, and community environmental and neighborhood organizations. The organizing meeting, hosted at the First United Methodist Church in Elkin, made special plea to religious communities: "Congregations will be inspired to take better care of the earth by understanding where we are in the watershed. Without fully embracing [humanity's] part in our watershed, people are separated from their impact to the water and natural resources they rely on in their daily lives and in worship."[32] Although WatershedNOW is not itself a religious organization, its leaders' roots remain deeply theological. In fact, a promotional video for the project opens with the images and sounds of a quietly burbling stream and Stuart Taylor's voice: "We cannot take water for granted. Water is sacred. Water is life."[33] That language would be familiar to members of Elkin Presbyterian, who heard him make the same affirmations in a sermon titled "A River Flows through Us." In that sermon Taylor recounted the story of the Baptism of Jesus, wondering aloud what the River Jordan might have to do with the Yadkin Pee Dee Watershed. He recalled his first impression of the small town where he had now been for two years: "I thought, Wow—a river running through it. And then once here, I began to learn more and more about the wonders of this, our Yadkin River, and the surrounding watershed." Interpreting the gospel story of Jesus' baptism, Taylor went on to relate the biblical context of the Jordan River to the Yadkin River:

> What would it mean for us as baptized Christians, to move from an understanding of the sacred water of our baptism to an understanding

of the sacredness of all water? . . . If you were to retell the story of Jesus' baptism here and now what river would you choose—the Mitchell, Big Elkin Creek, and the Yadkin? And who would be our John the Baptist? And what bird would you choose for the Holy Spirit? Instead of a dove we could pick a kingfisher, a wood duck, a hummingbird.[34]

Demonstrated over a series of sermons in the course of two years, Taylor's intimate and detailed knowledge of the Yadkin Valley, the watershed, and the community in which he is serving becomes readily apparent. His ongoing invitations to the congregation to locate their Christian faith more precisely within that place are clear and compelling. And if congregational and ecumenical decisions and practices are any indication, there are many people of faith now learning, in new ways, how to become inhabitants of that place. Elkin Presbyterian Church started with a general two-year mission emphasis on the stewardship of creation that rather quickly converged around the theme of watershed discipleship. While these practices certainly respond to environmental challenges in the broader Yadkin Valley—population growth and development have contributed to soil erosion and sediment run-off into the rivers and lakes in the watershed, for example—the beating heart of watershed discipleship is, in short, love and a fierce urge to protect the river that is the source of life, beauty, and joy in the community.

And yet one must be careful not to romanticize the idea of place. Elkin is a small town in a rather rural part of North Carolina. Green space abounds, and the rolling hills of the Yadkin Valley beckon inhabitants and appreciative visitors to know more about the river, the hills, and the landscape. People who grew up in Elkin recall it with love and affection. It is as if Elkin is the kind of community that many who write about nurturing a consciousness of place have in mind. It is understandable, then, that for some, calls to attend to "place" smack of atavism, a rural ideal, and the economic privilege wrapped up in land ownership. It may also sound like a summons to an earlier era that feels quite removed from and even at odds with important gains in women's, human, and labor rights.

Indeed, the appeal to a rural ideal is sometimes quite explicit.[35] There are, however, many ways in which the rural ideal inadequately represents the work of cultivating a sense of place. First, residents in many rural communities, particularly agricultural communities, are not any more place-conscious than other communities. Indeed, the exodus of industry, public services, and even grocery stores from rural communities means that many rural residents must commute great distances for work and basic household needs. Second, to think only of the rural when thinking about a sense of place is to ignore the plain fact that humans are *part of nature*. Thus, the built environment, the humans who construct and live within it, and the bioregional context are together aspects of a place.[36] The theological vocation of inhabitance turns on the idea of the human as a member of the ecosystem. A member with disproportionate power, but a member, nonetheless.

CRITICAL PEDAGOGIES OF PLACE

Rather than a rural ideal of place, perhaps what is needed is a critical pedagogy of place that takes as its primary objective the nurture of the well-being of persons *and* the places they inhabit.[37] This is what a good inhabitant does. As such, place-based education is community-based, taking into account all of the resources, beauty, and struggles in a given place, whether that place be rural, wilderness, urban, small town, or suburban. It is not romantic, idealistic, or necessarily old-fashioned. In many religious communities, ecological faith is born in a deep awareness of the beauty *and* wounds of the particular communities and ecosystems in which they are situated. Religious education that attends seriously to particular places, and that nurtures a sense of love and commitment toward particular places, must take into account these diverse places and the diverse relationships that persons and communities have to these places.

Critical place-based pedagogies do exactly this. They bring together the relatively recently developed concepts of place-based pedagogy and the long and powerful legacies of Paulo Freire and the broader field of critical pedagogy. Many tensions between place-based and critical pedagogies are immediately apparent: place-based pedagogies sometimes emphasize rural and ecological contexts to the exclusion of urban, cultural, and economic concerns, while critical pedagogies sometimes fail to recognize that the human, political, and economic systems they seek to address are embedded in ecological systems.[38] The two approaches, however, share a concern for knowing and understanding the context—the *situation*—in which learning is happening. "[Human beings] *are* because they *are in* a situation," Paulo Freire observed.[39] While Freire primarily meant the sociocultural and economic situation, critical *place*-based learning expands the pedagogical imagination to include the ecological situation. A critical pedagogy of place encourages learners to understand and analyze their socioecological places, and it encourages learners to "reinhabit" those places with the intention of living well within them, seeking the well-being of the place and all of its inhabitants.[40] Thus critical place-consciousness is needed in urban places just as urgently as it is needed in rural places. It is needed in Yadkin County, North Carolina, and it is needed in Chicago, Illinois.

"BY ANY GREENS NECESSARY"

Trinity United Church of Christ

As members, neighbors, and visitors approach Trinity United Church of Christ on 95th Street on the historic South Side of Chicago, they are greeted with one of two vibrant billboards. One of the billboards reads, "Taste and See," and features an image of a smiling child eating a perfectly ripe strawberry, while the other reads, "By Any Greens Necessary," and features an image of a table overflowing with fresh produce. Both signs, funded by a grant from the U.S. Department of Agriculture, are advertising the Trinity UCC Farmers Markets. The two messages are reflective of the congregation's identity, mission, and relationship to its neighborhood and bioregion. Trinity and its pastoral leadership comprise a religious community deeply embedded in and committed to the well-being of its larger socioecological context.

Trinity United Church of Christ, a historical, social, and political force on the South Side of Chicago, is perhaps best known to many as the home congregation of former president Barack Obama and former first lady Michelle Obama. Trinity was established in the apex of the civil rights movement in 1961 as a congregation in the United Church of Christ focused on liberation and social justice, with the motto "Unashamedly Black, Unapologetically Christian." Trinity's history and theological identity is rooted in the black liberation tradition, drawing on political and intellectual figures like Stokely Carmichael and W. E. B. DuBois. Rev. Dr. Jeremiah Wright arrived as pastor in 1972, serving for more than thirty-five years until his retirement in 2008. During his tenure the congregation's membership grew from fewer than one hundred persons to more than eight thousand. True to its mission, the congregation has established some seventy ministries, many of which have sought to strengthen the local community through education, housing, healthcare, and community development. The congregation's worship, education, and arts ministries are deeply committed to the recounting and celebration of African and African American cultures.

This historic legacy of community service and social justice was entrusted to Rev. Dr. Otis Moss III when Wright retired in 2008. Moss and his spouse, Monica Moss, brought with them a vision to extend the social justice of the congregation to include environmental justice and community development. Right away, they established a Green Team, whose work has been very closely aligned with the congregation's identity. During Moss's tenure, in addition to the Green Team, the congregation has established a community garden, water barrel distribution, a home winterization initiative, a green building initiative, and the weekly farmers markets. The most ambitious ecological project, however, is the planned Imani Village, a multiuse community a few blocks east of Trinity. Imani Village promises green building, a food hub and urban agriculture, affordable housing, educational and recreational programming, and accessible health care. Built upon the foundation of a "theo-social vision of sustainable, ethical economic development, designed to nurture the economic character of the neighborhood and deepen the ecological commitment of the community," Imani Village will boast affordable LEED certified housing, green job training, "culturally relevant" education for black children, and a sports complex. These planned "sectors" of Imani Village demonstrate a clear consciousness of the place in which it is being built.

Trinity is a congregation deeply embedded in its place with an intuitive and carefully studied understanding of the social, cultural, economic, and environmental histories and needs of the South Side. Whereas Elkin Presbyterian Church has pursued a very specific focus on riverkeeping and watershed discipleship in light of the particular needs of that place, Trinity's ecological practices are intersectional in light of the particular needs of their own place, calling for a *holistic* view of Christian faith in ecological context. For example, the establishment of an urban agricultural center at Imani Village will reclaim a former "brownfield" as a five-acre urban farm, provide agricultural job training, create ten to fifteen jobs, offer community residents a green social space, and increase access to healthy produce and prepared foods.[41]

The urban agricultural center will strategically partner with African American farmers to begin this work. Partnering with African American farmers has been a core practice of Trinity's "green" ministries for about a decade now, originating with the congregation's farmers market and community garden initiatives. The farmers market billboard taglines, "by any greens necessary" and "taste and see," connect deeply to the two commitments in the congregation's motto of "Unashamedly Black, Unapologetically Christian." The first is a play on the phrase popularized by Malcolm X, "By any means necessary." The second, of course, is an allusion to Psalm 34: "Taste and see that the Lord is good" (v. 8). Together, these two phrases bespeak a congregation deeply situated in the Christian and black liberation traditions. For the past seven or eight years, Trinity has hosted black farmers from the Black Oaks cooperative in Pembroke, Illinois, about seventy miles south of Chicago, to bring fresh and healthy food to a neighborhood short on grocery outlets and long on junk food. Although recent research on food access might describe such a context as a "food desert," Adrienne Wynn, chair of the congregation's Green Committee, prefers to describe it as a "food swamp."[42]

The farmers markets and the George Washington Carver community garden are motivated by and contribute to a sense of place. First, practices like the farmers markets are motivated by both a clear understanding of resources in the community and a careful assessment of what the community needs. Here, the more immediate urban environment of the South Side of Chicago comes into view. The South Side, dubbed the "Black Metropolis" by sociologists St. Clair Drake and Horace Clayton in 1945, is an economically diverse area, comprising many neighborhoods.[43] The South Side both is the historical home of the black middle class in Chicago and suffers from inadequate access to healthy and affordable food. The farmers markets work in a place like the South Side because they meet a need, they draw on historical and economic resources, and they provide a gathering place for community members.

Second, the markets and garden are necessarily bioregional practices. That is, through these two initiatives, inhabitants in the urban context of the South Side of Chicago learn about their extended bioregions. A city of Chicago's size relies on relationships with a much broader ecosystem for water, waste, and food systems. For example, in Chicago and other dense urban centers, the region from which food might come and still be understood as "local" currently stretches as far as four hundred miles from the city.[44] Thus, Trinity has drawn on the wisdom, expertise, and resources of black farmers in rural central Illinois, establishing networks not only in their city but in the broader "Central Corn Belt Plains" bioregion, as defined by the Environmental Protection Agency.[45] The network connects inhabitants of the "Chicago Lake Plain" subecoregion with the subecoregion just south of the Kankakee River, which the EPA has labeled starkly the "Sand Area."[46] Along the way Chicagoans learn where their food comes from, what grows where, and how. Although the soil in Pembroke is a sandy challenge and resources are few, Pembroke has attracted African American farmers for 150 years since it was established by formerly enslaved persons in the mid-nineteenth century.[47] In recent years it has attracted a new influx of black organic farmers.[48]

MEMORY, MOVEMENT, AND PLACE

One contributing factor to the formation of both Pembroke and the booming Black Metropolis was the Great Migration of the twentieth century. During the period between the First World War and the 1970s, approximately six million African Americans migrated from the southern United States to the North and the West. Violence, Jim Crow laws, and the economic injustice of the sharecropping system pushed black farmers especially northward where jobs were available and paid a just wage.[49] When the Great Migration began,

ninety percent of all African Americans were living in the U.S. South. By the
second half of the twentieth century, almost half of African Americans lived in
northern and western states.[50] Families who moved north and west during the
Great Migration left behind the virtual slavery and theft of the sharecropping
system, the political and physical violence of Jim Crow laws, and untenable
economic conditions. They also left behind, however, the complicated place
that had become home. This was the case even for those who thrived after the
move north, like novelist Richard Wright: "We look up at the high southern
sky and remember all the sunshine and rain and we feel a sense of loss, but
we are leaving. We look out at the wide green fields which our eyes saw when
we first came into the world and we feel full of regret, but we are leaving. We
scan the kind black faces we have looked upon since we first saw the light of
day, and, though pain is in our hearts, we are leaving.'"[51]

For many who made the trek north and west, the grief of leaving a homeplace was compounded by the struggle to find adequate and safe housing in
their new communities when neighborhoods, the housing market, and policies proved inhospitable to the influx of African Americans. Historian of the
Great Migration Isabel Wilkerson put it starkly: "Thus the eternal question
is: Where can African-Americans go?"[52] Place-consciousness necessarily
functions quite differently for persons who have been displaced, who have
migrated, or who are far away from the places that carry their familial and
ecological memory. This would certainly be true of the original inhabitants
of northeastern and central Illinois, including the Illinois and Miami tribes,
driven out by European settlers in the late eighteenth century.[53] Additionally,
place-consciousness must take into account places and communities that are
inhospitable or even violent toward already vulnerable groups. Indeed, bell
hooks describes the perhaps unintended consequences for African Americans
who moved from the agrarian south to the industrial north during the Great
Migration as a kind of "psychic genocide."[54] Mourning homeplaces, reckoning with the experience of displacement, and establishing relationship with
a new—sometimes even inhospitable—place must all be incorporated into
place-based religious education.

BECOMING NATIVE TO A (NEW) PLACE

San Jose Parish, Beloit, Wisconsin

"Build houses and settle down; plant gardens and eat what they produce. Marry
and have sons and daughters . . . seek the peace and prosperity of the city to
which I have carried you into exile. Pray to the LORD for it, because if it

prospers, you too will prosper" (Jer 29:5-7).[55] These words from the prophet Jeremiah greet visitors to the webpage for the San Jose Parish. Founding pastor Rev. Neddy Astudillo, herself an immigrant from Venezuela (having come to the United States for her seminary degree), sees a resonance between Jeremiah's words of comfort and challenge to exiles and a revisioning of place-conscious ministry among immigrants. That revisioning, she argues, must honor and even draw on the "tension between our environmental responsibility and the social structures that move us away from that same environment."[56]

San Jose is a predominantly immigrant worshipping community of approximately 150 persons, including fifty children. Established by local governing bodies in the Evangelical Lutheran Church in America and the Presbyterian Church (U.S.A.), the community worships in space shared with another Lutheran congregation in Beloit, Wisconsin. Astudillo (who now, after fourteen years as pastor of San Jose, works full-time with Green Faith as the Latin America Director) brought with her to the infant community a passion for ecojustice and her experience as a cofounder of the Angelic Organics Learning Center, an experiential education project associated with the Angelic Organics farm in nearby Caledonia, Illinois. Despite these theological and ministry-shaping commitments, Astudillo is disinclined to use language like "environmental" or "ecological" to describe her approach to ministry with the San Jose community, as members in the community face urgent economic and personal crises related to their vulnerable status as largely non-English-speaking immigrants in low-paying jobs.

The educational and pastoral practices Astudillo introduced in the community, however, are deeply ecological in the most holistic sense, located in relationship to both the community members' places of origin and the new place in which they find themselves. It is a sacred and fearsome time for them, a psychological and social experience of *liminality*. To describe this moment of transition as a "liminal" state is to recognize its ambiguities in which the familiar, old place has fallen away, and the new place is not yet familiar or understood. In this liminal moment, immigrants are "neither here nor there; they are betwixt and between."[57] Astudillo understands the liminal experience of migrants because she experienced it herself when she arrived from Venezuela: "My heart was still tied to the natural landscape of my homeland—to the point of not allowing me to be present in full to the new land and to my responsibility in it."[58] One means by which San Jose community members are learning to love this new place is the regular visits to the Angelic Organics Learning Center, just fifteen minutes from the church. At the farm they take classes and learn about agriculture in the midwestern United States, and they spend time on the farm, encountering goats and chickens, harvesting and gleaning from the fields. Many of the community members who visit the farm regularly are deeply concerned about food quality, particularly for their children, and visits to the farm (and what they learn there) make quality food more accessible.

These visits to the farm are a form of ecological education in the explicit sense because participants learn about farming and raising chickens (and subsequently petitioned the city of Beloit to change an ordinance so that families could keep a few chickens on their property!). Astudillo observes, "We're all immigrant and part of the learning experience is—how do we care for this place? How can I grow? If we're going to do this organically, how do we compost? What do we eat? . . . It's not done in any large way, just to raise awareness." The visits to the farm also fit into a larger emphasis on health and wholeness, essential in a community that lacks consistent access to good health care. The church hosts three Zumba classes a day and nutrition classes, and it has hired a member to offer free Reiki for members: "People receive healing through her—I don't know how it happens, but it does. Reina has really caught on this idea of healing the earth and healing ourselves."

The challenge from Jeremiah is poignant for members of a community like San Jose who continue to grieve the places from which they have come. The migrant experience, however, "challenges us to open our hearts to a new place and to its people."[59] The experience of displacement and migration disrupts simplistic summons to "become native" to a place, as if the "place" is a fixed location or phenomenon. Political and personal histories, economic situations, and familial relationships change and thereby reorient human relationships to places of significance. While this is true for migrants in a visceral way, it is true for any human being who lives and seeks to make commitments in a world unfinished.[60] Landscapes are transformed, encountered anew, and sometimes left behind. In the process human beings are profoundly *dis*located even as they seek to be profoundly located. Those who have mourned leaving a place know this is true: Place is more than geographical location. It also is biographical location. By weaving together opportunities to learn a new place with the human story and the promise of meeting real human needs like food and health care, San Jose Parish is honoring the places from which immigrants have come, making space for those real losses, and yet gently inviting a new relationship. "For migrants," Astudillo affirms in a sermon, "this calling has a redeeming and healing effect: 'I can now begin to love again! I can now relate and live my spirituality in this place!'"[61] This place—in southern Wisconsin— includes the histories of the Ho-Chunk and Potawatomi nations.[62]

One of the reasons that Christians can courageously move from past to future, from grief to love, even in a deeply ambiguous and liminal context, is the affirmation that God is active in and redeems history. Stories of love for a homeplace, of wounds inflicted by inhospitable places, of loss, of dislocation, of delight and discovery are all held and remembered by God. They are held with integrity and folded into the unfolding narrative of a complex and unfinished world permeated with the love of God.

Such is the path of inhabitance: located, dislocated, and relocated. Holistic ecological practices that take into account human, community, and ecological resources and needs have the capacity to resituate human life in particular places. Educational and ecclesial practices that take into account the whole span of human relationships to place thus have the power to free Christians to live fully, honestly, and consciously in their habitats, experiencing and expressing the full range of human affective dispositions.

LOCATED LIVING

Proposals for Educational and Ecclesial Practice

In Elkin, North Carolina, in Chicago, Illinois, and in Beloit, Wisconsin, the place-based practices that nurture inhabitance look quite different. This is necessarily the case, for religious education that locates itself in a particular place must also be specific. A practice that nurtures inhabitance in one place will not work the same way in another place. Indeed, it may not even be possible! The particularities of the geographical landscape, the community's history, the distribution of economic and social resources all must be taken into account. Each religious leader and each faith community must encounter their place in some detail, with curiosity and commitment. Despite the diversity and particularity that distinguishes one approach to place-based religious education from another, some common principles and practices do present themselves. Religious education that is attentive to place incorporates practices of memory, encounter, and commitment.

Practices of Memory

Pedagogical theories of place often emphasize the role that *present* place plays in education: what the present place has to teach the learner, what commitments the present place requires from learners. However, human encounters with place are deeply biographical. All the places in which people have lived have formative effects upon them. One does not arrive to a new place, a new context for learning, as a blank slate. The new place is not the only place that matters in the formation of a person or even a whole community. Certainly, the experience of migration and longing for a lost homeplace figure prominently in biblical narratives.[63] Persons and communities who grieve leaving even the most complicated of places can find in these biblical narratives communities who share that experience, even as they move toward a divinely promised future. Religious education for inhabitance needs practices that respect and honor the powerful role that particular places occupy in human memory and identity.

Powerful emotional responses to lost or left-behind places of significance serve as a reminder that persons already often have learned how to love a place in the specific. Loving a particular place is something that many *already* know how to do. Certainly, the immigrant members of the San Jose Parish understand what it means to love and grieve a place. Although practices of inhabitance often organically elicit participants' stories of their homeplaces, ecological religious education can nurture place-consciousness by explicitly creating space for these stories to emerge. Religious education that nurtures a sense of place is helpfully expanded by storytelling practices that invite participants to describe a place that formed them, or to tell a story about a photograph of such a place, or to recall a formative experience and the place in which that experience took place.

Practices of Encounter

To become knowledgeable and loving inhabitants, Christians must, of course, encounter the places in which they live. Although learning *about* the place— its plant and animal life, its watershed, its soil, its culture—is an essential step in developing place-consciousness, it is only in encounter, body to body, that a relationship is built between person and place. Floating down a river, visiting a farm, and walking a neighborhood all locate in an embodied way whatever demographics, facts, or economic and environmental trends might be learned about that place. When members of Elkin Presbyterian church together float down the Yadkin River on a lazy Saturday afternoon, they understand their watershed in a different way—it not only demands moral care and stewardship but also *gives* delight and life to its inhabitants, including the human ones. Thereby, God's creating and loving presence in creation is made "flesh," palpable to human beings in their very bodies.

Absent practices of recreation and encounter, inhabitants might well take appropriate care of a place, but they will struggle to see how their identity, their very lives, are shaped and given meaning by it. In the interest of expediency, forgoing practices of recreation and encounter might be tempting. They

might smack of indulgence, practices for human beings who still prioritize
their own desires and delight over the urgent needs of the planet. They are,
however, the only way to cultivate an affective relationship to a place. No data
factsheets, no Cliffs notes, provide a shortcut to allowing a place to locate its
human inhabitants.

Practices of Commitment

Insofar as places carry narrative meaning for their human inhabitants, they
are the site for understanding the past, present, and future. Alongside storytelling practices that invite inhabitants to recall and express gratitude for
places of memory and embodied practices that invite inhabitants to encounter
present places, ecological religious education needs practices that anticipate
the future well-being of a place. Such practices serve as a means for human
beings to reinhabit a place, to recognize its wounds and envision a future in
which humans can direct their wonder, love, and hope. Such practices reorient
human life in the interest of a shared good future, incorporating elements of
conservation and appreciation, agriculture and food distribution, relationship
building and community renewal.[64]

Trinity UCC, through its practices of growing and distributing fresh
food and supporting black farmers practicing sustainable agriculture, imagines and works diligently toward the strengthening and establishing of a
thriving community. They emerge from a deep and affectionate knowledge
of the community's needs: fresh food, energy savings, job training, and spaces
for gathering. And they envision and work toward a future marked by the
mutual flourishing of individuals, of the community, and of the bioregion.[65]
It is not a technical or calculated hope, however, that assumes that by some
environmental calculus, human beings can forestall an ecological apocalypse.
No, in committing to the future well-being of a place, inhabitants embody
Christian hope for a future in which God's creative and living presence is
making all things new.

6

EMBRACING VULNERABILITY

Religious Education, Embodiment, and the Ecological Affections

Approaching Yellowstone National Park from Montana Highway 191, through the Gallatin Canyon, is something of a spiritual experience. Formidable mountains cropping up on either side and in the distance, the bright blue canopy above, and expansive plains stretching all around elicit gasps of wonder and delight. There is a reason it is called Big Sky. Inside the park slow but majestic bison, elk, and grizzly bears move about freely, hot springs gurgle and steam, and human beings from around the world watch in silence as they encounter this protected wilderness. They wait expectantly for geysers to erupt, the powerful explosions of water and steam anticipated by rumblings born deep in the earth and experienced deep in the body. Few places in the world offer such immediate, embodied, and spectacular knowledge of the creative power at work in nature. It is an invitation to embrace vulnerability in body and in spirit.

But, as powerful as it is, Yellowstone National Park also is vulnerable. Indeed, the park and its ecosystem are in trouble. Ann Rodman, a park scientist who has studied ecosystem and weather changes in the park for thirty years, is alarmed by what she is seeing: "When I first started doing it, I really thought climate change was something that was going to happen to us in the future. But it is one of those things where the more you study it, the more you realize how much is changing and how fast."[1] Longer and hotter summers and decreased snowpack are drastically changing the ecosystem, killing off native plants and making the park vulnerable to invasive species; raising the temperature and slowing the flow of the region's rivers; exacerbating more frequent and damaging fires; and leaving less foraging material for animals, pushing them to seek other sources of food inside and outside the park.

At Yellowstone the vulnerability of the human being, small and in awe, meets the vulnerability of the ecosystem: large, complex, and suffering. The same poignant space that humans inhabit between life and death is reflected in the whole ecosystem on a larger scale. Religious education for inhabitance courageously dwells in the space between life and death, between wonder and grief. It honors the ways in which, as members of a living and dying world, human beings in body and soul are exposed to wonder, love, grief, suffering, and indeed, hope. Living as an inhabitant in a living and dying world knits together the deep pain of human and ecological loss and the soaring thrill of being alive in a wondrous and beautiful world pulsating with the heart of God. In so dwelling, inhabitants welcome vulnerability.

WELCOMING VULNERABILITY

Between Death and Rebirth, the San Jose Parish

When members of the San Jose Parish make the fifteen-minute trip to the farm and educational center at Angelic Organics, they are doing something more than an ordinary field trip.[2] As migrants, they are relocating themselves in the upper Midwest, learning about the place that now has become the provisional terminus for their migration experience. To get to the farm, they drive from Beloit, Wisconsin, their new city of approximately forty thousand, across flat plains, passing miles of corn and prairie grass underneath an expansive canopy of open blue sky. The landscape is simultaneously beautiful and stark, still unfamiliar and not yet "home" by any stretch of the imagination. Beloved family members, places, and landscapes all have been left behind. The life that they knew has in some ways died. And while rebirth is promised in this new place, this season between death and birth rightly evokes feelings of grief and vulnerability. The vulnerability is not only emotional but material: immigrants in the United States find their status in this country quite tenuous in the face of profoundly inhospitable and inhumane enacted policies and voiced sentiments.

The trip to Angelic Organics promises more than fresh produce, time outdoors, and an opportunity to connect with the land in a new place, however important those benefits are. Angelic Organics' story resonates with migrants because it has its own story of death and rebirth, a narrative that mirrors their own. Farmer and founder John Peterson inherited his family farm just outside of Beloit, in the 1970s. Upon his return to the farm, like many other farmers, he lost large swaths of the land, the equipment, and his history in the early 1980s during the transformation to large-scale agriculture.[3] Peterson's family farm, as it had existed since the 1930s, had died, and with it, seemingly, his own identity. The loss was paralyzing for Peterson. He sunk into a deep depression, something like grief:

> It seemed impossible that my life could fall apart like that. I had been with all those fields my whole life. I had the deepest sense of eternity about them. They were part of me. It was incomprehensible that I had to sell them. It was like selling an arm. No, more like selling a child. . . . For two years after the sale, I could hardly get out of bed. I hardly recognized myself. Land gone. Friends gone. Money gone. Rashes over my body. I was terribly weakened.[4]

In his body, spirit, and landscape, Peterson experienced the material loss of the farm. He managed to hold on to one small patch of it, however. And in 1990, Angelic Organics was born out of Peterson's dream to grow and share food in a way that is responsive to the soil and to nature. They instituted biodynamic farming practices, an agricultural model that understands the farm as an organism, an integrated whole, made up of land, trees, plants, animals, soil, and, importantly, human beings. It also attends to what biodynamic farmers call "the spirit of the place."[5] The farm at Angelic Organics, then, is a kind of resurrected body, its spirit reenlivened with a new mission and purpose. Several years after the loss of the farm and his own identity, John Peterson saw death and grief give way to new life and hope.

The immigrant parishioners of San Jose and the farmers at Angelic Organics share this story of rebirth and reestablishing roots in new (or resurrected) soil. But one does not get to resurrection without first dying. The immigrant experience is one rooted in memories of beloved places, grief upon leaving (and thus losing) those places, and the hard and hopeful work of becoming inhabitants in a new place. In this immigrants are profoundly vulnerable, unmoored from what is familiar, experiencing deep and powerful emotional responses and even acclimating their bodies to this new place and the ways in which it confronts their senses and even their health.[6] The vulnerability of relating to a place, the vulnerability required to become inhabitants, is cast in sharp relief in the immigrant experience. They encounter these emotions, new sensory experiences, their own memories, and even the poignant dance between life and death with a high degree of immediacy. In some way this vulnerability is thrust upon immigrants, many of whom would happily have

stayed in their familiar places had circumstances been different. The vulnerability that inheres in the immigrant experience is particular, but it also binds
all persons together in a common humanity.

After all, to be human is to be vulnerable.

No one lives a fully human life absent vulnerability. Human beings live
in bodies that feel, move, hurt, and die.[7] They have souls that wonder, love,
grieve, and hope. Despite their most well-established defenses, they will fall
in love, they will be wounded, they will be afraid, they will die. Ecological
faith is embedded in this poignant dance between death and life: seed germination, birth, illness, injury, decline, and death. Human beings encounter
these rhythms in the natural world even as they experience them personally
and intimately in their own lives. The work of becoming an inhabitant thus
requires the whole self: body, memory, and emotions. Inhabitance is a holistic
way of being in God's world, seeking integration between what is experienced
in the body; what is respected, loved, grieved, and hoped for; and the complexities, wonders, and sufferings of the "more-than-human" world.[8] It is to find
one's own vulnerability wrapped up in the vulnerability of God's world and
to be open to the emotional implications of that vulnerability.

ECOLOGICAL GRIEF AND ECOLOGICAL COMMITMENT

When human beings must leave a homeplace, when they witness the loss of
a homeplace, or even when they daily monitor the symptoms of a sick and
dying ecosystem, they are not often afforded room to acknowledge and tend
the emotional responses that might well up in the face of such losses. But
losses they are. As the changes in Yellowstone sink in, Ann Rodman and other
scientists acknowledge that the work is beginning to take a toll: "You begin
to go through this stage, I don't know if it is like the stages of grief. . . . All
of a sudden it hits you that this is a really, really big deal and we aren't really
talking about it and we aren't really thinking about it."[9] Ecological grief is a
complicated emotional space because grief is not often a word used to describe
the loss of something, some being, other than human. Many individuals and
communities, however, experience just such a deep grief when confronted
with the loss of animal life, sacred places, landscapes, and even a way of life
that appears now foreclosed as a result of ecological crises facing the planet.
For most environmental scientists and ecologists, encountering ecological
loss is part of the job. Seldom are persons who spend their lives documenting
and trying to mitigate ecological loss afforded an opportunity to acknowledge
the toll exacted by daily facing ecological and human suffering. The grief is
real, however. Researcher Ashlee Cunsolo experienced it on a deep level

when she was studying climate change impacts among the Inuit in Labrador. As she conducted interviews with people in the community who sometimes cried in her presence, she was struck by their own sense of loss:

> In 2011, I was bereft. I was at a loss intellectually and emotionally. I felt adrift in waves of sadness, grief, loss, and pain, unanchored from my life, isolated from those around me, and unsure of how to process what I was experiencing. . . . It was a grief I did not expect or anticipate. . . . It was transformative, changing me in ways that I still do not know if I would label "good" or "bad." . . . I realized the deep importance of understanding, experiencing, and thinking about ecological grief and mourning, and about the power that comes from having a deep connection to the land and environment in such a way as to leave you completely vulnerable, completely raw.[10]

And yet an understanding of what it means to mourn the "more than human" does not come easily. It is a different kind of mourning because ecological grief is complicated by the fact that it often is nonspecific: what is mourned in ecological grief is often not a particular life with a name and a known history. If humans were to open themselves up to all kinds of ecological grief—the loss of places, of species, of futures, of ways of life—could they truly bear the weight of that much grief?[11] To be an inhabitant, however, is to grieve.

Another distinction between grieving human loss and grieving ecological loss resides in the recognition that human beings bear varying degrees of responsibility for the very ecological losses that they grieve. When engaged with honesty and courage, ecological longing and lamentation often eventually give way to ecological guilt and repentance. The posture of repentance may be as subtle as an acknowledgment of the ways in which living in the anthropocene implicates human beings in the destruction of nature and ecosystems, particularly human beings with economic privilege in developed countries like the United States.[12] Ecological grief is complicated because "we must mourn not only what we have lost, but also what we have destroyed."[13] While grief at personal and environmental loss is a powerful emotion, the work of mourning asks human beings to honor and sit with that feeling, face it, and tell its story in a culture that often studiously avoids real engagement with loss.[14] By doing so, the work of mourning requires "understanding our shared vulnerability and our shared finiteness; embracing the responsibility of the labours of grief that this entails; and understanding that all we have to give to the dead, to what we have lost, is our own living and our own acts of mourning and remembrance."[15] Honestly engaged, ecological grief necessarily leads to a consideration of the commitments implied by the life of inhabitance.

It is a process of *metanoia*, or repentance, in its truest sense. *Metanoia* means literally to turn around, toward God and a new life. When repen- tance is cast merely as remorse, "being sorry," or even a change of mind and belief, its full theological, embodied, and emotional meaning is diminished. *Metanoia*, understood as an ecological conversion, includes a turning away from complicity in ecological harm and death but also a turning *toward* a life made full with ecological awareness and hope.[16] Pope Francis uses inviting language to describe the life of faith awaiting persons on the other side of ecological conversion:

> This conversion calls for a number of attitudes which together foster a spirit of generous care, full of tenderness. First, it entails gratitude and gratuitousness, a recognition that the world is God's loving gift, and that we are called quietly to imitate his generosity in self-sacrifice and good works. . . . It also entails a loving awareness that we are not dis- connected from the rest of creatures, but joined in a splendid universal communion.[17]

Ecological conversion makes possible the birth of ecological hope, even out of ecological death. New life springs forth from what has died. Ecological communion heals ecological alienation. Together soil and human being are resurrected in body and spirit. Suffering, alienation, and death do not have the last word. However, one cannot truly live without encountering death. This is the tension that inheres in Christian faith generally: that resurrection does not come absent encounters with death.

LIFE, DEATH, AND COMPOST

Church of the Pilgrims

Living beings are always also dying beings. Wendell Berry once described an experience in which he recognized the way in which his own dying body might be swallowed up in the decaying earth in the Kentucky landscape most familiar to him:

> I have been walking in the woods, and have lain down on the ground to rest. It is the middle of October, and all around me, all through the woods, the leaves are quietly sifting down. The newly fallen leaves make a dry, comfortable bed, and I lie easy, coming to rest within myself as I seem to do nowadays only when I am in the woods.

And now a leaf, spiraling down in wild flight, lands on my shirt at
about the third button below the collar. . . . Suddenly, I apprehend in it
the dark proposal of the ground. Under the fallen leaf my breastbone
burns with imminent decay. Other leaves fall. My body begins its long
shudder into the humus. I feel my substance escape me, carried into the
mold by beetles and worms. Days, winds, seasons pass over me as I sink
under the leaves. For a time only sight is left me, a passive awareness of
the sky overhead, birds crossing, the mazed interreaching of the treetops,
the leaves falling—and then, that, too, sinks away. It is acceptable to me,
and I am at peace.

When I move to go, it is as though I rise up out of the world.[18]

In this moment of rest, Berry imagines his own human body's response to the
earth's "dark proposal." In the same way that leaves and other living things
decay and sink away, the human body dies and returns to the earth. Staring
death in the face, whether it is one's own or that of a loved one, summons
both vulnerability and courage. In death as in life, with all of its joys, surprises,
and suffering, human bodies have a share with the earth. Human beings
already know what it is to grieve the loss of a loved one, and a peculiar kind
of consolation is promised in making sense of that particular loss in the midst
of a vulnerable world. Christians thus need practices that link human living
and dying with the living and dying of the planet.

In the Christian tradition, All Saints' Day is a liturgical commemoration
in which worshippers remember and give thanks for all the members and
loved ones who have died in a given year. A few years ago at the Church of the
Pilgrims in Washington, D.C., Rev. Ashley Goff developed a new liturgy to
commemorate All Saints' Day, a liturgy that asked those gathered to lean into
human and earthly vulnerability in an embodied and personal way. During
the time in which one might expect one of the pastors to deliver a sermon,
three women led the congregation in a "litany for all saints." Following the
litany, Rev. Goff invited the gathered community to share "stories of memory
and hope," sharing her own story of loss and reminding the community that
"in this place, we tell the truth . . . the truth about what death brought to us."

Although later she said that she had felt hesitant sharing it, one of
the three women liturgists, Mary, poignantly and matter-of-factly shared
with the gathered community a story that very few people in the sanctuary had heard: earlier that spring, she had suffered a miscarriage.[19] The
experience was as confusing as it was sad because until she miscarried,
she did not know that she was pregnant. However, Mary found herself
longing for some way to honor the infant who was not to be, whom she

named Agape. She chose that name because through this experience, she said, she had learned that she had love to give to the world.

After the miscarriage happened, Mary sought out Rev. Goff, who served as Minister for Spiritual Formation at the church, for guidance in processing the loss. Having read some blogs written by other women who had faced a similar experience, she knew she wanted a ritual to honor her own experience and to honor the life that never came to be. Together with Rev. Goff, she decided to plant something in the church garden, nourishing it with water, a symbolic gesture reminiscent of baptism, a recognition that "in life and in death, we belong to God."[20] On a Sunday morning right before worship, Mary, Rev. Goff, and a couple of friends gathered in the pastor's office. They said some prayers and blessings as water was poured into a bowl, then went out behind the church to the garden. There the young woman planted an azalea, watering it from the bowl over which they had just offered their prayers. Mary placed her love, her loss, her memory, and her hope there into the soil. "[Rev. Goff] said, 'We're creating a memory here,' because I didn't get a chance to do that. I didn't know I was pregnant. I didn't get a chance to hold my baby or anything like that. It was sad obviously, but being able to create some sort of positive memory out of that was incredibly therapeutic." And not only for her. One of the friends she invited asked if she could also bring her own mother, who had experienced two miscarriages herself. As the planting and blessing concluded, Mary recalls, the woman said, "This was . . . therapeutic for me even though this happened thirty-plus years ago. I never did anything like you did." To call the practice therapeutic perhaps underplays the theological significance of the ritual, developed in response to the deepest kind of human vulnerability: the gestation and subsequent loss of life or the potential for life. The ritual blessing with water of these most profound and mysterious aspects of human embodiment and loss, together with the nurturing of a new living thing, would continue to resonate with others. A few weeks later, Rev. Goff reached out to Mary, letting her know that the small ritual that had transpired in her office a few weeks earlier had inspired ideas for a ritual for the entire community on All Saints' Day, and inviting her to help lead some aspects of the service.

Members affectionately joke that Rev. Goff is always asking them to conspire with her in some creative and surprising worship practices.[21] A few times, for example, piles of compost from the church garden, worms and all, have appeared in the sanctuary, filling the baptismal font or as a makeshift communion table. The material presence of the "natural world" in the built and sacred space of the sanctuary—indeed, as sacramental element—is a degree of integration deeper than the more common incorporation of ecological liturgical language. As one member recalls, "[It was] something incredibly controversial. . . . We've had an enormous pile of dirt in the middle of the sanctuary. . . . Some people hated it. . . . We also had compost mixed in, too, which was super gross. It didn't smell too bad, it just looked like, 'ugh!' but that was also part of the environmental cycle." Another member recalls that "we had a big pile of compost in the middle of the congregation . . . worms crawling off of it into the congregation. I think that works better for some people than for other people. I was cool with it." The sensory language of scent, sight, and even touch demonstrates that worshippers relate to the earth in a visceral way when the elements are present in the sacred space, sensory knowledge bearing the capacity to deepen the ecological awareness that might be prompted by ecological language in ordinary liturgy.

This same principle of placing human bodies in direct relationship to the elements of soil, water, stones, and plants was at work in the All Saints liturgy. In this case, however, participants also were invited to bring their own stories and even grief into that relationship. Bodies, stories, suffering, and earth would be woven together in this practice. After Mary and others gathered shared "Stories of Memory and Hope," the congregation celebrated communion together, standing around the communion table that is at the center of the worship space.[22] Having shared the sacred meal, at the end of the worship service the congregation was invited to respond to God's word to remember and draw strength from the "great cloud of witnesses."[23] Led by a single drummer, the worshippers processed out of the sanctuary, down the sidewalk, and into the backyard of the church, which hosts the church's community garden, native plants, beehives, and several picnic tables around which sat several homeless neighbors, some of whom remained as the congregation gathered.[24]

One liturgist invited those gathered to plant a pansy (interestingly, an annual, not perennial, plant), write the name of a deceased loved one on a stone, and place it alongside the plant in the garden. Liturgists introduced and interpreted the practice by saying,

> In the planting and in the writing of names we will create a space where love and relationships and memories are planted. It will be a place where we can visit and remember. The plants and rocks won't last forever. But neither do we. . . . While the mystery of death remains hidden from us, the living, we can be aware of death in our lives and how death can drive the beauty of this garden. . . . We can remember, as we plant the flowers in the soil and place the rocks, that life doesn't disappear; it just changes shape and form.

In this simple liturgical practice, the members of the gathered community were invited to encounter and feel the interplay between life and death. Anyone who gardens—even if it is just a simple potted plant—understands this dance on an intuitive level. One must sometimes "thin" seedlings, removing infant salad greens or pea shoots in order to make room for a neighboring seedling to thrive. Sometimes the weather is too cold for too long, too hot too soon, too wet, or too dry. Sometimes bugs, worms, and larger, furrier creatures help themselves to bounties of greens, squash, and fruits before they can be harvested. And sometimes for a yet unknown reason, a plant simply fails to thrive, slowly disintegrating back into the earth from which it sprung forth. Indeed, in such patterns of decomposition, "death can drive the beauty of this garden."

Rev. Goff has considered the theological implications of life and death in the garden perhaps more than most pastors. She has worked with master gardeners, beekeepers, and arborists to think through and practice what she calls an agrarian spirituality. A symbol and practice central to agrarian spirituality is the generation and use of compost, which holds together decay, death, and new life in its pungent layers. Rev. Goff elucidates the metaphor:

> Composted soil absorbs death, or decomposition, and sets the groundwork for new life, the resurrection, to begin again. Compost holds together the process of death and resurrection. When our hands are covered with the dark, rich soil and compost of our garden, we are, in essence, covered with the resurrection. Our skin cells feel the fusion of life and death. Covered in compost, the resurrection is literally getting under our skin. . . . Digging in the dirt, trying to figure out the best place to plant the tomatoes, feeling sadness over our honeybees dying over the winter, and anticipating our first harvest of blackberries is embodied faith. When I spend time amending the soil for the garden and I look down at the compost running through my fingers, I think, "Crap, this is me in 50 years." I want to bring that symbol of resurrection into the sanctuary where we liturgically experience mutual care and love.[25]

In the All Saints planting liturgy, the theology of compost is apparent. The affirmation that "death can drive the beauty of this garden" invites participants to bring human experience of life, love, grief, and hope in direct contact with the earth, so made only by the decay and reabsorption of ecological death.

More deeply, however, the perichoretic dance between life and death in both human being and soil is grounded in ancient wisdom about life and death before God. It is an intersection of human, ecological, and theological truth. Such ecological, embodied, and emotional practices elicit more than

an immediate response of feeling, which might be quite powerful but fleeting.[26] By joining ecological, embodied, narrative, and liturgical experience,
a practice like the All Saints planting taps into deep reservoirs of spiritual
wisdom. The ongoing cultivation of human capacities for vulnerability, grief,
and repentance is appropriately described as the nurturing of religious affection, "a basic attunement which lies at the heart of a person's way of being
and acting."[27] The Christian life is governed by such patterns of being, and
one way in which the affections are formed and transformed in Christian
life is through liturgical practices like the All Saints liturgy at the Church
of the Pilgrims. These ecological affections are shaped when in prayer and
embodied action one joins her grief over the death of a loved one with the
deep pattern of life, death, and decay in a church garden's soil, and in light of
the presence of God in life and in death. It is under the dark cover of soil that
seeds germinate and bring forth life, as Wendell Berry succinctly describes
in this brief poem:

> The seed is in the ground.
> Now may we rest in hope
> While darkness does its work.[28]

THE BODY'S KNOWLEDGE

ECOLOGICAL FAITH IS INCARNATIONAL

Ecological practices like the All Saints planting at the Church of the Pilgrims
are powerful for two reasons: First, they connect with the deep streams of religious knowing in Christian liturgical traditions to deal with the fundamental
tension in human life: that of living and dying in a living and dying world.
Second, like liturgical traditions, these practices are embodied. The body is
located somewhere specific; assumes particular postures; and touches, hears,
sees, smells, perhaps even tastes the material "body" of the world. In liturgical
and ecological practice, the body's wisdom is needed. The body matters deeply,
whether it be what the body knows when confronted with the power of a geyser,
when learning a new landscape, when planting a vulnerable seedling as an act
of remembrance and grief, or when standing alongside the banks of a polluted
river. The body matters theologically, ecologically, and pedagogically.

The Body in Theological Perspective

The theological claim at the heart of Christianity is this: God came to the world
in human flesh, joining the heart of God with human embodied experiences of

birth, joy, play, love, fear, pain, suffering, death, and healing. Thus, Christians know God not only through their minds or ethereal spirits but also through their very bodies, the same substance indwelled by divine love. Although Christian traditions are grounded in a theology of incarnation, of divine love in human flesh, they have sometimes expressed degrees of ambivalence about the human body.[29] Even the apostle Paul struggled to understand the meaning of the body for Christian faith. He alternately understood the human body as a vessel for Christ's own body, life, and death (2 Cor 4:10); an earthly, perishable "tent" assumed only until resurrected human beings receive their "spiritual bodies" (2 Cor 5:1-4; 1 Cor 15:35-58); a source of tension and incapacity for good, a "body of death" (Rom 7:18, 24); and even, metaphorically and in a collective sense, the body of Christ (Rom 12:4-5).[30] The gnostic tradition worried that the body would interfere with the true wisdom available to the spirit. The puritans feared that bodily pleasures would distract believers from the love of God. Even now, Christians argue about dress, sex, and food as means of honoring, respecting, and sometimes suspecting the human body. In U.S. political and social contexts, some bodies are deemed more worthy of love and protection than other bodies. All of these arguments, ambiguities, and tensions testify that the human body is important, theologically speaking.

Doctrinal arguments among the earliest Christians and theologians would turn on whether and how the human body of Christ was significant. In docetic Christianity, for example, later to be determined a heresy, Christ's human body was assumed to be an apparition.[31] Others, like Nestorius, granted that Christ indwelled a real human body but argued that the human and divine natures of Christ really constituted two distinct persons.[32] The divine nature of Christ thus avoids running the risk of being contaminated by the base human nature of Christ. For many of the early Christians who held these views, the idea of God suffering the pains and indignities of a human body was too much. However, the Christian tradition would not even exist, save for the human body. Absent the enfleshing of divine love, the incarnation of God, the redemptive love of God would be limited or so spiritualized as to be ephemeral. In Christ, God became human, with a human body capable of love, rest, work, fatigue, sensory delight, pain, and even death. In so inhabiting a material body, God redeems this body in all of its sacredness and vulnerability.[33] The body matters, theologically speaking.

The Body in Ecological Perspective

The body matters ecologically, too. The body's ecological significance resides in its materiality, which it shares with other human beings, nonhuman life, and earthly matter. It is in the body that humans find themselves connected to their social and ecological habitat. Take, for example, the liturgical practice of foot-washing. Although many traditions have focused on cognitively interpreting the social and spiritual meaning of Jesus' washing of the disciples' feet, the practice's real power is in its radically embodied character. This practice involving real water, body parts, and human interaction affords a different kind of knowledge, like "the startling, excessively intimate experience of handling the feet of another and putting our own feet in another's hands."[34] Through such embodied experience, human beings have a share in life with other human beings and, indeed, other living creatures.

The embodied experiences of human beings are, furthermore, a means of relating with nonhuman life. When Beatrice, a sign language teacher for the female chimpanzee Washoe, suffered a miscarriage, she had to miss several weeks of work. Once she returned, she found Washoe distant and aloof. Beatrice finally decided to try to share with Washoe what had happened. When she signed, "My baby died," Washoe, who had miscarried two pregnancies herself, met her gaze with intensity and made one simple gesture: a finger tracing her own cheek, indicating the fall of a tear. In this brief exchange, two embodied beings shared a common (if differently processed) experience.[35] Indeed, humans encounter the whole sweep of creation through their bodies, even forms of life with whom they neither communicate nor relate on emotional terms. The body understands the bracing splash of a waterfall, the moldering scent of decaying wood, the shock of spring leaves and the whimsy of fall ones, and the sounds of chattering birds and silent earth. The body understands in an aching gardener's back the earth's work in bringing forth vegetation, and in the roar of a rising river the power of the earth's elements. Absent the body's knowledge, how would humans know their habitats?

The Body in Pedagogical Perspective

Finally, the body matters pedagogically. Environmental education that privileges the intellectual processing of data at the expense of experiential learning that recruits the body and the senses short-changes itself. It fails to recognize that learning processes that incorporate bodily memory tend to "stick" in a more powerful way. Teachers of languages know this, as research in the scholarship of teaching affirms the central role played by embodied cognition in the learning of languages.[36] So, too, do ecological educators understand the crucial role embodied knowledge plays in the cultivation of ecological knowing. Members of Elkin Presbyterian Church are afforded a renewed understanding of the meaning of water in their faith tradition and in their community after paddling down the Yadkin River. Members of the Church of the Pilgrims encounter the presence of the Holy Spirit in the space between life and death when they hold decaying earth in their hands even as it nourishes plant seedlings—new life.

What becomes apparent as one considers the role of the body in ecological learning and ecological consciousness is that it quickly and often concurrently summons learners' emotional attention, as well.[37] What human beings experience through their bodies—excitement, labor, fatigue, health, pain, sensory experiences—are often implicitly or imperceptibly linked to their emotions, their self-understandings, and their religious identities. San Jose's practice of visiting the farm at Angelic Organics and the Church of the Pilgrims' practice of planting on All Saints recruit the body in the process of faith formation. By beginning with what the body knows, unmediated, these embodied practices open a way to the formation of ecological affections: wonder, love, grief, and hope. The body knows how to be a living, dying, and vulnerable being in a vulnerable world.

FOOD FOR LIFE

Conetoe Missionary Baptist Church

For many, ecological and human vulnerability are readily apparent, experienced in the very bodies of poor and marginalized communities around the world. Migrants grieve homeplaces lost to political and economic upheaval and conflict; poor communities (and often communities of color) are left with few options as land in their communities becomes a dumping ground for toxic waste; and rural communities have long since lost access to healthy, fresh food and basic preventative health care as a result of transformations in food production and distribution.[38] In such cases a congregation's practices need not rely solely on human imagination to name and respond to ecological grief; the members of the community already know that grief in their bodies and in their hearts.

This has certainly proved true in Conetoe, North Carolina.[39] There, in 2014, Rev. Richard Joyner was exhausted. In a single year, he had conducted some thirty funerals, often for people in the region who had died from nutrition-related disease such as diabetes or high blood pressure.[40] As a volunteer chaplain at the Vidant Edgecombe hospital, he saw even more illness related to poor diet and insufficient physical activity. The tiny community of Conetoe, population three hundred, sits in the eastern part of the state in the midst of a rural and agricultural region. The area, despite being in the midst of farmland, lacks secure access to healthy food, the nearest grocery store being about eight miles away. Eight miles is a nearly insurmountable distance without reliable transportation.[41] Pleading to God for an idea of what to do, Joyner heard an unexpected divine response: "Look around you."

"I looked around," he says, "and there was nothing but land."[42] Joyner jokes that he almost asked to speak to someone else, having held a long and understandable resentment of agriculture after watching his father (and grandparents, before him) suffer economic exploitation and an erosion of dignity during the era of sharecropping. His great-grandparents had been forced to work the land as enslaved laborers.[43] With time and imagination, however, the landscape that once reverberated with familial memory of exploitation and violence in systems of slavery and sharecropping transformed, becoming a landscape of promise. Rev. Joyner, together with community members (many of them adolescent), successfully petitioned local landowners to let them farm their unused acres.

Convincing other members of the congregation and community of his agrarian vision, however, was not a simple matter. They carried the same memories that Joyner carried and were reluctant to send their children into fields, given the wounded histories that were rooted there. But the children, who had not lived through these histories, had other ideas. About sixty adolescents from the church and neighborhood participated in the first gardening summer camp in 2005, working with Rev. Joyner to cultivate two acres of land. Two years later, the Conetoe Family Life Center was born, now boasting twenty-five acres of farmland and 150 hives for a booming beekeeping and honey-production program. Since the founding of the center, visits to the local emergency room, often the primary site of primary care for the poor, and spending on prescription medications have dropped rather dramatically.[44]

The Conetoe Family Life Center demonstrates a holistic approach to ecological faith that attends to human vulnerability in an intersectional way. These ecological practices address human relationships to the earth while they *also* address human health, economic stability, leadership development, and community fellowship. Through these practices of farming, beekeeping, local commerce, summer camps, and sharing healthy meals, participants learn that the health of the earth is bound up with the health of the community and all of its members. "Ecological" concern may strike some ears as something that only communities who do not face more basic and immediate threats to their well-being (such as poverty, racism, violence, and health disparities) have the luxury to address. The ministry of the center, however, is ecological in its most holistic sense, attending to questions of economic resilience, race, human health, and spirituality. It embodies the relationships of interdependence that bind humans, communities, and the land together in one household.

Farming and beekeeping is not easy work, and yet the youth continue to invest their energy and joy in the Conetoe Family Life Center's projects. Rev. Joyner recalls that it was the youth who came up with the song they often sing together when they are working in the gardens:

> We are on the garden field, for my Lord.
> Oh, we are on the garden field, for my Lord.
> We promise Him that I would eat healthy 'til I die,
> and I'm on the garden field, for my Lord.[45]

Along the way, Joyner has noticed, the youth have established a strong and resilient community among themselves. Perhaps this is because by engaging their whole bodies and imagination their vulnerability is encouraged without being explicitly summoned. Through play, physical exertion, and collectively imagining a different and healthy future, the youth experience and express joy, frustration, and hope. It is an unexpected space of mutual encouragement where young people can share their struggles, breaking through a social challenge described by youth participant Tobias Hopkins: "How do we get the youth out of their shell? How do we crack them open so that they can really pour out what's really in their heart about their lives?"[46]

The whole sweep of human experience is honored and welcomed in a holistic ecological ministry like the Conetoe Family Life Center. Rev. Joyner celebrates the transformative power of these ministries: "The garden is a beautiful, spiritual sanctuary that we play in, eat in, educate in and change our lives in."[47] In this sanctuary the sacred mysteries of life, flourishing, struggle, and death are palpably present.[48] In the relationship between human being and soil, human being and animal, participants see that their own joy, wonder, grief, and love are bound up with the flourishing of the ecosystem, the well-being of their habitat. While their parents may have long ago concluded, with cause, that the land was an oppressive and even threatening place, these children are forging a new relationship to the land in their community and have become community and agricultural leaders in the process.

CHILDREN AND YOUTH AS LEARNERS
AND LEADERS OF INHABITANCE

For many faith communities cultivating ecological faith, children and youth play a central role in the awakening of the whole community to the gifts and responsibilities of inhabitance. Certainly, this is true in a quite obvious way for the youth of Conetoe. On a basic, material level, members of that community are healthier as a result of the adolescents' efforts: with improved access to healthy food, they face fewer medical crises and take fewer medications. The youth also demonstrate for the whole community, however, the joys and gifts discovered in their agricultural labors. The Conetoe Family Life Center is "youth-planned, youth-led, and sowing the seeds of change."[49] Much of the farming, beekeeping, and even food distribution in local shops and to local families in need is coordinated by youth. For some of them, the work is deeply personal, as they worry about family members who struggle with nutrition and fitness-related illness or grieve family members who have died at ages far too young. In these practices of ecological formation, the histories, voices, agency, and imagination of young people are honored. They are the leaders in these initiatives and already make significant contributions to their communities.[50] In their work the painful historical memory of agricultural labor is being transformed into practices of community uplift and self-sufficiency.

In fact, children are leading the way in many places. At the San Jose immigrant parish in Beloit, the children, who make up about one-third of the worshipping community, are already developing dispositions and skills of inhabitance in their schools. They bring that awareness with them to San Jose and their trips to Angelic Organics. Berea Mennonite Church in Atlanta, Georgia, hosts a "Peace and Carrots" camp each summer, where children learn agriculture on the church farm alongside the principles of nonviolence. Children also participate in worship leadership at Berea, often drawing on ecological themes. For instance, during an outdoor worship service in the church's pumpkin patch, the children prepared and shared stone soup over a campfire as the worship service progressed. The gathered congregation feasted on that meal when the worship service concluded. At Trinity United Church of Christ, youth took leadership in winterizing and installing rain barrels at older members' homes. The Wilderness Way community has from the beginning held a central place for children's learning and leadership during and in addition to their weekly gatherings. They host a "Children's School" for children in the WWC and broader communities during their weekly gatherings, a space for children to deepen their "connection with the sacred earth."[51] On Earth Day 2017, the community worked with Eloheh Farm to plant 150 trees as part of an international, children-led movement called "Plant for the Planet."[52] One child in the community, E'llee, aged nine, describes Wilderness Way as follows: "The Wilderness Way community is so kind and loving. . . . And we go on hikes and walks and trails and go camping. . . . Instead of kneeling, standing and sitting we go on field trips, camp, explore trails and experience nature.... It is more active, we sing and dance and laugh. Everyone plays the way they want."[53]

The significance of children's experiences with the outdoors cannot be overstated. In the first place, and perhaps most obviously, children's sensory, cognitive, and social development are strengthened and made more resilient by experiences in the outdoors. The research on these benefits of outdoor play led one environmental educator to propose that children in the United States suffer from a "nature-deficit disorder." Nature-deficit disorder, the cost of being alienated from nature, affects children's physical and emotional health as well as their capacities to use their senses and focus their attention.[54] And second, the planet needs adults who had early and formative childhood experiences in the outdoors, as numerous studies suggest that environmental commitment may originate in just such encounters.[55] Early encounters shape how human beings understand their place, relationships, and purpose in the world. They are essential to cultivating a sense of inhabitance that translates into a lifelong commitment to and enjoyment of God's world. Children who encounter and play in nature are more likely to understand themselves to be a part of it.

Neddy Astudillo, founding pastor of the San Jose Parish, recalls taking walks with her father on the beach as a child in Argentina: "Nature was a peaceful place that was away from the social unrest and tension and it was my upbringing." Farmworker activist Cesar Chavez relied on a deep connection to nature nurtured in his childhood experiences on a farm by the Gila River. From his father he learned about soil and water systems, and from his mother he learned about herbs.[56] And Lauret Savoy recalls standing with her parents, her Kodak Instamatic in hand, at the edge of the Grand Canyon during her family's cross-country move when she was seven years old:

> Decades have passed, nearly my entire life, since a seven-year-old stood with her family at a remote point on the North Rim. I hadn't known what to expect at road's end. The memory of what we found shapes me still.... The Kaibab Plateau ended and limestone cliffs fell oh so far away to inconceivable depth and distance. The suddenness stunned. No single camera frame could contain the expanse or play of light.... I felt no 'troubled sense of immensity' but wonder—at the dance of light on rock, at ravens and white-throated swifts untethered from Earth, at serenity unbroken.[57]

Wonder and joy perhaps come a little more easily for children. They carry a capacity for transcendence unimpeded by self-consciousness or suspicion, their relationship to the environment marked by a high degree of flexibility and resilience.[58] As renowned natural scientist Rachel Carson observed, "A child's world is fresh and new and beautiful, full of wonder and excitement. It is our misfortune that for most of us that clear-eyed vision, that true instinct for what is beautiful and awe-inspiring, is dimmed and even lost before we reach adulthood."[59] Although Carson's objective was to encourage adults to nurture wonder and an appreciation for beauty in the minds and hearts of their children, there is a subtheme: perhaps it is precisely the other way around—perhaps it is the child who helps the adult to wonder and be caught up in beauty and mystery. Adults accompanied by children in encounters with nature find themselves invited into a space of wonder and delight.

Adults do not outgrow their capacity and need for wonder and recreation. One of the threats to ecological faith and commitment is despair. Wonder is the "antidote" to ecological despair: "Once the emotions have been aroused—a sense of the beautiful, the excitement, of the new and the unknown, a feeling of sympathy, pity, admiration or love—then we wish for knowledge about the object of our emotional response. Once found, it has lasting meaning."[60] Accompanied by and experiencing a familiar place through her nephew Roger's eyes, his hearing, his eagerness to touch, Carson recalled a kind of self-forgetting wonder, a capacity to become lost in and surprised by the intricacies of the world:

> One stormy autumn night when my nephew Roger was about 20 months old I wrapped him in a blanket and carried him down to the beach in the rainy darkness. Out there, just at the edge of where-we-couldn't-see, big waves were thundering in, dimly seen white shapes that boomed and shouted and threw great handfuls of froth at us. Together we laughed for pure joy—he a baby meeting for the first time the wild tumult of Oceanus, I with the salt of half a lifetime of sea love in me. But I think we felt the same spine tingling response to the vast, roaring ocean and the wild night around us.[61]

Together, children and adults learn how to delight in God's world. When it comes to the cultivation of inhabitance, delight and wonder, nurtured in play, are as serious as grief. Without the heights of joy and the depths of suffering, humanity fails to live at "full stretch before God."

RECREATION AS A MEANS OF ECOLOGICAL KNOWING

Importantly, the youth of the Conetoe Family Life Center are invested in holistic ecological practices that engage both their own bodies in practices of play, agriculture, and beekeeping and the bodies of their family and community members whose nutritional and physical health outcomes are at stake. Practices that engage, use, and even heal the body are essential to the cultivation of inhabitance. The body is the unmediated locus of human vulnerability, in that breath, blood, senses, pulse, and cognition demarcate the distinction and relationship between life and death. The emotional responses to embodied experience further deepen human understanding and interpretation of such vulnerable existence. Both human and ecological vulnerability are bound together in the poignant interplay between life and death, to be sure. Consequently, the vulnerability of human and nonhuman life is to be held with reverence and care. Grief, lamentation, and repentance are born in and given meaning, however, by the recognition that human beings live in and love a wondrous, beautiful, and wounded world. Human experiences of wonder, awe, joy, beauty, and love are the conditions in which the seeds of commitment to the world are nurtured such that real grief is possible. Thus, embodied experience is a pedagogical key to cultivating the dispositions inherent in being good inhabitants.

The perhaps clearest examples of embodied ecological practices are recreational practices. Indeed, the work in the Conetoe gardens and in the beehives becomes a kind of recreation. "They're bringing food to people who need it," Joyner observes. "They enjoy the process. They're *playing* out there."[62] The story of the Conetoe Family Life Center cannot be told without naming the enlivening and transformative power of play. Play, in its recruitment and honoring of the body, *is* revelatory. The revelatory power of play is not predicated upon the comprehension of a passively received divine revelation but upon how human beings "encounter divine mystery, themselves, and others in new, life-giving ways."[63] Although the Conetoe gardens and hives are spaces for play, they should not be discounted as something less than serious or transformative. Play is powerful, the site for wonder and deep and dramatic encounters with God.[64]

Just like the youth of Conetoe and children in gardens, at camps, on playgrounds, and in the woods all over the place, adults need opportunities to engage the nonhuman world with their bodies, playing and seeking restoration as they encounter the elements of their habitats. Many communities invite members to participate in recreational practices that place their bodies in direct relationship to nature: floating down a river, fishing, hiking, gardening. Such practices of recreation are saturated with theological meaning related to bodies, creativity, and joy. Many congregations recognize the gifts of recreation for the building up of Christian community, for spiritual nurture, and for glorifying God.

The Sweaty Sheep Christian community, with sites in Louisville, Kentucky, and Santa Cruz, California, takes recreation very seriously. The community invites housed and homeless persons, yoga enthusiasts, fishers, hikers, persons with mental illness, and gardeners together to participate in recreational practices in the outdoors. They garden together, go hiking, and even took a fishing boat out on the Pacific Ocean, followed by a cookout on the beach. Bobby Marchessault, who pastors the Missio Dei Community (one of Sweaty Sheep's partnering communities), describes such recreational experience in the outdoors as an "equalizing" force in the face of social stratification. Sweaty Sheep takes recreation so seriously, in fact, that it is at the theological center of their vision:

> I wonder *when*,
> in the course of the Christian experience,
> we decided that church,
> that worship,
> meant *sitting still*?
> When did we decide that faith
> was a *passive experience*?
>
> If you believe that worship is movement,
> in the acting out of our faith
> through a mixture of service and play,
> then maybe you are a
> **Sweaty Sheep**.
>
> If you connect with God
> through laughter and activity,
> through hiking a trail as well as sitting in a pew,
>
> . . . if your understanding of "baptism" is the crest of a
> crashing wave
> then maybe you are a
> **Sweaty Sheep**.
>
> If you believe that God is bigger than a name and calls us
> to squeeze every ounce out of life,
> smell every flower,

and dance every chance we get,
then maybe you are a
Sweaty Sheep.[65]

Fishing, cooking out, hiking, paddling, laughter, and play—at first blush such practices may seem a luxury, given the urgent ecological situation we face. The data is in, after all. People of faith and conscience must act fast and with clear eyes and courageous hearts. Hiking, floating, gazing, and even gardening are to some degree pleasures, divine gifts worthy of human attention, but may seem hardly robust enough to stem the tide of ecological change. Stubbornly, however, Baba Dioum, Stephen Gould, and a host of others insist that humans will not—perhaps, cannot—fight to save what they do not love.[66] Although ecological challenges are knocking at the door with increasing urgency, they do not necessarily bring with them the cultivation of ecological love. Humans learn to love by diving into vulnerability, the pleasures and the pains of being living and dying beings in the world. They learn to love by opening themselves up, body and spirit, to profound encounters with the world. Ecological faith is embodied and honors recreation as an essential practice of Christian and ecological life.

The ecological work ahead is long and hard. Human hearts may very well break in response to the embodied awareness of suffering creatures, radically altered landscapes, dying ways of life, and an unknown and even unsure future for human life. And yet human life still unfolds in a wondrous world, filled with openings for delight, shock, and profound connection. Although sometimes assumed to be frivolous or irrelevant to the cultivation of ecological consciousness and commitment, such openings are bedrock. They are the antidote to despair. They are the only path to ecological resilience and hope.

CONCLUSION

Christian Hope in the Anthropocene

For Christians who want to draw nearer to the creative, loving, and pulsing heart of God, inhabitance is the way. In the willing embrace of its attendant vulnerability and commitment, we discover the wonder, joy, and love inherent in being alive. Indeed, it just might be the path by which we truly come alive. Inhabitance summons Christians' memories of sacred origin stories, remembering that we are from the start ecological beings. It also summons the imaginings of what shall be: the liberation of a groaning creation, which awaits the "revealing of the children of God" (Rom 8:19-24). In this way inhabitance is a path of sanctification, halting and incomplete and absolutely dependent on the love and creativity of God to transform human life and, indeed, the whole household of God. And yet, the healing of the world is not something for which we have a blueprint or even a map: "See what love the Father has given us, that we should be called children of God; and that is what we are. . . . Beloved, we are God's children now; what we will be has not yet been revealed" (1 John 3:1-2). Christians already are called inhabitants of the household of God. The *way* of inhabitance is the process of formation and transformation by which we discover *how* we shall be inhabitants in God's unfolding future. This is the source and direction of ecological hope for Christians.

ECOLOGICAL HOPE IN THE ANTHROPOCENE

Hope seems a strange disposition to cultivate in what scientists and environmentally inclined thinkers call the age of the anthropocene, when ecosystems

and the planet are radically and perhaps irrevocably altered by human presence and activity. Responsible Christian hope requires holding two dispositions in tension: a full and unflinching examination of the challenges that
inhere in the anthropocene, and a courageous and resilient resistance to
the despair that threatens to swallow up human imagination.[1] In a time in
which Yellowstone, and the coral reefs, and rural communities, and even
faith communities are dying, largely due to human action or inaction—a
time in which we do not yet know what will be, only that what *is* shall soon
be a memory—in this time, how shall Christians speak of coming alive? Of
hope for a future more wondrous than we can imagine?

The path to inhabitance is a vulnerable one whereby we are confronted
by the thrill and despair of being living and dying beings. It is vulnerable
because when human beings risk loving a place well with their whole hearts,
losing that place can introduce deep grief and suffering. In this vulnerability,
however, is the deepest promise of Christian faith for inhabitance. Practices
of inhabitance anticipate a future in which divine creativity and love flourish
unbound. They invite participants to reimagine themselves as loving and just
inhabitants of that future, opening themselves to wonder, love, and trust in
God's creativity and provision. The theological and moral imagination necessary for this work is born, nurtured, and sustained in communities of hope.[2]

In the stories told above—Elkin Presbyterian Church's watershed
discipleship, Trinity United Church of Christ's sustainable community
development, San Jose Parish's farm visits for new immigrants, Church of
the Pilgrim's agrarian liturgy, Conetoe Missionary Baptist Church's youth
farming and public health initiatives—in each of these stories, one thing is
clear: Inhabitance does not happen in isolation. It takes a faith community,
and sometimes it even takes a broader community. These communities are
marked by love for particular places, a deep sense for the interdependence of
creation, the courage to confront ecological injustice, and a spirit of hopeful
resilience, a trust in God's creative power in the unfolding world, as not yet
fully known.

One of the peculiar aspects of the environmental movement in the United
States is its prioritizing of individual, private action: drive the right car, forego
the straws, use less water, grow your own food, and recycle, for God's sake!
Research has now established, however, that these efforts, though perhaps
formative of ecological character (and thus, not without benefit), will not
right the environmental ship. What is more, they falsely leave the person
who longs to be an inhabitant finally alone and singularly culpable for the
planet's distress. Inhabitants need communities of love, accountability, and

imagination—communities of hope. Communities of hope are communities of formation whose practices expand the sense of what is theologically and morally possible through sets of practices that engage the body, the affections, and the imagination.[3] They envision and live into a way of inhabitance that may not yet be entirely possible, where relationships between human beings and between humans and the ecosystem are marked by wonder, longing, reverence, and mutual dependence. Together, these communities can imagine and even *do* and *become* that which one person cannot on their own. A brief and personal example: When my mother was dying of cancer in 2006, I was a negligible member of the choir in my local congregation. I was never a particularly strong singer, but during that season, I found that I could not utter even the faintest sound. And yet, the choir director and the choir members allowed me to show up and sit among them on Wednesday nights and Sunday mornings, where I sometimes pretended to sing and sometimes stood there and wept. That choir made the most beautiful sound, together. It was even my own sound, though I could not contribute a note to it. The beauty of that sound carried me for months. Communities of hope can do that.

They also are places where one's personal path of inhabitance is supported and inspired by the community: its traditions, its texts, its practices, its people. When one struggles or falls down on the way toward becoming a loving and just inhabitant, the community lovingly restores that person to community. If inhabitance is the way to come alive, a community practicing inhabitance provides the conditions necessary for living. If human lives are bound up in a deadly mess of alienation, harm, and ecological despair in the anthropocene, a community practicing inhabitance offers the promise of resurrection: of coming back to life. Ecological religious education is made up of just such practices in just such communities, forming human beings into thriving inhabitants even in the most ecologically challenging contexts and times.

INHABITANCE AS SACRED AND WONDROUS VOCATION

When the son Christians call "prodigal" reappears after wandering alone, being careless with the provisions from his parent, and suffering himself from others' exploitative practices, his father cannot contain his joy: "[T]his son of mine was dead and is alive again!" (Luke 15:24a). The one who was dead is alive. The one who was lost is found. And the one who wandered alone in a series of unfamiliar places, the one who has alienated himself from the place that formed him, has now been restored to his home, his family, and his community. A father weeps with joy. A child, estranged and repentant, is embraced. And almost the entire household (save, of course, the resentful brother) rejoices as the community is restored, and an extravagant banquet commences. This parable, perhaps one of the most familiar in the whole biblical narrative, teaches hearers about God's grace, God's inexhaustible welcome. To read it only as a story of the redemption of the individual, however, misses its ecological themes. The son, now penniless and vulnerable, has lived an unrooted life, at least initially by choice, failing to understand himself as a loving and responsible participant in the communities in which he has landed. He has failed to be a just and loving inhabitant. And he has been alienated from both his homeplace and the new places in which he has found himself. When the repentant wanderer returns home, however, he is woven back into the fabric of the place. And thus, he lives again. It is a story of resurrection, a soul returned to itself. And thus is the path of inhabitance. Importantly, this is not a simple story of return. Time has passed. The wanderer has changed, and certainly the household to which he returns, ashamed, has changed without his presence as a loving and responsible member. Perhaps this is why the father calls it not a homecoming but a resurrection. The restoration of the community brings those who are dead back to life.

The unbounded love and unlimited creativity of God mean that no amount of suffering, wandering, apathy, wastefulness, disregard, or even despair can separate Christians from the promise of the full-throated, vulnerable, and wondrous life of inhabitance. The promise of an ecological conversion, a kind of *metanoia* profound enough to traverse the space from death to life, perpetually summons human beings to not only their origins but also their yet-to-be-revealed future. It sets the path, or the trail, or the way toward humanity's deepest vocation, inhabitance. It is to consider in detail the beauty and struggle of the world, to wonder about and seek our place in it, and to live together with courage and hope in spite of all that threatens to silence the deepest longings of the human heart. This. This is what inhabitants do with their "one wild and precious life."[4]

NOTES

INTRODUCTION

1   Baba Dioum, "Paper Presented at the General Assembly of the International Union for the Conservation of Nature and Natural Resources" (New Delhi, 1968); cited in Joann M. Valenti and Gaugau Tavana, "Continuing Science Education for Environmental Journalists and Science Writers," *Science Communication* 27, no. 2 (2005): 308.

2   "Habitats—The Great Barrier Reef," MESA, Marine Education Society of Australasia, accessed December 11, 2018, http://www.mesa.edu.au/habitat/gbr01.asp.

3   "Home," Million Pollinator Garden Challenge, National Pollinator Garden Network, accessed December 11, 2018, http://millionpollinatorgardens.org/.

4   It must be stated, clearly and frequently, that human beings and human communities are not uniformly culpable for our ecological crises. First, some cultures and religious traditions actually *do* nurture the way of inhabitance, cultivating an awareness of human embeddedness in the ecosystem, inspiring deep reverence and love for the natural world, and assuming an ethic of restraint and simplicity. Second, the structures and practices that most drastically harm ecosystems—agriculture, transportation, consumer capitalism—inequitably enrich and benefit some human beings while they economically and ecologically exploit and oppress other human beings. This is true on a local and regional scale: take, for example, the placement near poor communities of landfills and other waste facilities, which hides, far from the view of those most responsible for it, the evidence of pathological

patterns of consumption. On a global scale, consider the effects of human-caused climate change, globalized agriculture, and transnational commerce and waste: Some human beings are shielded from the effects of, and even benefit financially from, the practices that deplete natural resources, create waste and pollution, and damage ecosystems. Conversely, some communities and even countries find themselves the receptacles for electronic waste and other garbage, while their resources are extracted, enriching business owners and shareholders on the other side of the world. While human beings might *collectively* be destructive inhabitants, they are not *universally* or *equally* destructive inhabitants.

5   This quote is attributed to Thurman, though it does not seem to appear in any of his published writings. The quote resonates with some of the themes in his baccalaureate address at Spelman College, often identified as "The Sound of the Genuine." Howard Thurman, "The Sound of the Genuine: Baccalaureate Address," *Spelman Messenger*, Summer 1980.

Chapter 1: Longing for Home

1   Pope Francis, *Laudato Si': On Care for Our Common Home* (Huntington, Ind.: Our Sunday Visitor, 2015), 3.

2   Technically, Pope Francis' first encyclical was the concluding encyclical of a three-part series on the theological virtues of charity, hope, and faith. The encyclicals on charity (*Deus Caritas Est*) and hope (*Spe Salvi*) were penned by Pope Benedict XVI. The third encyclical on faith, entitled *Lumen Fidei*, was originally drafted by Benedict and edited and expanded by Francis. See Pope Francis, *Lumen Fidei* (New York: Crown Publishing Group, 2013), 8. *Laudato Si'*, however, is the first encyclical envisioned and penned by Francis. It is notable that Francis chose our ecological responsibility as the first theological case to make in his papacy, and that he addressed this encyclical to not only Catholics, or even Christians, but to the whole human family. See *Laudato Si'*, 8, 14, 45.

3   Theodore Hiebert, *The Yahwist's Landscape* (New York: Oxford University Press, 1996), 65–66.

4   Botanist Aldo Leopold recognized that humans need to expand the concept of social belonging so that we understand ourselves as belonging also to the land, a claim discussed in more detail below. Leopold, "The Land Ethic," in *A Sand County Almanac and Other Writings on Ecology and Conservation* (New York: Literary Classics of the United States, 2013), 171.

5   The web of interdependence as a theological anthropological image is discussed at length in Jennifer R. Ayres, *Waiting for a Glacier to Move: Practicing Social Witness* (Eugene, Ore.: Wipf and Stock, 2011).

6   Pope Francis, *Laudato Si'*, 3.

7   Interestingly, from a theological perspective, the term "ecumenical" derives
      from the same root. In New Testament Greek, *oikoumene* refers to the whole
      "inhabited earth." More recently, the term has been Anglicized and now also
      refers to the worldwide, multitraditioned Christian communion: ecumen-
      ical. Just as we inhabit our communities and our planet with attention and
      care for the connections that bind us together, so too might intentional and
      just inhabitance characterize our life together across Christian traditions.

8   Gillian Judson, *A New Approach to Ecological Education: Engaging Students'
      Imaginations in Their World* (New York: Peter Lang, 2010); Neil Evernden,
      The Natural Alien (Toronto: University of Toronto Press, 1985), 124–26.

9   The same tension is being worked out in the theory and practice of environ-
      mental and ecological education, discussed in a later chapter.

10   Jürgen Moltmann, *God in Creation: A New Theology of Creation and the Spirit
      of God* (Minneapolis: Fortress, 1993), 184. This chapter engages the ecologi-
      cal theology of Jürgen Moltmann with some depth. For a more focused study
      of Moltmann's ecological eschatology, see Jennifer R. Ayres, "Cultivating
      the 'Unquiet Heart': Ecology, Education, and Christian Faith," *Theology
      Today* 74, no. 1 (2017): 57–65.

11   Gerald G. May, *Will and Spirit: A Contemplative Psychology* (San Francisco:
      HarperOne, 1987), 52.

12   After extolling God's majesty in creation and humanity's correlatively
      small stature, however, even this psalmist also moves quickly to humani-
      ty's dominion over nature: "Yet you have made them a little lower than God,
      and crowned them with glory and honor. You have given them dominion
      over the works of your hands; you have put all things under their feet . . ."
      (Ps 8:5-6).

13   Pope Francis, *Laudato Si'*, 58–59.

14   Sallie McFague, *Super, Natural Christians: How We Should Love Nature*
      (Minneapolis: Augsburg Fortress, 1997), 34.

15   McFague, *Super, Natural Christians*, 155.

16   Indeed, McFague would argue that "landscape" is the wrong metaphor
      altogether, as it presumes a distanced "spectator" with a privileged view
      rather than a participant who knows a place up close and from the inside.
      She argues that the "maze," therefore, is the better metaphor. See McFague,
      Super, Natural Christians, 68.

17   Some of the best nature writers poignantly show readers how to love a place
      in the specific. So intimate is their knowledge of their homeplaces, that it
      is not always clear whether they extol the virtues of a landscape or a lover.
      And is that not how it ought to be? To love the earth and one's place in it is
      to notice every contour, every blemish, every movement, and every cry up
      close, and with a loving, compassionate, and deeply integrated eye.

Mary Oliver knows, perhaps instinctively, how to live well in a place, loving it in detail, extolling its beauty, respecting its limits, grieving its deaths. She began writing poetry at the age of ten in the woods near her small-town Ohio home. Her later poetry would invite readers into the particulars of the dramatic landscape of Cape Cod, where she made her home for fifty years. About the mystery of the world that inspires her poetry, Oliver has said: "The world is pretty much—everything is mortal. It dies. But its parts don't die. Its parts become something else. And we know that when we bury a dog in the garden. And with a rose bush on top of it. We know that there is replenishment. And that's pretty amazing." "Listening to the World: Mary Oliver," interview by Krista Tippet, *On Being*, October 15, 2015, accessed March 21, 2019, https://onbeing.org/programs/mary-oliver-listening-to-the-world/. Oliver shares this commitment to be fully present and loving in a place with many other "nature writers," such as Wendell Berry, who recounts his return to his native Kentucky with stunning detail, culminating in an instinctive desire even to lie down and allow his body to seep into the humus of the place he loves so well. See Berry, "A Native Hill," in *The Art of the Commonplace: The Agrarian Essays of Wendell Berry*, ed. Norman Wirzba (Berkeley, Calif.: Counterpoint, 2002). Also a prodigal returned to Kentucky, black feminist scholar and essayist bell hooks evocatively describes the longing she held for her verdant and broken Appalachian homeland, all while finding professional success in urban settings ostensibly more "hospitable" to black intellectuals. See hooks, *Belonging: A Culture of Place* (New York: Routledge, 2009). Annie Dillard, too, commits to knowing a place, seeking to interpret its mysterious language and symbol. See Annie Dillard, *Pilgrim at Tinker Creek*, 5th ed. (New York: HarperCollins, 1988). Oliver, Berry, hooks, and Dillard are virtuosos in the art of inhabiting a place well.

18   See, for example, Ernst Conradie, *An Ecological Christian Anthropology: At Home on Earth?* (Burlington, Vt.: Ashgate, 2005).

19   Moltmann, *God in Creation*, 207.

20   The second creation account, which appears in the second chapter of Genesis, is attributed to the "Yahwist" writer, who demonstrates an intimate familiarity with agricultural language and systems, in contrast with the "Priestly" of the first creation account in Genesis 1, who demonstrates a preoccupation with order and categories.

21   For an extended treatment of the anthropological implications of the language in the Genesis creation accounts, see Hiebert, *Yahwist's Landscape*; Theodore Hiebert, "The Human Vocation: Origins and Transformations in Christian Traditions," in *Christianity and Ecology*, ed. Dieter T. Hessel and Rosemary Radford Ruether (Cambridge, Mass.: Harvard/CSWR, 2000), 135–54.

22 In fact, most of the other appearances of this verb are in reference to how humans are to serve and worship God, or, more troublingly, how slaves are to relate to their owners. It is a problematic and dramatic verb, written in a different time and describing hierarchical, subservient, and, in some cases, oppressive relationships. Without valorizing subservience, however, readers might allow the force of this verb to disrupt and indeed invert simple assumptions about human power to rule over or even steward the land.

23 Hiebert, *Yahwist's Landscape*, 140–41. These conflicting images of the human relationship to the land foreshadow a long and complicated story that unfolds in the Hebrew bible. Already in the third chapter of Genesis, God describes the humans' *return* to the "fertile land, since from it you were taken; you are soil, to the soil you will return" (Gen 3:19, CEB). During most of Deuteronomic history, the Israelites are a landless people. God's promise of a land for the Israelites animates their self-understanding and fortifies them through generations of transience. Then, once established in the promised land, they find it difficult to live in just and righteous ways, eventually finding themselves once again exiled from the land in what the prophets interpret as divine judgment. Indeed, even the manner by which Deuteronomic history recounts the narrative of the Israelites' anticipation of the promised land demonstrates the tensions implicit in the relationships between human beings, human cultures, and the land. Since these texts were likely written during the period of Persian exile, the promise is recounted through the lens of memory, a longing to return. When the Israelites do return to the land, they do so by force. These complicated accounts raise crucial questions for theological anthropology: Are human beings members, tenders, managers, or even exploiters or occupiers of the land? Do they have a *right* to the land, or an obligation to it? How shall humans of different religions, cultures, or political and economic status live together on the land? See Walter Brueggemann, *The Land: Place as Gift, Promise, and Challenge in Biblical Faith*, 2nd ed. (Minneapolis: Fortress, 2002).

24 "Land," here, must be read broadly. When Aldo Leopold describes humans as members of the "land community," he does not mean possession of land, nor does he necessarily mean what we commonly call "nature," bringing to mind peaceful pastoral landscapes that stand in contrast with urban contexts. It is a set of values that holds in view the interdependent relationships between all living things, from soil microbes to human beings, everywhere that life is present. See Leopold, "Land Ethic," 180–83.

25 Larry Rasmussen, *Earth-Honoring Faith: Religious Ethics in a New Key* (New York: Oxford University Press, 2012), 12.

26 Scientists in the field of ecology, too, worry somewhat about the broad and diffuse use of the term "ecology" by new agrarians, poets, and otherwise sentimental nature lovers. See Evernden, *Natural Alien*, 5.

27 Moltmann, *God in Creation*, 207.

28 How do we make sense of the instances of violence and suffering that permeate life on this planet, for example? Is it appropriate to pray that the wolf might lie down with the lamb when predation and survival are woven into the fabric of nature? While some ecological suffering is surely bound up in human sin and exploitation of the earth, an idealized vision of the earth as peaceable kingdom does not resonate with the experience of natural disaster, creaturely violence, or the general finitude of creation. See Conradie, *Ecological Christian Anthropology?* 44–51.

29 John Calvin, *Institutes of the Christian Religion*, trans. Ford Lewis Battles, Library of Christian Classics (Philadelphia: Westminster, 1960), 2.1.8.

30 Moltmann, *God in Creation*, 197.

31 In a recent conference hosted by Candler School of Theology on the occasion of Jürgen Moltmann's ninetieth birthday, presenters were invited to reflect on the theme, proposed by Moltmann, of "Unfinished Worlds."

32 Russ Pierson and John Roe, "Marc Driscoll: Gas Guzzlers a Mark of Masculinity," *Sojourners*, October 18, 2016.

33 Jürgen Moltmann, *Theology of Hope: On the Ground and the Implications of a Christian Eschatology*, trans. James W. Leitch, 5th ed. (San Francisco: HarperSanFrancisco, 1967).

34 Moltmann, *God in Creation*, 206–14.

35 Conradie, *Ecological Christian Anthropology?* 13.

36 The same might be said about our social relationships. Technical knowledge of a community only gets us so far toward real understanding. It is only when we seek to establish and nurture our relationships to the persons we seek to "know" that we can approach comprehending the emotional, moral, and material complexities that shape their lives.

37 McFague, *Super, Natural Christians*, 33.

38 Dominant epistemological frameworks over the past two centuries have been deeply shaped by the Baconian scientific method, Cartesian enlightenment philosophy, and Kantian ethics. These influences have prized objectivity, universality, and rationalism as means toward producing knowledge that is trustworthy, verifiable, predictable, and free of influence from mythologies or religion. These laudable commitments, however, have some liabilities. In their quest toward order and generalizable knowledge, they risk excluding divergent sources of understanding, atomizing data and insights that should be held together, and instrumentalizing nature so that it is more easily used—or worse, exploited. See Carolyn Merchant, *The Death of Nature: Women, Ecology, and the Scientific Revolution*, 2nd ed. (New York: HarperOne, 1990); Val Plumwood, "Nature, Self, and Gender: Feminism, Environmental Philosophy, and the Critique of Rationalism," in *Environmental Philosophy: From Animal Rights to Radical Ecology*, ed. Michael E. Zimmerman et al.,

2nd ed. (Upper Saddle River, N.J.: Prentice Hall, 1998); Lorraine Code, *Ecological Thinking: The Politics of Epistemic Location* (New York: Oxford University Press, 2006).

39 Code, *Ecological Thinking*, 49.

40 David W. Orr, "Ecological Literacy," in *Ecological Literacy: Education and the Transition to a Postmodern World*, SUNY Series in Constructive Postmodern Thought (Albany, N.Y.: SUNY Press, 1992), 90.

41 David Orr draws an extended contrast between the way of the resident and the way of the inhabitant. For example, "To *reside* is to live as a transient and as a stranger to one's place, . . . to become merely 'consumers' supplied by invisible networks that damage their places and those of others. . . . The life of the *inhabitant* is governed by the boundaries of sufficiency, organic harmony, and by the discipline of paying attention to minute particulars." Orr, "An Alternative to Bloom's Vision of Education," in *Ecological Literacy*, 102.

42 Luke 15:11-32. Although many translations have associated it with "riotous living" or "debauchery," ζων ασωτως could also express a more central concern with waste. Walter Arndt William Bauer, *A Greek-English Lexicon of the New Testament and Other Early Christian Literature* (Chicago: University of Chicago Press, 1979), 798.

43 Pope Francis, *Laudato Si'*, 13.

44 David W. Orr, *Hope Is an Imperative: The Essential David Orr* (Washington, D.C.: Island Press, 2011), 3. Indeed, popes and ecological educators are not the only ones who are imploring us to consider the planet our "home." In his presentation of the recent report of the Intergovernmental Panel on Climate Change, cochair Thomas F. Stocker said, "Climate change is the greatest challenge of our time. . . . In short, it threatens our planet, our only home." Justin Gillis, "U.N. Climate Panel Endorses Ceiling on Global Emissions," *New York Times*, September 27, 2013.

45 Frederick Buechner, *Wishful Thinking: A Seeker's ABC*, rev. and expanded (New York: HarperOne, 1993), 119.

46 Serene Jones, "Graced Practices: Excellence and Freedom in the Christian Life," in *Practicing Theology: Beliefs and Practices in Christian Life*, ed. Dorothy Bass and Miroslav Volf (Grand Rapids: Eerdmans, 2002), 51–77.

47 Calvin, *Institutes*, 1.5.8.

Chapter 2: Becoming Inhabitants

1 My colleague Steven Kraftchick has helpfully pointed out that since approximately two-thirds of the surface of the planet is covered in water, perhaps a more apt descriptor is "wet faith." This is all the more true when we think about the primary practice used to mark theological identity— baptism. Here, however, I understand "dirt" and "soil" in somewhat the

same symbolic way that Aldo Leopold redefines the "land," including "soils, waters, plants, and animals." Leopold, "Land Ethic," 172.

2   Calvin, *Institutes*, 2.6.1.

3   Recent studies demonstrate, for example, that a microbe called *Mycobacterium vaccae* triggers mouse brains to produce serotonin. See Barbara Damrosch, "The Healing Powers of the Earth," *Washington Post*, April 23, 2015.

4   One of the advantages of this approach, Blanchard and O'Brien argue, is that it does not require agreement on environmental practice or policy—indeed, it assumes a diversity of perspectives on these issues without attributing environmental antagonism or indifference to those who propose conflicting responses to the same challenges. Kathryn D. Blanchard and Kevin J. O'Brien, *An Introduction to Christian Environmentalism* (Waco, Tex.: Baylor University Press, 2014), 12.

5   Blanchard and O'Brien, *Christian Environmentalism*, 18, 23–24.

6   Blanchard and O'Brien, *Christian Environmentalism*, 13.

7   Certainly, Alasdair MacIntyre, Craig Dykstra, and others have something broader in mind when they turn to the categories of virtue and character in human life and responsibility. Indeed, MacIntyre would resist the urge to develop a definitive list of virtues, instead arguing that it is the process by which virtues are cultivated that demands our attention. This cultivation of virtues and their concomitant dispositions results in the development of a *habitus*, a way of being in the world that becomes "second nature," a way of responding and acting that transcends rational decision-making. For Christian practical theologians, this is the promise of virtue ethics and, more particularly, practices as a vehicle for cultivating virtue. See MacIntyre, *After Virtue: A Study in Moral Theory*, 2nd ed. (London: Duckworth, 1984); Dykstra, "Reconceiving Practice," in *Shifting Boundaries: Contextual Approaches to the Structure of Theological Education*, ed. Barbara G. Wheeler and Edward Farley (Louisville, Ky.: Westminster John Knox, 1991), 35–90; Dykstra, *Growing in the Life of Faith: Education and Christian Practices*, 2nd ed. (Louisville, Ky.: Westminster John Knox, 2005). In contrast, critical theorists worry somewhat about this suprarational character of *habitus* and the ways in which it might serve to dull human capacities of critical analysis. See Dykstra, "Reconceiving Practice"; Pierre Nice Richard Bourdieu, *The Logic of Practice* (Stanford, Calif.: Stanford University Press, 1992).

8   These principles are at the heart of permaculture. See David Holmgren and Richard Telford, "Permaculture Design Principles," Permaculture Principles, accessed January 30, 2019, https://permacultureprinciples.com/principles/.

9   Bernard J. Lee, "Practical Theology as Phronetic: A Working Paper from/for Those in Ministry Education," *Association of Practical Theology Occasional Papers* 1 (1997): 1–16.

10   Aristotle, *Nicomachean Ethics*, trans. Joe Sachs (Newburyport, Mass.: Focus, 2002), 106.

11   Aristotle, *Nicomachean Ethics*, 114. This quality of "second nature," or way of being, is actively cultivated through participation in practices that shape human character and virtue, often described as *habitus* (47).

12   Aristotle, *Nicomachean Ethics*, 109.

13   This is the interpretation of *phronesis* offered by Joe Sachs in his commentary on *Nichomachean Ethics* (209).

14   The idea of divine persuasion in the world signifies the relational dimension of ecological consciousness. Persuasion figures prominently in process thought, though it also appears in some reformed feminist arguments. See Anna Case-Winters, *Reconstructing a Christian Theology of Nature: Down to Earth* (Burlington, Vt.: Ashgate, 2007).

15   Rasmussen, *Earth-Honoring Faith*, 5–6.

16   Larry Rasmussen, with ecologists and ecological philosophers, has argued that the current epoch should be described as the *anthropocene*, as geological and biological systems have been so radically affected by the presence and power of human beings. The moral challenge, he concludes, is to participate in the dawning of a new epoch: the *ecozoic* age (*Earth-Honoring Faith*, 55, 81).

17   McFague, *Super, Natural Christians*, 33.

18   Donna Haraway, "Situated Knowledges: The Science Question in Feminism and the Privilege of Partial Perspective," *Feminist Studies* 14, no. 3 (1988): 582–83. This moral and pedagogical challenge implies an examination of what constitutes knowledge and how one goes about "knowing." These epistemological issues are taken up in more detail in the discussion of the philosophical assumptions of an ecological theory of religious education below.

19   David Orr states the quandary succinctly: "Why is it so hard to talk about love, the most powerful of human emotions, in relation to science, the most powerful and far-reaching of human activities? . . . Perhaps it is only embarrassment about what does or does not move us personally." Orr, "Love," in *Hope Is an Imperative*, 31. The pedagogical critique introduced here will be presented in more detail below.

20   Pope Francis, *Laudato Si'*, 12–13.

21   Elliott Eisner has argued that modes of understanding and fields of study absent from school curricula constitute a "null curriculum." Null curricula have pedagogical outcomes, in that learners are unable to understand or employ that which is absent in their educational experience. Eisner, "The Three Curricula That All Schools Teach," in *The Educational Imagination: On the Design and Evaluation of School Programs*, ed. Elliott Eisner (Upper Saddle River, N.J.: Merrill Prentice Hall, 2002), 87–107.

22 Don E. Saliers argues that true spirituality implicates the whole person: it is "humanity at full stretch before God." Saliers, *Worship and Spirituality* (Akron, Ohio: OSL Publications, 1996), 1.

23 Rachel Carson, "Help Your Child to Wonder," *Women's Home Companion,* July 1956, 46. Published in 1956, Rachel Carson's prescient essay, later republished as *The Sense of Wonder,* describes in evocative terms the cultivation of wonder in children, identifying the ways in which wonder works among adults, even scientists, too.

24 Gerald R. McDermott, "Jonathan Edwards on the Affections and the Spirit," in *The Spirit, the Affections, and the Christian Tradition,* ed. Dale M. Coulter and Amos Yong (Notre Dame, Ind.: University of Notre Dame Press, 2016), 281.

25 Martin Ostrow and Terry Kay Rockefeller, *Renewal: Stories from America's Religious-Environmental Movement* (Fine Cut Productions, 2007).

26 Walter Brueggemann observes that we sometimes accept and even welcome a degree of numbness in exchange for being spared the full weight of consciousness of suffering, oppression, and even death. See Brueggemann, *The Prophetic Imagination,* 2nd ed. (Minneapolis: Fortress, 2001). In search of an "unfailing antidote" to human numbness, Rachel Carson longed for an "indestructible" sense of wonder that could withstand the "disenchantments of later years" whereby adults are alienated "from the source of our strength." Interestingly, Carson describes children's capacities for wonder as "clear-eyed vision, that true instinct for what is beautiful and awe-inspiring, [which] is dimmer and even lost before we reach adulthood." In a posture sometimes dismissed as naïve or childish, Carson stands in marked contrast to the tone of pessimistic realism often associated with something like "clear-eyed vision." In other words, wonder is the correct response to the rightly perceived infinite beauty and power of the world. Carson, "Help Your Child," 46.

27 William P. Brown, *Wisdom's Wonder: Character, Creation, and Crisis in the Bible's Wisdom Literature* (Grand Rapids: Eerdmans, 2014), 21.

28 Carson, "Help Your Child," 46.

29 Carson describes in great detail how Roger could lose himself gazing at and encountering lichens and all manner of life during walks in the Maine woods ("Help Your Child," 46).

30 Brown, *Wisdom's Wonder,* 21. Brown writes: "In its fullness, wonder exhibits an irresistible pull that may begin with a centrifugal push of fear, the push away from the perceived source or object of fear, but ultimately wonder attracts rather than repels. In wonder, fascination overcomes fear, desire overcomes dread."

31 Dianne D. Glave, *Rooted in the Earth: Reclaiming the African American Environmental Heritage* (Chicago: Lawrence Hill Books, 2010), 41, 59.

32 Alphonso Saville, "Where Are Our Brush Harbors Today??" *Patheos: Rhet-oric, Race and Religion,* August 1, 2017, accessed September 1, 2018, http://www.patheos.com/blogs/rhetoricraceandreligion/2017/08/brush-harbors -today.html. See also Anthony E. Kaye, *Joining Places: Slave Neighborhoods in the Old South* (Chapel Hill: University of North Carolina Press, 2009), 40–41; Janet Duitsman Cornelius, *Slave Missions and the Black Church in the Antebellum South* (Columbia: University of South Carolina Press, 1999), 8–12.

33 Stephen Jay Gould, "Unenchanted Evening," in *Eight Little Piggies: Reflec-tions in Natural History* (New York: W. W. Norton, 1993), 40. Gould's appeal to ecological love echoes the words of Senegalese conservationist and forestry engineer Baba Dioum, who told the 1968 General Assembly of the International Union for the Conservation of Nature and Natural Resources, "In the end we will conserve only what we love, we will love only what we understand, and we will understand only what we are taught." Joann M. Valenti and Gaugau Tavana, "Continuing Science Education for Environmental Journalists and Science Writers," *Science Communication* 27, no. 2 (2005): 308.

34 Edward O. Wilson, *Biophilia* (Cambridge, Mass.: Harvard University Press, 1984), 85. Although it is notable that a scientist coined this term, Wilson's hypothesis has proved notoriously difficult to prove, and few published scientific studies have explored it with any depth. See Sharon Begley, "Do We Really Need Nature?" *Mindful,* August 12, 2015, accessed September 3, 2018, https://www.mindful.org/do-we-really-need-nature/. Here, Wilson's hypothesis is treated as an important constructive category for ecological theology, ethics, and philosophy.

35 Rasmussen, *Earth-Honoring Faith,* 22.

36 George Sessions, "Deep Ecology: Introduction," in Zimmerman et al., *Envi-ronmental Philosophy,* 167.

37 Arne Naess, "The Deep Ecological Movement: Some Philosophical Aspects," in Zimmerman et al., *Environmental Philosophy,* 196.

38 Carolyn Merchant, "The Death of Nature," in Zimmerman et al., *Environ-mental Philosophy,* 280.

39 Indeed, this is the question implied in the very subtitle of *Super, Natural Christians* and explored in depth in the second chapter of that book: "How Should Christians Love Nature?" Assuming that Christians *should* love nature, McFague tries to describe in that book *how* they should go about this work.

40 Bauer, *Greek-English Lexicon,* 859.

41 For example, Timothy P. Jackson has argued that *agape* has three central features: "(1) unconditional willing of the good for the other, (2) equal regard for the well-being of the other, and (3) passionate service open to

self-sacrifice for the sake of the other." Jackson, *The Priority of Love: Christian Charity and Social Justice* (Princeton, N.J.: Princeton University Press, 2002), 10.

42   Thomas Aquinas, *Summa Theologica*, vol. 3 (Allen, Tex.: Christian Classics, Thomas More Publishing, 1981), Question 23, Article 1, pp. 1280–81.

43   Anders Nygren, *Agape and Eros*, trans. Philip S. Watson (London: S.P.C.K., 1957), 210.

44   Nygren, *Agape and Eros*, 75–78.

45   Nygren, *Agape and Eros*, 91. Perhaps no modern theologian has devoted as careful and exhaustive attention to the historical interpretations of *agape* and what he understands to be its inverse, *eros*, as Anders Nygren. Nygren argued that *agape* is thus a fundamental motif of the New Testament, a core idea manifest in all parts of the Christian tradition (35). The *agape* motif stands in tension with another fundamental motif: *eros* (209).

46   Nygren, *Agape and Eros*, 91.

47   Nygren, *Agape and Eros*, 91. It is, as Nygren put it, "spontaneous and unmotivated, uncalculating, unlimited, and unconditional."

48   This longing and desire is in part what concerns Nygren about *eros*: he describes *eros* as always an acquisitive love, a longing born out of lacking something, which leads one to strive to satisfy that need by acquiring the object of desire. It is the "will to get and possess which depends on want and need" (*Agape and Eros*, 210). Some have argued that these two conceptions of love are in the end incompatible and that there is no correspondence between the two. Nygren is sharply critical of what he describes as "syncretic" theologies that seek to connect the idea of love as self-giving abundance with the idea of love as longing desire. This is a strong theme throughout *Agape and Eros*, but also it is clearly summarized and critiqued by Virginia Burrus. Burrus, "Introduction: Theology and Eros after Nygren," in *Toward a Theology of Eros: Transfiguring Passion at the Limits of Discipline*, ed. Virginia Burrus and Catherine Keller (New York: Fordham University Press, 2006), xiv. The object of desire might be sensual and material (human sexual desire falls into this category), but in his reading of the Platonic sense of *eros*, material beauty and goodness are a mere shadow of ideal Beauty and the Good. He writes, "The sight of the beautiful, which comes to man in the sense-world, has for its function to awaken Eros in his soul; not, however, in order that his love may be fixed on the beautiful object, but rather than it may pass beyond it in the continual ascent which is of the very essence of Eros." See Nygren, *Agape and Eros*, 173. Other readers of Plato's *Symposium* do not read such a clear distinction between love for the sensual and love for the sublime. For them, love for the sensual, material world is not something to be escaped but intimately woven together with love for divine beauty and goodness. See Mark D. Jordan, "Flesh in the Confession: Alcibiades beside

Augustine," in Burrus and Keller, *Toward a Theology of Eros*, 23–37; Catherine Keller, "Afterword: A Theology of Eros, after Transfiguring Passion,"
in Burrus and Keller, *Toward a Theology of Eros*, 366–74. Whether sensual
or sublime, however, Nygren dismisses *eros* as a Christian framework for
love. Even heavenly *eros* is always egocentric, he worries, because it is the
human being's desire, even what might be called "love for God," that must be
satisfied. It ultimately and always serves the self and the self's ascent toward
God. Even theologians who seek to retrieve conceptions of *eros* often agree
that, absent *agape*, *eros* becomes a "greedy grasp." Keller, "Afterword," 373.

49 Such perspectives hold a rather limited view of *eros*, identifying it with
Nygren's reading of "vulgar" *eros*: when lovers become preoccupied with
the acquisition of a material good, this constitutes "vulgar" *eros*. When lovers
pass through and are thus "delivered" from the material good, Nygren understands this to be a sublimation of desire for the sensual good by "heavenly"
or ascetic *eros* (*Agape and Eros*, 51).

50 Audre Lorde famously argued that *eros* is the personification of love, creative
power, and harmony born of chaos. It is the deepest kind of knowledge, even
as it is nonrational. Sometimes confused with the pornographic, it has been
suppressed and suspected as a source of power: "For the bridge is sensual—
those physical, emotional, and psychic expressions of what is deepest, and
strongest, and richest within us." Lorde, "Uses of the Erotic: The Erotic as
Power," in *Sister Outsider: Essays and Speeches*, reprint ed. (Berkeley, Calif.:
Crossing Press, 2007), 56.

51 Matthew Henry, "Song of Solomon," in *Commentary on the Whole Bible*,
vol. 3, *Job to Song of Solomon* (1710), online at Christian Classics Ethereal
Library, https://www.ccel.org/ccel/henry/mhc3.html.

52 Keller, "Afterword," 368.

53 Nygren, *Agape and Eros*, 210.

54 Plumwood, "Nature, Self, and Gender," 294.

55 Catherine Keller argues that Nygren is mistaken to presume that *Eros* is
predicated on lack. Associating *eros* with the yearning for that which is
lacking risks confusing *eros* with covetousness, which presumes a context of
scarcity. Certainly, as a creative—indeed, procreative—force in the world,
eros is generative, rather than deleterious: "But what about creative desire:
the desire to make something beautiful, something new? The desire to create
cannot, I suggest, be reduced to lack. Rather creativity bespeaks fullness
that overflows, that wants to give of its resources, to express itself." Keller,
"Afterword," 369.

56 Karmen MacKendrick, "Carthage Didn't Burn Hot Enough: Saint Augustine's Divine Seduction," in Burrus and Keller, *Toward a Theology of Eros*, 212.

57 Mayra Rivera notes that Luce Irigaray somewhat problematically situates
these phenomena of wonder, surprise, and astonishment in sexual difference,

perhaps reinscribing sexual hierarchies and gender binaries. Perhaps the deeper principle holds, however: that it is in the desire of another and the embodied relationship to another body that humans are opened to wonder, surprise, and astonishment. This principle might thereby extend to embodied encounters with nature. Rivera, "Ethical Desires: Toward a Theology of Relational Transcendence," in Burrus and Keller, *Toward a Theology of Eros*, 262. Erotic love, Rivera observes, is a means by which humans seek to transcend themselves. It is not always, however, a narcissistic, individual ascent but often a "relational transcendence" ("Ethical Desires," 253).

58 Emmanuel Levinas would argue that the encounter with the other, face to face, confronts one with the irreducible separation between beings. The other is always exterior. In contrast, Irigaray would argue that the encounter with the other, body to body, confronts us with the paradox that the very drawing nearer to another—even to the point of drawing another into the self, or being drawn into the body of another—implies an insurmountable distancing, even in the most intimate of approaches. Rivera, "Ethical Desires," 260–62. Here, erotic longing is poignant, an "elusive mystery of which the preservation is necessary . . . [it] welcomes touch; it envelops bodies, within and without." Rivera, "Ethical Desires," 260. Rather than perpetuating a separation, however, the "elusive mystery" functions alluringly, even seductively, "whisper[ing], 'Wait, there's more.'" MacKendrick, "Carthage Didn't Burn," 212.

59 This is what Sallie McFague describes as the "Loving Eye," which stands in direct contrast with the "Arrogant Eye" (*Super, Natural Christians*, 33–34).

60 The concept of "erotic education" is explored below. See Rosemary P. Carbine, "Erotic Education: Elaborating a Feminist and Faith-Based Pedagogy for Experiential Learning in Religious Studies," *Teaching Theology & Religion* 13, no. 4 (2010): 320–38.

61 See "Love. Not Loss," International Union for Conservation of Nature Commission on Education and Communication, last modified 2018, accessed March 13, 2019, https://www.iucn.org/commissions/commission -education-and-communication/cec-resources/love-not-loss; Ronne Randall and Nicola Evans, *Chicken Little* (New York: Parragon Books, 2015).

62 Colin Murray Parkes and Holly G. Prigerson, *Bereavement: Studies of Grief in Adult Life*, 4th ed. (New York: Routledge, 2010), 6.

63 Robert Saler, personal conversation.

64 Ashlee Cunsolo and Neville R. Ellis, "Ecological Grief as a Mental Health Response to Climate Change-Related Loss," *Nature Climate Change* 8 (2018): 275.

65 Aldo Leopold, "The Round River—A Parable," in *Round River: From the Journals of Aldo Leopold* (New York: Oxford University Press, 1993), 165.

66 Phyllis Windle, "The Ecology of Grief," *BioScience* 42, no. 5 (1992): 366.

67   Cunsolo and Ellis, "Ecological Grief," 276.

68   An emerging field of study considers the effect of "environmental grief" in human consciousness and action: Jordan Rosenfeld, "Facing Down 'Environmental Grief,'" *Scientific American*, July 21, 2016; Windle, "Ecology of Grief."

69   Calvin, *Institutes*, 2.1.8. I have written elsewhere on the relationship between moral action and doctrines of sin. See Ayres, *Waiting for a Glacier*.

70   See McFague, *Super, Natural Christians*; Rasmussen, *Earth-Honoring Faith*. Reinhold Niebuhr perhaps most famously articulated the fundamental human tension between finitude and transcendence. Human nature is marked by both the boundaries of finitude (limits) and a transcendent awareness of and desire to reach beyond these same boundaries. The desire to test, stretch, and even transcend human finitude, however, cannot be directly equated with human sin. Reinhold Niebuhr, *The Nature and Destiny of Man: A Christian Interpretation*, vol. 1, Library of Theological Ethics (Louisville, Ky.: Westminster John Knox, 1996).

71   Niebuhr, *Nature and Destiny*, 17.

72   Andrew Linzey (among others) levied a critique against ecotheological preoccupation with interdependence, which he argues fails to account for disproportionate human power. Linzey, *Creatures of the Same God: Explorations in Animal Theology* (Brooklyn: Lantern Books, 2009); Linzey, "Is Christianity Irredeemably Speciesist?" in *Animals on the Agenda: Questions about Animals for Theology and Ethics*, ed. Andrew Linzey and Dorothy Yamamoto (Chicago: University of Illinois Press, 1998).

73   Matthew Humphrey, "Lived Theology in the Little Campbell Watershed," in *Rooted and Grounded: Essays on Land and Christian Discipleship*, ed. Ryan Dallas Harker and Janeen Bertsche Johnson (Eugene, Ore.: Wipf and Stock, 2016), 119.

74   Moltmann, *God in Creation*, 207.

75   Richard A. Floyd, *Down to Earth: Christian Hope and Climate Change* (Eugene, Ore.: Cascade Books, 2015), 19.

76   Moltmann, *Theology of Hope*, 21.

77   John B. Cobb Jr., *Sustainability: Economics, Ecology, and Justice* (Maryknoll, N.Y.: Orbis Books, 1992), 13, 51, 123.

78   Nathaniel Rich, "Losing Earth: The Decade We Almost Stopped Climate Change," *New York Times*, August 1, 2018, sec. Magazine, accessed September 5, 2018, https://www.nytimes.com/interactive/2018/08/01/magazine/climate-change-losing-earth.html.

79   Andrew Zolli, "Learning to Bounce Back," *New York Times*, October 18, 2016.

CHAPTER 3: RELIGIOUS EDUCATION FOR INHABITANCE

1   Pope Francis, *Laudato Si'*, 140–44.

2   Saliers, *Worship and Spirituality*, 1.

3   Rasmussen, *Earth-Honoring Faith*, 104. Rasmussen describes human beings
     as "biosocial" creatures, our existence dependent on the "Earth community"
     (23). Sallie McFague has argued that Christians' proper way of engaging
     nature is through the gaze of the "loving eye" (*Super, Natural Christians*, 30).
4   Rasmussen, *Earth-Honoring Faith*, 103–9.
5   Werner Jaeger, *Paideia: The Ideals of Greek Culture*, vol. 1 (New York: Oxford
     University Press, 1945), 286.
6   Several religious education scholars already seriously theorize, evaluate,
     and propose constructive approaches to the ecological dimensions of reli-
     gious education. See Mary Elizabeth Moore, *Ministering with the Earth* (St.
     Louis: Chalice Press, 1998); Timothy L. Van Meter, *Created in Delight:
     Youth, Church, and the Mending of the World* (Eugene, Ore.: Wipf and Stock,
     2013); Miriam K. Martin, "Religious Education and a New Earth Conscious-
     ness: 'Let Us Play,'" *Theoforum* 41, no. 1 (2010): 93–112. Up to this point,
     however, there has been little attention to the body of literature in environ-
     mental educational theory and practice, although Van Meter incorporates
     the work of Chet Bowers. See C. A. Bowers, *Educating for Eco-Justice and
     Community* (Athens: University of Georgia Press, 2001). A growing field,
     environmental education refers broadly to all those educational theories
     (and there is an incredible amount of diversity within the field) that set as
     their goal the nurturing of environmental awareness of learners. The field
     includes attention to best practices of teaching and learning, educational
     theory, and environmental science, among other intersections. Although
     one might trace strands of environmental education through many eras and
     contexts of learning, the contemporary field of "environmental education"
     as we know it identifies as a key developmental moment the publication of
     Rachel Carson's essay, "Help Your Child to Wonder" in 1956. See Carson,
     "Help Your Child." The field of environmental education is well-established,
     diverse, and situated across a variety of learning contexts: early childhood
     education, primary and secondary schools, colleges and universities, busi-
     ness, government, and nonprofit institutions. The North American Associa-
     tion for Environmental Education reports a membership of sixteen thousand.
     Each year, more than a thousand members and affiliates gather for an annual
     conference. The NAAEE defines environmental education as the process by
     which learners develop the skills necessary to "learn about and investigate
     their environment, and to make intelligent, informed decisions about how
     they can take care of it." See "About EE and Why It Matters," NAAEE, North
     American Association for Environmental Education, last modified May 19,
     2015, accessed September 1, 2018, https://naaee.org/about-us/about-ee
     -and-why-it-matters. Generally speaking, while there are many particular
     ways of approaching environmental education, all of these programs might
     be said to share an "interest in planetary well-being." The many terms used

to describe what they are doing by theorists and practitioners who share this goal include "ecological education, environmental education, environmental learning, bioregional education, nature education, place-based education, education for sustainability, and education for sustainable living." See Judson, *New Approach*, 9.

7   Some of the current literature in environmental education has taken up the task of assessing the state of that field, now half a century old, and some scholars lament the limited successes that environmental education efforts might claim when it comes to measuring the environmental commitments in the general population. If environmental education has been successful, they argue, would we not see increased understanding of issues like climate change, pollution, and waste reduction? Some attribute the unrealized purposes of environmental education to a gap between theory and practice in the field. These gaps may very well be emotional and even spiritual in character, dimensions of a comprehensive model of education as *paideia* that is at the heart of some theories of religious education.

8   David W. Orr, for example, notes that some traditional capacities like description and analysis, the cultivation of which have been at the heart of environmental education, are limited: "The cultivation of the sense of wonder, however, takes us to the edge, where language loses its power to describe and where analysis, the taking apart of things, goes limp before the mystery of Creation, where the only appropriate response is prayerful silence." Orr, "Place as Teacher," in *Hope Is an Imperative*, 228. His appeal to mystery echoes that of nature writer and philosopher Wendell Berry, who observed that ecological questions, generally, are also "religious, because they are asked at the limit of what I know; they acknowledge mystery and honor its presence in the creation; they are spoken in reverence for the order and grace that I see, and that I trust beyond my power to see" ("Native Hill," 22–23).

9   Grant P. Wiggins and Jay McTighe, *Understanding by Design* (Alexandria, Va.: Association for Supervision and Curriculum Development, 2005).

10   This way of thinking about theories of religious education was first introduced to me by my mentor, Pamela Mitchell Legg, at the Presbyterian School of Christian Education. More than twenty years later, I find this approach still extraordinarily helpful in grounding approaches to religious education.

11   Since sometime around 2000, many climate scientists, geologists, and other scientists have argued that human influence on the ecosystems of the planet actually has ushered in a new epoch: the anthropocene age. "From their trawlers scraping the floors of the seas to their dams impounding sediment by the gigatonne, from their stripping of forests to their irrigation of farms, from their mile-deep mines to their melting of glaciers, humans were bringing about an age of planetary change. With a colleague, Eugene Stoermer, Dr

Crutzen suggested this age be called the Anthropocene—'the recent age of man.'" "A Man-Made World—The Anthropocene," *Economist*, last modified May 26, 2011, accessed September 2, 2018, https://www.economist.com/briefing/2011/05/26/a-man-made-world.

12   Lisa Friedman and Glenn Thrush, "U.S. Report Says Humans Cause Climate Change, Contradicting Top Trump Officials," *New York Times*, November 3, 2017, accessed September 2, 2018, https://www.nytimes.com/2017/11/03/climate/us-climate-report.html. It is notable that this report was released one year into the presidential term of Donald J. Trump, an administration vocally critical of the conclusions of climate research.

13   John Sutter, "Sixth Extinction: The Era of 'Biological Annihilation,'" *CNN*, last modified July 11, 2017, accessed September 2, 2018, https://www.cnn.com/2017/07/11/world/sutter-mass-extinction-ceballos-study/index.html. Other scientists, similarly alarmed about human-caused loss of biodiversity, caution against using language like "mass extinction," arguing that such an assessment can be made only in hindsight and usually describes a more catastrophic scenario than what the planet faces today. Peter Brannen, "Earth Is Not in the Midst of a Sixth Mass Extinction," *Atlantic*, last modified June 13, 2017, accessed September 2, 2018, https://www.theatlantic.com/science/archive/2017/06/the-ends-of-the-world/529545/.

14   See, for example, the 130-ton "fatberg," a mass comprising primarily wet wipes and cooking fat dislodged from London's sewer system in 2017. Jason Slotkin, "Behold the Fatberg: London's 130-Ton, 'Rock-Solid' Sewer Blockage," *NPR.Org*, last modified September 12, 2017, accessed September 2, 2018, https://www.npr.org/sections/thetwo-way/2017/09/12/550465000/behold-the-fatberg-london-s-130-ton-rock-solid-sewer-blockage. Other majority world countries are buried in exported e-waste from the United States, waste that consumers believe is recycled but often finds its way to pyres and landfills in other parts of the world. Stephen Leahy, "Each U.S. Family Trashes 400 iPhones' Worth of E-Waste a Year," *National Geographic*, last modified December 13, 2017, accessed September 2, 2018, https://news.nationalgeographic.com/2017/12/e-waste-monitor-report-glut/.

15   With the provocative title, "What Is Education For?" David W. Orr interrogates the fundamental purposes of education, arguing that several myths undergird current approaches to education. For example, an educational emphasis on the mastery of knowledge assumes that "ignorance is a solvable problem . . . [but] ignorance is not a solvable problem; it is rather an inescapable part of the human condition." Orr, "What Is Education For?" in *Hope Is an Imperative*, 239.

16   Orr, "What Is Education For?" 242.

17   Eisner, "Three Curricula," 97.

18 Orr, "Ecological Literacy," 92. The educational goal of ecological literacy is examined in more detail alongside other ecological capacities below.

19 Seth Motel, "Polls Show Most Americans Believe in Climate Change, but Give It Low Priority," *Pew Research Center*, September 23, 2014, accessed September 2, 2018, http://www.pewresearch.org/fact-tank/2014/09/23/most-americans-believe-in-climate-change-but-give-it-low-priority/.

20 Orr, "Ecological Literacy," 89–90. Orr, notably not a theologian, describes this failure as a "sin of omission and of commission" (85).

21 Eric Holthaus, "Stop Scaring People about Climate Change. It Doesn't Work," *Grist*, July 11, 2017, accessed September 5, 2018, https://grist.org/climate-energy/stop-scaring-people-about-climate-change-it-doesnt-work/.

22 MacKendrick, "Carthage Didn't Burn," 213. Erotic love cast in ecological terms is discussed at length above.

23 "The hallmark of networked individualism is that people function more as connected individuals and less as embedded group members." Harrison Rainie and Barry Wellman, *Networked: The New Social Operating System* (Cambridge, Mass.: MIT Press, 2012), 26.

24 John Cacioppo and Stephanie Cacioppo, "Loneliness Is a Modern Epidemic in Need of Treatment," *New Scientist*, last modified December 30, 2014, accessed September 5, 2018, https://www.newscientist.com/article/dn26739-loneliness-is-a-modern-epidemic-in-need-of-treatment/.

25 Both British Health Secretary Jeremy Hunt (in 2013) and former U.S. surgeon general Vivek Murthy (in 2017) identified loneliness as a public health issue. See "Hunt Highlights Plight of the Lonely," *BBC News*, October 18, 2013, sec. UK Politics, accessed September 6, 2018, https://www.bbc.co.uk/news/uk-politics-24572231; Murthy, "Work and the Loneliness Epidemic," *Harvard Business Review*, September 26, 2017, accessed September 6, 2018, https://hbr.org/2017/09/work-and-the-loneliness-epidemic.

26 Murthy, "Work and the Loneliness Epidemic." See also Robert Stuart Weiss, *Loneliness: The Experience of Emotional and Social Isolation* (Cambridge, Mass.: MIT Press, 1974).

27 "The Lonely Society?" *Mental Health Foundation*, last modified May 2, 2010, accessed September 6, 2018, https://www.mentalhealth.org.uk/publications/the-lonely-society.

28 See Robert N. Bellah, *Habits of the Heart: Individualism and Commitment in American Life* (Berkeley: University of California Press, 1985); Robert D. Putnam, *Bowling Alone: The Collapse and Revival of American Community* (New York: Simon & Schuster, 2000); Sherry Turkle, *Alone Together: Why We Expect More from Technology and Less from Each Other* (New York: Basic Books, 2012). Unpacking these arguments is beyond the purview of this book, and valid critiques have been made of each of these arguments. Salient for ecological religious education, however, is the perennial struggle to make

       meaningful connections, a struggle that is at the very least exacerbated by a digital milieu.

29   Religious education and youth ministry scholar Andrew Zirschky contrasts networked individualism with the Christian theological concept of *koinonia*, which he describes as communities of presence. Zirschky, *Beyond the Screen: Youth Ministry for the Connected but Alone Generation* (Nashville: Youth Ministry Partners and Abingdon Press, 2015), 16. Networked individuals bear the burden of maintaining social relationships, while communities of presence are spaces where individuals are drawn into the Body of Christ, inviting a different quality of relationship. Networked individuals are "the hub and center of their networks as they try to attract enough diverse connections to give them security and social support" (83). In contrast, "communion is a matter of being with, for, and within each other" (95).

30   Judson, *New Approach*, 9.

31   Gillis, "U.N. Climate Panel Endorses Ceiling"; Pope Francis, *Laudato Si'*, 3.

32   Orr, "What Is Education For?" 242. Ecological education suggests that the formation of the affections, the imagination, and the moral self are the very purpose of education. This is why, Orr argues, we must ask ourselves, "What is education for?" When framed this way, education is a kind of *paideia*, a learning that forms the whole person. As such, it implicates not only the character of individual persons and learning communities but also the visions and commitments that they hold.

33   Thomas Berry calls for a transition to an "Ecozoic Age," in which "humans will be present to the planet as participating members of the comprehensive Earth community. This is our Great Work . . ." Berry, *The Great Work: Our Way into the Future* (New York: Random House, 1999), 8.

34   Here I mean "land" in the same broad sense that Aldo Leopold used the term: "to include soils, waters, plants, and animals, or collectively: the land" ("Land Ethic," 172).

35   Ecological understanding, in this sense, is a broad and general capacity that applies to both the natural world and its sociocultural dynamics. In a more particular sense, ecological understanding might also refer to the science of ecology and its key principles: understanding, at least at an elementary level, how biosystems work or the basic principles of climate science, for example. Judson, *New Approach*, 13–14. Ecological understanding, construed in this way, mirrors the most foundational elements of learning categorized by education scholar Benjamin Bloom. In Bloom's taxonomy, learning begins with the processes of recalling and remembering key concepts and data, and a subsequent capacity to understand the significance of those concepts. Patricia Armstrong, "Bloom's Taxonomy," *Vanderbilt University*, last modified June 10, 2010, accessed September 6, 2018, https://wp0.vanderbilt.edu/cft/guides-sub-pages/blooms-taxonomy/.

36 David Orr calls this "ecological literacy," which shares many theoretical assumptions with what other scholars call "ecological consciousness." Here, the term "consciousness" is preferred because of its implication that the learner's perception and way of understanding the *self* are at stake. Orr's category of ecological literacy clearly shares this deeper understanding of learning, but consciousness makes it clearer. Indeed, many of the scholars in the field of ecological education use these diverse terms to refer to the same purpose. Orr, "Ecological Literacy," 87.

37 Judson, *New Approach*, 13–14. Ecological consciousness challenges grounding assumptions of what it means to "know." This epistemological challenge is addressed below.

38 Judson, *New Approach*, 14. An ecologically conscious person "feels an affinity between the natural other and the self."

39 Orr, "Ecological Literacy," 86.

40 Rasmussen, *Earth-Honoring Faith*, 12.

41 Judson, *New Approach*, 30. In a well-known critique of standard taxonomies of learning, Lee S. Shulman argued that while defining and understanding basic concepts is an early moment in the learning process, first learners must be engaged and motivated by the question at hand. See Shulman, "Making Differences: A Table of Learning," *Change* 34 (2002): 36–44.

42 Leopold, "Land Ethic," 172.

43 Leopold, "Land Ethic," 181. Freya Mathews calls this awareness the realization of the ecological self, the self-perception that encourages human beings to see and experience the correspondence between the love and protection they have for their own bodies, and "a loving and protective attitude to the world." Mathews, *The Ecological Self* (London: Routledge, 1991), 149. Love for ecological context, in Mathews' view, is a full expression of self-love.

44 Orr, "Ecological Literacy," 86.

45 One example described by Judson, and judged yet wanting, is the Edible Schoolyard program. The Edible Schoolyard, established at Martin Luther King Jr. Middle School in Berkeley, California, uses a school garden, landscape, and kitchen as a multidisciplinary and multisensory setting for learning. The themes of cultivation and preparation of food are integrated across the curriculum: in science, math, and humanities classes. While they are perhaps not yet established enough to be evaluated according to their effectiveness, Judson worries that even these programs that meet current "best practice" standards fail to engage adequately the emotional and imaginative capacities of learners: "These 'good' programs are not good enough when it comes to supporting the emotional and imaginative core of ecological understanding." Judson, *New Approach*, 23.

46 Judson, *New Approach*, 4. In recent years imagination has gained some traction as a key descriptive category in theology, ethics, and educational

theory and now is finding a place in ecological educational theory. Defining imagination theoretically is beyond the purview of this book, but a few explanatory words and conceptual connections are in order.

47 Maxine Greene, *Releasing the Imagination: Essays on Education, the Arts, and Social Change* (San Francisco: Jossey-Bass, 2000), 19.

48 Greene, *Releasing the Imagination*, 35; Amy Levad, *Restorative Justice: Theories and Practices of Moral Imagination*, Criminal Justice: Recent Scholarship (El Paso: LFB Scholarly Publishing, 2012), 70–72.

49 Greene, *Releasing the Imagination*, 28.

50 Greene, *Releasing the Imagination*, 3. The economic sufferings of farmers in another country, for example, might seem a distant if unfortunate set of circumstances that demand little from persons in the United States besides sympathy and well-wishes for a better future. However, when one is able to perceive, emotionally and in coherent detail, the often invisible global economic, political, and agricultural connections that make this suffering persist, the relationship takes on a different character. An inhabitant can imagine how, in the context of interdependence, one is a participant in this system and has a role to play in the alleviation of this suffering.

51 Although one might argue that imagination is, in its very interconnected character, ecological by default, we might put a sharper point on it by defining ecological imagination as "a flexibility of mind oriented toward interdependence and pattern, to the diversity and complexity that characterize natural- and human-world relationships. This type of imaginative process is inspired by one's emotional connection to the natural environment." Judson, *New Approach*, 5.

52 Woody Hickox, personal correspondence.

53 Given that imagination bears within it these relational, connectional, and moral capacities, its role in the formation of ecological consciousness emerges as an obvious and organic component. Interestingly, few ecological education theorists treat imagination with any degree of specificity. Judson, *New Approach*, 31.

54 Stuart Taylor, "A River Flows Through Us" (Sermon, Elkin Presbyterian Church, Elkin, N.C., January 11, 2015), accessed September 12, 2018, https://elkinpres.podbean.com/e/a-river-flows-through-us/.

55 The Church of the Pilgrim's ecological liturgical practices are discussed in more detail below. For more on the ecological and social aspects of the Eucharist, see Jennifer R. Ayres, *Good Food: Grounded Practical Theology* (Waco, Tex.: Baylor University Press, 2013).

56 Robert W. Pazmiño has argued that there are six sets of "foundational issues" in Christian religious education that shape what we understand education to be, what it is for, and how it unfolds. These foundational issues are theological (what do we believe about God and God's relationship to the world?),

biblical (what role does sacred text play in religious education, and how does learning happen in biblical settings?), psychological (how does the inner life and development of the learner affect the process of learning?), sociological (how does learning engage social settings, and how does education form and transform social groups?), historical (what historical commitments or practices shall be retrieved, reformed, or rejected?), and philosophical (what basic questions of human life and meaning are at stake?). In any theory and practice of Christian religious education, one might be able to locate and analyze all six of these "foundational issues," but often two or three more substantively shape the theory and hold the context, purpose, and practices together. Pazmiño, *Foundational Issues in Christian Education: An Introduction in Evangelical Perspective*, 3rd ed. (Grand Rapids: Baker Academic, 2008).

57 Focusing on moments of formal instruction to the exclusion of all of the ways in which the practices of a faith community shape religious identity and character would prove an inadequate foundation for more comprehensive theories of religious education. John Westerhoff, for example, lamented the segregation of children and youth from the rest of the life of the church, especially during corporate worship. He argued that it is in worshipping together that the faith is transmitted from generation to generation. See John H. Westerhoff III, *Will Our Children Have Faith?* (New York: Seabury Press, 1976), 52–57. Maria Harris made a correlative point, appreciatively identifying all the ministries of the church that contribute to the formation of individual Christians and a Christian community as a whole: formal instruction (*didache*) undoubtedly does this, but so do practices of service (*diakonia*), preaching (*kerygma*), worship (*leitourgia*), and fellowship (*koinonia*). Harris, *Teaching and Religious Imagination: An Essay in the Theology of Teaching* (San Francisco: Harper and Row, 1987).

58 Dykstra, *Growing in the Life of Faith*, 12.

59 MacIntyre, *After Virtue*, 187. Practices are discussed in more detail below.

60 MacIntyre, *After Virtue*, 222.

61 Leopold, "Land Ethic," 172.

62 Feminist philosopher Lorraine Code compares ecological knowing to the knowing between two human beings: "[Ecological] knowledge is not primarily propositional . . . knowing all such facts about another person might not warrant claiming to know her." Code, *Ecological Thinking*, 49.

63 Edmund V. O'Sullivan and Marilyn M. Taylor, "Glimpses of an Ecological Consciousness," in *Learning Toward an Ecological Consciousness: Selected Transformative Practices*, ed. Edmund V. O'Sullivan and Marilyn M. Taylor (New York: Palgrave MacMillan, 2004), 8.

64 Sallie McFague calls this way of encountering the world the "arrogant eye." McFague, *The Body of God: An Ecological Theology* (Nashville: Augsburg Fortress, 1993), 88.

65   Carbine, "Erotic Education," 323. Rosemary Carbine describes this
     approach to education as "erotic," resonating with the call to cultivate an
     erotic relationship to the ecosystem presented in chapter 2.
66   Ostrow and Rockefeller, *Renewal.*
67   Dykstra, "Reconceiving Practice," 45.
68   Although here employed primarily as a pedagogical category, the concept
     of practice is a key aspect of larger conversations about moral formation
     and character education. Indeed, Alasdair MacIntyre concludes that one
     of the factors in the breakdown of moral discourse and disagreement in
     societies is the decline of the formative influence of traditions, encountered
     in communities of practice, in persons' lives. It is through traditions, he
     argues, that human beings develop shared conceptions of a good life. And
     they discover these conceptions of the good life by participating in social
     practices. See Ayres, *Waiting for a Glacier.*
69   As described above, religious education scholar John Westerhoff would call
     this process "enculturation." Westerhoff, *Will Our Children Have Faith?* 80.
70   This is the question preoccupying Werner Jaeger in his three-volume explo-
     ration of the concept and historical trajectory of *paideia.* As envisioned by
     the Greeks, beginning with Homeric epic poetry in the eighth and seventh
     centuries B.C.E. and through Sophocles and Plato, education was a means
     of creating and nurturing a culture. Jaeger, *Paideia,* vol. 1.
71   Jaeger, *Paideia,* 1:21, 274.
72   In Homer's *Iliad* and *Odyssey,* Jaeger traces the evolution of virtue from
     the heroic and courageous fulfillment of one's duty in the context of battle
     to the establishment of nobility in aristocratic civilization. In both cases,
     Jaeger notes, the poetic *form* is essential for understanding *how* education
     in the virtues happens. It is not merely the content of the heroic and epic
     poetry that is educative; indeed, the form itself awakens the aesthetic and
     moral potentialities of humanity. It can bridge abstract concepts of the ideal,
     such as beauty, and the personal experience of the reader or hearer. Poetic
     narrative has the power to touch the human soul in this way. While Jaeger
     is especially concerned with the poetic form, we might also ask how other
     literary forms, and indeed other art forms, might also be a way of "releasing
     the powers of a young soul, breaking down the restraints which hampered
     it, and leading it into a glad activity." Jaeger, *Paideia,* 1:31.
73   While early Homeric literature valorized individually embodied virtue
     of the battle hero, later Homeric poetry and especially the followers of
     Sophocles, some time later, would emphasize the social aspects of virtue
     formation. The Sophists move from the cultivation of virtue via kinship to
     the more conscious and intellectual cultivation of virtue in the commu-
     nity, or the polis. Such virtues would have included intellectual power and
     oratorical ability and would prepare learners to be leaders in society. These

leaders might still be understood to be an aristocratic class of sorts. Jaeger, *Paideia*, 1:288.

74   Werner Jaeger, *Early Christianity and Greek Paideia* (Cambridge, Mass.: Belknap Press of Harvard University Press, 1965), 22–23, 25. Later, Clement's student Origen (and Origen's own students) would use the literary principles of *paideia* to engage biblical texts with an allegorical method, as "transparent illustrations of great metaphysical or ethical truths. This was for them striking proof of the pedagogy of the Holy Spirit." Jaeger, *Early Christianity*, 53.

75   Aristotle, *Nicomachean Ethics*, 4.

76   Although Jaeger's treatment of the historical development of *paideia* remains the most extensive and well-known, it is importantly limited by its culturally narrow reading of the concept. First, Jaeger has rightly been criticized for his "hellenocentric" privileging of Greek culture and history, to the point of erroneously arguing that other historically significant places and peoples did not produce "cultures" and do not constitute "civilizations." See Jaeger, *Paideia*, 1:xiv–xv, xix. Second, Jaeger assumes some agreement on what ideals should shape society and thus education for that society. If education is meant to cultivate the ideal human being with a virtuous character that contributes to the building and maintenance of a just civilization, Jaeger rhetorically asks, "But what is the ideal man? It is the universally valid model of humanity which all individuals are bound to imitate" (1:xxiv). The assumption of a "universally valid model of humanity," coupled with critical suspicion of *whose* model is deemed universally valid, gives the contemporary educator pause. Mortimer Adler and the *Paideia* group would revisit this component of the *paideia* model of education, arguing that, as resistance to unjust hierarchical educational systems and a corresponding stratification in the education of the populace, education should offer one set of educational objectives and one curriculum for all, including a reading list populated by "individual works of merit." In the original *paideia* proposal, the texts prescribed are four: the Declaration of Independence, the Constitution, selections from the Federalist Papers, and the Gettysburg Address. See Mortimer Jerome Adler, *The Paideia Proposal: An Educational Manifesto*, 1st paperback ed. (New York: Macmillan, 1982). Elsewhere, however, Adler cultivated a list of texts that would be used in a variety of educational settings, including the "great books" curricula of some colleges and secondary schools. Those other lists comprise predominantly Western works of literature and philosophy written almost exclusively by men, so the question remains: Whose ideals? Whose culture? See, for example, "Mortimer Adler's Reading List," *Thinking as Leverage*, October 5, 2012, accessed September 6, 2018, https://thinkingasleverage.wordpress.com/book-lists/mortimer-adlers-reading-list/. Finally, a perhaps corollary critique of Jaeger's framework relates to the

way in which Greek conceptions of *paideia* relied on elite classes, aristocracy, and identified "leaders" as the primary embodiers and transmitters of noble virtues. Jaeger's argument for a retrieval of *paideia* thus depends on a hierarchical social structure, which contemporary liberative pedagogy seeks to challenge. All members of a society (or a faith community, for that matter), not just its leaders, are in need of moral formation for just and responsible participation in community, decision-making, and political structures. This is the core conviction at the heart of John Dewey and Paulo Freire's work. See Dewey, *Democracy and Education: An Introduction to the Philosophy of Education* (New York: Free Press, 1966); Freire, *Pedagogy of the Oppressed*, trans. Myra Bergman Ramos (New York: Continuum, 1982).

77 Brazilian educator Paulo Freire would argue that the development of critical consciousness, as an opening toward full humanity, is the purpose of education. Education that does not cultivate the critical faculties, he insists, serves only the interests of the privileged elite because it ultimately oppresses learners, making of them automatons unable to question systems of harm or injustice. Freire, *Pedagogy of the Oppressed*, 71–72.

78 James W. Fowler, *Becoming Adult, Becoming Christian: Adult Development and Christian Faith* (New York: Harper and Row, 1984), 81; Fowler, *Weaving the New Creation: Stages of Faith and the Public Church* (Eugene, Ore.: Wipf and Stock, 1991), 187–88; Edward Farley, *Theologia: The Fragmentation and Unity of Theological Education* (Minneapolis: Augsburg Fortress, 1994), 152–56.

79 Orr, "What Is Education For?" 243.

CHAPTER 4: EDUCATIONAL PRACTICES FOR INHABITANCE

1 Monica Davey and Mitch Smith, "2 Former Flint Emergency Managers Charged over Tainted Water," *New York Times*, December 22, 2017, sec. U.S., accessed September 6, 2018, https://www.nytimes.com/2016/12/20/us/flint-water-charges.html.

2 Julie Bosman, "Flint Water Crisis Inquiry Finds State Ignored Warning Signs," *New York Times*, January 19, 2018, sec. U.S., accessed September 6, 2018, https://www.nytimes.com/2016/03/24/us/flint-water-crisis.html; "QuickFacts: Flint City, Michigan," U.S. Census Bureau, accessed September 6, 2018, https://www.census.gov/quickfacts/fact/table/flintcitymichigan/PST045217.

3 Matthew Haag, "64 Pounds of Trash Killed a Sperm Whale in Spain, Scientists Say," *New York Times*, April 13, 2018, sec. Science, accessed September 6, 2018, https://www.nytimes.com/2018/04/12/science/sperm-whale-death-spain.html.

4 Wiggins and McTighe, *Understanding by Design*, 16–17.

5 Wiggins and McTighe, *Understanding by Design*, 17–18.

6   There is an important and creative tension between the reflective develop-
     ment of learning outcomes and the critique levied against "banking" models
     of education by scholars of critical and liberative pedagogy like Paulo Freire.
     The tension lies in the question of whether a teacher (or institution) should
     be the arbiter of what constitutes learning. A critical pedagogical approach
     seeks to disrupt unidirectional exertions of power in educational systems
     and to establish that teachers and learners alike are always simultaneously
     "teacher-students." Freire, *Pedagogy of the Oppressed*, 59. I believe it is a
     misreading of Freire, however, to reject the use of learning outcomes alto-
     gether. Outcomes concerned with the development of capacities (rather
     than content), especially, are hospitable to critical pedagogy's principle
     goal of the humanization of learners. Becoming an inhabitant is entirely
     about becoming more human—in emotional, intellectual, theological, and
     moral perspective. Certainly, however, educational approaches that priv-
     ilege content acquisition above all else more perilously tread the line of
     reducing learning to the point where "the scope of action allowed to the
     students extends only as far as receiving, filing, and storing the deposits."
     Freire, *Pedagogy of the Oppressed*, 58.
7   Armstrong, "Bloom's Taxonomy."
8   Bloom and colleagues did develop what they described as an "affective
     taxonomy," considering the important role played by learners' receptivity,
     response to, and internalization of cognitive learning. Shulman, "Making
     Differences," 39.
9   Shulman, "Making Differences," 38.
10   Shulman, "Making Differences," 38, 41 (emphasis in original).
11   David W. Orr, "Slow Knowledge," in *Hope Is an Imperative*, 14.
12   The epistemological assumptions undergirding education for inhabitance
     were proposed in the previous chapter. Orr, "Slow Knowledge," 14.
13   Orr, "Slow Knowledge," 15.
14   David Orr writes that slow knowledge is "shaped and calibrated to fit a particu-
     lar ecological and cultural context. It does not imply lethargy, but rather care-
     fulness and patience. The aim of slow knowledge is resilience, harmony, and
     the preservation of . . . 'the patterns that connect'" ("Slow Knowledge," 16).
15   Orr, "Slow Knowledge," 17.
16   Pope Francis, *Laudato Si'*, 13.
17   Judson, *New Approach*, 69.
18   Judson, *New Approach*, 69.
19   Sharon Daloz Parks argues that faith is itself the process of meaning-making.
     Parks, *Big Questions, Worthy Dreams: Mentoring Emerging Adults in Their
     Search for Meaning, Purpose, and Faith*, rev. ed. (San Francisco: Jossey-Bass,
     2011), 27–37.

20 Howard E. Gardner, "In a Nutshell," in *Multiple Intelligences: New Horizons* (New York: Basic Books, 2006), 3–24. Multiple intelligences theory, developed by educational psychologist Howard Gardner, holds that an intelligence is "the ability to solve problems or fashion products that are of consequence in a particular cultural setting or community" (6). Our schooling in the United States, however, tends to privilege only some forms of intelligence, ignoring the cultivation of other capacities for knowing. Gardner originally identified seven intelligences: linguistic, logical-mathematical, bodily-kinesthetic, visual-spatial, musical, interpersonal, and intrapersonal. Interestingly, other scholars suggested to Gardner that he add an eighth intelligence, the "naturalist" intelligence. Gardner agreed that the capacities described did meet the criteria to constitute a discrete intelligence. While the naturalist intelligence includes capacities that might resonate with ecological educational concepts of understanding, Gardner's description of it still seems to privilege the more "indoor" cognitive skills of classification and identification above more relational capacities that characterize ecological consciousness or imagination, capacities that implicate the emotions and the body (18–19).

21 Orr, "Ecological Literacy," 87. Elliott Eisner understood that the architecture of an educational space, coupled with the time and approach afforded to any given topic, "teaches" as much as does the explicit content and learning objectives. He described this as the "implicit curriculum." Eisner, "Three Curricula," 92–93.

22 Orr, "What Is Education For?" 244.

23 Some describe this as "activeness," arguing that it requires intentional embodied experience in connection with nature, accompanied by intentional efforts to make sense of that experience. Activeness in this usage is distinguished from activity, which is the mere experience of kinesthetic movement. It requires the "attunement of our senses with our surroundings." Judson, *New Approach*, 69.

24 Judson, *New Approach*, 69.

25 Wiggins and McTighe, *Understanding by Design*, 16. As described above, curriculum theorists Wiggins and McTighe were concerned about the temptation to vacillate between these poles of curriculum design: fixating on either the content to be "covered" or the selection of interesting and engaging activities. Instead, they argue, teachers must begin with intended outcomes for the learners: what we hope learners will be able to understand or do as a result of the learning event, which in terms of ecological education would be the cultivation of skills and capacities indicative of ecological consciousness or imagination.

26 John Dewey, *Experience and Education* (New York: Touchstone, 1938).

27 Among such writers is David Orr, who observes: "First, in the lives of most, if not all, people who define themselves as environmentalists, there is experience in the natural world at an early age. . . . Second, and not surprisingly, there is often an older teacher or mentor as a role model: a grandfather, a neighbor, an older brother, a parent, or a teacher." To these two factors, Orr adds a third: "Seminal books that explain, heighten, and say what we have felt deeply but not said so well" ("Ecological Literacy," 88).

28 Ostrow and Rockefeller, *Renewal*.

29 Carson, "Help Your Child," 46.

30 These ecological affections were introduced above.

31 Rosemary Carbine understands this desire to be the root of *eros*, the "joyful, creative energy of shared connections between the self and other" ("Erotic Education," 323).

32 Lorde, "Uses of the Erotic," 56.

33 Greene, *Releasing the Imagination*, 27.

34 Courtney T. Goto, *The Grace of Playing: Pedagogies for Leaning into God's New Creation*, Horizons in Religious Education (Eugene, Ore.: Pickwick, 2016), 21.

35 Goto, *Grace of Playing*, 3, 19.

36 Goto, *Grace of Playing*, 20.

37 Furthermore, students in economically depressed school districts are more likely to have no recess time at all. Nicholas Day, "The Rebirth of Recess," *Slate*, August 29, 2012, accessed September 6, 2018, http://www.slate .com/articles/life/family/2012/08/recess_in_schools_research_shows _it_benefits_children_.html.

38 For a brief and accessible summary of recent research and policy analysis of the standardized testing fortified by No Child Left Behind, see Alia Wong, "So Many Tests, So Little Information," *Atlantic*, last modified October 28, 2015, accessed September 6, 2018, https://www.theatlantic.com/education/ archive/2015/10/testing-testing/412735/.

39 Recess promotes "social interaction, exploration and creativity." Eric Westervelt, "Trim Recess? Some Schools Hold On to Child's Play," *NPR.Org*, last modified November 7, 2013, accessed September 6, 2018, https://www.npr.org/2013/ 11/07/243713419/trim-recess-some-schools-hold-on-to-childs-play.

40 Louise Chawla et al., "Green Schoolyards as Havens from Stress and Resources for Resilience in Childhood and Adolescence," *Health & Place* 28 (2014): 6. "Students in grades 1–4 voted for their choice of woods play with their feet. During three fall seasons, 96% of the students in these early grades were observed to head for the woods as their regular recess location."

41 Chawla et al., "Green Schoolyards," 6.

42 Kit Harrington, "Magic, Wonder, Science and Exploration: The Educational Value of Fairy Villages," *Natural Start Alliance*, last modified July

2015, accessed December 19, 2018, https://naturalstart.org/feature-stories/
magic-wonder-science-and-exploration-educational-value-fairy-villages;
Lisa Davis, "Pixie Sticks: Fairy Houses Are Popping Up in Backyards and
along a New Permanent Trail," *Anniston Star* (Anniston, Ala.), May 3, 2015,
accessed March 15, 2019, https://www.annistonstar.com/features/pixie
-sticks-fairy-houses-are-popping-up-in-backyards-and/article_a7887de2
-f070-11e4-bab0-6f725d2bb443.html.

43 See Orr, "What Is Education For?"

44 Carson, "Help Your Child"; Richard Louv, *The Last Child in the Woods:
Saving Our Children from Nature-Deficit Disorder*, rev. and updated (Chapel
Hill, N.C.: Algonquin Books of Chapel Hill, 2008).

45 MacIntyre, *After Virtue*; Dorothy C. Bass and Craig Dykstra, "A Theological
Understanding of Christian Practices," in Bass and Volf, *Practicing Theology*, 13–32.

46 Orr, "Ecological Literacy," 92.

47 David W. Orr, "Epilogue," in *Ecological Literacy*, 182.

48 Robert Saler, personal conversation, January 25, 2017.

49 A note here on religious leadership: in some congregations, the minister or
other professional religious leader is the primary originator and carrier of
the ecological vision. In other settings, a group of passionate congregation
members are the ecological conscience and innovators of the community,
pushing the congregation and its leaders to consider the ecological implications of ministries of social justice, service, and worship. Inhabitance is
nurtured by diverse models of religious leadership. No one model of leadership is more ecological than others, though the most sustainable practices
are valued by clergy and laity alike.

50 Inhabitance often relates to economic systems in conflicted ways. Some
congregations or communities adopt an ethic of nonparticipation in and
prophetic critique of a consumption-driven capitalist economy. Others see
just and sustainable economic development to be an important critical and
constructive means of engaging local and regional economies. Still other
communities rely on fundraising to sustain their work, thus placing them
in a somewhat complicated relationship to economic systems.

CHAPTER 5: LOCATED, DISLOCATED, RELOCATED

1 Orr, "Place as Teacher," 224.

2 Stuart Taylor, "St. Francis and the Canticle of Creation" (Sermon, Elkin
Presbyterian Church, Elkin, N.C., October 6, 2013), accessed September
12, 2018, https://elkinpres.podbean.com/e/st-francis-and-the-canticle-of
-creation/.

3 Wallace Stegner, "The Sense of Place," in *Where the Bluebird Sings to the Lemonade Springs: Living and Writing in the West*, repr. (New York: Modern Library, 2002), 199.

4 Although Berry writes prolifically on the theme of place, and his theorizing about place is deeply dependent on the sentiment expressed by this quote used by Stegner and innumerable scholars in place-based education, tracking down the source of the quotation leads not to Berry but to Ralph Ellison's *Invisible Man*. "If You Don't Know Where You Are, You Probably Don't Know Who You Are," *Quote Investigator*, September 29, 2017, accessed September 24, 2018, https://quoteinvestigator.com/2017/09/29/where-who/.

5 hooks, *Belonging*, 65.

6 Wendell Berry, "It All Turns on Affection" (presented at the National Endowment for the Humanities Jefferson Lecture, Washington, D.C., April 23, 2012), https://www.neh.gov/about/awards/jefferson-lecture/wendell -e-berry-biography.

7 Berry, "Native Hill," 5.

8 Orr, "What Is Education For?" 241–42; Wes Jackson, *Becoming Native to This Place* (Washington, D.C.: Counterpoint, 1996), 5, 97.

9 Berry, "Native Hill," 6; hooks, *Belonging*, xx.

10 David W. Orr, "Foreword," in Hutchison, *Natural History*, ix.

11 David W. Orr, "Place and Pedagogy," in *Ecological Literacy*, 263.

12 See Orr, "Place as Teacher," 224; McFague, *Super, Natural Christians*, 43; Pope Francis, *Laudato Si'*, 58–59.

13 Berry, "Native Hill," 5.

14 Orr, "Place as Teacher," 220.

15 David Hutchison, *A Natural History of Place in Education* (New York: Teachers College Press, 2004), 12.

16 Hutchison, *Natural History*, 11–12. In attending to the histories of places in the United States, a tension immediately presents itself: many histories, particularly those of indigenous peoples, have been ignored and forgotten. Many communities trace their histories back to a "founding date," which might mark the historical moment in which European settlers established a town or county, thus eclipsing the centuries of indigenous cultural and social histories in that place. Where possible, in this chapter, I have tried to acknowledge the indigenous histories of each place described.

17 Jackson, *Becoming Native*, 97.

18 The very word "vocation" derives from the Latin *vocare*, which literally means "to call." In theological terms a faithful response to a divine call has often precluded an ostensibly self-serving desire to stay in one place. See Jennifer R. Ayres, "Memories of Home: Theological Education, Place-Based Pedagogy, and Inhabitance," in *Grounding Education in the Environmental*

Humanities: Exploring Place-Based Pedagogies in the South, ed. David Aftan-dilian and Lucas Johnston (New York: Routledge, 2019).

19 David Orr argues that to this end we need to reimagine the purposes of education: "We do not need more successful people. We need peacemakers, healers, restorers, storytellers, and lovers of every kind. [We] need people who live well in their places. . . . And these qualities have little to do with success as our culture defines it" ("What Is Education For?" 242).

20 "Visit the Yadkin Valley Region of North Carolina," accessed September 24, 2018, http://visittheyadkinvalley.com/.

21 As a point of comparison, in 2016, Donald Trump, the Republican candi-date for president, received just under half of the popular vote, statewide. In Surry, Wilkes, and Yadkin Counties, the counties surrounding Elkin, he received more than seventy-five percent of the popular vote. "North Carolina Election Results 2016," *New York Times*, August 1, 2017, sec. U.S., accessed September 24, 2018, http://www.nytimes.com/elections/results/north-carolina.

22 United States Environmental Protection Agency, "Healthy Watersheds Protection: Basic Information and Answers to Frequent Questions," accessed September 26, 2018, https://www.epa.gov/hwp/basic-information -and-answers-frequent-questions.

23 Theda Perdue, *Native Carolinians: The Indians of North Carolina* (Raleigh: Division of Archives and History, North Carolina Department of Cultural Resources, 1985), 5–10, 13; William A. Link, *North Carolina: Change and Tradition in a Southern State*, 2nd ed. (Hoboken, N.J.: John Wiley and Sons), 7–8. Many of these indigenous groups were decimated by disease and conflict brought by Spanish and English settlers in the sixteenth and seventeenth centuries (12–15).

24 This is the title and theme of a sermon Stuart Taylor preached on Baptism of the Lord Sunday, January 11, 2015. See Taylor, "A River Flows Through Us."

25 See, for example, "Welcome to the Yadkin Valley"; Tourism Partnership of Surry County, "Art & Soul of the Yadkin Valley," accessed September 26, 2018, https://www.yadkinvalleync.com/; Town of Elkin, N.C., "Town of Elkin, NC," accessed September 26, 2018, http://www.elkinnc.org/.

26 Yadkin Riverkeeper, "Yadkin Riverkeeper Protects the Yadkin Pee Dee River Basin," accessed September 26, 2018, http://www.yadkinriverkeeper.org/.

27 Yadkin Riverkeeper, "About," accessed September 26, 2018, http://www .yadkinriverkeeper.org/about.

28 Myers has written several articles developing the concept of watershed discipleship, many of which are posted on his blog or the Watershed Disci-pleship website. Ched Myers, "ChedMyers.Org," accessed September 26, 2018, https://www.chedmyers.org/; "Watershed Discipleship," accessed September 26, 2018, https://watersheddiscipleship.org/.

29 Here, Taylor alludes to "The Columbia River Watershed: Caring for Creation and the Common Good," a Pastoral Letter written and distributed by Catholic Bishops in the Pacific Northwest. That document was signed on the Feast of the Baptism of the Lord, the day on which Christians recognize Jesus' baptism in the Jordan River. See "The Columbia River Watershed: Caring for Creation and the Common Good," January 8, 2001, accessed September 26, 2018, http://www.inee.mu.edu/documents/30columbiariverwatershed_000.pdf.

30 Stuart Taylor, "The River of Life" (Sermon, Elkin Presbyterian Church, Elkin, N.C., April 28, 2013), accessed September 12, 2018, https://elkinpres.podbean.com/e/the-river-of-life/.

31 Laura Schmidt Roberts, "The Theological Place of Land: Watershed Discipleship as Re-placed Cultural Vision," in Harker and Johnson, *Rooted and Grounded*, 125. Roberts borrows and defines the term "watershed discipleship" from scholar-activist Ched Myers. See https://watersheddiscipleship.org.

32 From planning document "Watershed Discipleship: A Proposal for an Ecumenical Partnership in Elkin/Jonesville/Surry County," developed by Taylor in conversation with community partners in 2014.

33 "Watershed NOW," accessed September 26, 2018, https://www.watershednownc.com/.

34 Taylor, "A River Flows Through Us."

35 David Orr even questions whether one can become centered in a place when that place is an urban setting: "Can it happen in a city? Not likely, at least not likely in the cities that we've built. My urban friends would protest that they too have a sense of place. By my reckoning, however, what they have is a sense of habitat shaped by familiarity. The sense of place is the affinity for what nature, not humans, has done in a particular location and the competence to live accordingly." Orr, "Place as Teacher," 224.

36 T. J. Gorringe, *A Theology of the Built Environment: Justice, Empowerment, Redemption* (Cambridge: Cambridge University Press, 2002).

37 David A. Gruenewald, "The Best of Both Worlds: A Critical Pedagogy of Place," *Educational Researcher* 32, no. 4 (2003): 10.

38 Gruenewald, "Best of Both Worlds," 4.

39 Freire, *Pedagogy of the Oppressed*, 100 (emphasis in original).

40 David Gruenewald summarizes the dual purposes of critical pedagogies of place thusly: "A critical pedagogy of place aims to (a) identify, recover, and create material spaces and places that teach us how to live well in our total environments (reinhabitation); and (b) identify and change ways of thinking that injure and exploit other people and places (decolonization)" ("Best of Both Worlds," 9).

41 "Urban Agricultural Center," Imani Village, Trinity United Church of Christ, accessed September 18, 2018, https://www.imanivillage.com/urban -agricultural-center.

42 Interview with Adrienne Wynn. Many food justice activists and communities also resist the language of "food desert" because the term defines a neighborhood or region according to its deficits rather than its assets. For a fuller explanation of the limitations of the language of "food deserts," see Ayres, *Good Food*, 107–8, 172n32.

43 St. Clair Drake and Horace R. Cayton, *Black Metropolis: A Study of Negro Life in a Northern City* (New York: Harper and Row, 1962).

44 The 2008 U.S. Farm Bill defined the 400-mile radius for what constitutes "local food." The 2014 bill did not define the term. "Mailboxes, Mom and Pop Stands, and Markets: Local Foods Then and Now," *United States Department of Agriculture National Agricultural Library*, accessed September 25, 2018, https://www.nal.usda.gov/exhibits/ipd/localfoods/exhibits/show/food -locality/local-distance.

45 The EPA identifies eighty-five distinct "ecoregions" in the United States: "Ecoregions are areas where ecosystems (and the type, quality, and quantity of environmental resources) are generally similar. . . . Designed to serve as a spatial framework for the research, assessment, and monitoring of ecosystems and ecosystem components, ecoregions denote areas of similarity in the mosaic of biotic, abiotic, terrestrial, and aquatic ecosystem components, with humans considered as part of the biota." United States Environmental Protection Agency, "Ecoregions," last modified November 16, 2015, accessed September 18, 2018, https://www.epa.gov/eco-research/ ecoregions. The Central Corn Belt Plains ecoregion comprises the northeastern third of Illinois and the northwestern corner of Indiana. United States Environmental Protection Agency, "Level III and IV Ecoregions of the Continental United States," last modified November 25, 2015, accessed September 18, 2018, https://www.epa.gov/eco-research/level-iii-and-iv -ecoregions-continental-united-states.

46 US EPA, "Level III and IV Ecoregions."

47 Linnet Myers, "DIRT POOR," *Chicago Tribune* (February 28, 1999), accessed September 20, 2018, http://www.chicagotribune.com/news/ct -xpm-1999-02-28-9902280416-story.html.

48 Robert Themer, "Small Farms Grow in Pembroke," *Daily Journal* (Kankakee, Ill., September 13, 2008); Samuel G. Freedman, "A Chicago Church Sees Justice in Land's Bounty," *New York Times*, August 30, 2013.

49 See Isabel Wilkerson, *The Warmth of Other Suns: The Epic Story of America's Great Migration*, repr. (New York: Vintage, 2011).

50 Isabel Wilkerson, "The Long-Lasting Legacy of the Great Migration," *Smithsonian*, September 2016, accessed September 18, 2018, https://

www.smithsonianmag.com/history/long-lasting-legacy-great-migration
-180960118/.

51   Richard Wright, *12 Million Black Voices*, repr. (New York: Basic Books,
      2002), 100.

52   Wilkerson, "Long-Lasting Legacy."

53   "Native Americans: American Indian Tribes of Illinois," Illinois State
      Museum, accessed December 21, 2018, http://www.museum.state.il.us/
      muslink/nat_amer/post/.

54   hooks, *Belonging*, 43.

55   "Parroquia San José," September 2011, accessed April 1, 2018, http://
      sanjosebeloit.blogspot.com/2011/09/parroquia-san-jose-saint-josephs
      -parish.html.

56   Neddy Astudillo, "The Right to Love the Land," in *Earth and Word: Clas-
      sic Sermons on Saving the Planet*, ed. David Rhoads (New York: Contin-
      uum, 2007), 2.

57   Victor W. Turner, *The Ritual Process: Structure and Anti-structure* (Chicago:
      University of Chicago Press, 1969), 95. Turner develops the concept of
      liminality in his examination of rites of passage. The theory of liminality is
      in one way appropriate to the migrant experience because it understands
      the liminal experience to be marked changes in place, state, social position,
      age, or other conditions. Rituals and practices that accompany persons in
      these spaces of ambiguous transition are necessary. In the rites of passage
      that Turner studied, however, the liminal state often implies or demands
      anonymity, submissiveness and silence, and destruction of what has come
      before: "This theme is the stripping off of preliminal and postliminal attri-
      butes" (102–3). The place-based faith described here and below stands
      somewhat in tension with this "shedding" of former identity markers and
      social structures, calling for practices that *invite* recollection of personal
      histories and places of significance, even as persons immerse themselves
      in new histories and places.

58   Astudillo, "Right to Love the Land," 2.

59   Astudillo, "Right to Love the Land," 4.

60   Moltmann, *God in Creation*, 197.

61   Astudillo, "Right to Love the Land," 5.

62   "Map," *Wisconsin First Nations*, accessed December 21, 2018, https://
      wisconsinfirstnations.org/map/.

63   See, for example, narratives of sojourn, displacement, exodus, and exile in
      the Pentateuch, the call of prophets to leave a homeplace or journey to an
      unknown place, and the story of Jesus himself as well as the ambivalence
      Jesus' followers had about leaving behind the places and communities they
      loved and knew.

64   David Orr paints a portrait of a sustainable and thriving future that includes human, social, and environmental well-being: "What we must do to avert the worst effects of climate change are mostly the same things we would do to build sustainable communities, improve environmental quality, build prosperous economies, and improve the prospects for our children." David W. Orr, "Hope (in a Hotter Time)," in *Hope Is an Imperative*, 332.

65   Orr describes hope as "a verb with its sleeves rolled up" ("Hope," 324). Although this phrasing bears within it a perhaps optimistic suggestion that hope is something accomplished through human action, Orr's conception of hope does remind the reader that hope is not an abdication from responsible commitment in and to the world: "[People] should be taught the many disciplines of applied hope that include the skills necessary to grow food, build shelter, manage woodlots, make energy from sunlight and wind, develop local enterprises, cook a good meal, use tools skillfully, repair and reuse, and talk sensibly at a public meeting" (332).

Chapter 6: Embracing Vulnerability

1   Margaret Holloway, "Your Children's Yellowstone Will Be Radically Different," *New York Times*, November 15, 2018, accessed November 17, 2018, https://www.nytimes.com/interactive/2018/11/15/climate/yellowstone -global-warming.html.

2   The San Jose Parish was introduced in the previous chapter.

3   Taggart Siegel, *The Real Dirt on Farmer John* (CAVU Pictures, 2005).

4   John Peterson, "Glitter & Grease: I Don't Believe It," *Angelic Organics*, accessed November 28, 2018, https://www.angelicorganics.com/ao/index .php?option=com_content&task=view&id=125&Itemid=324.

5   "Biodynamic Principles and Practices," Biodynamic Association, accessed November 28, 2018, https://www.biodynamics.com/biodynamic-principles -and-practices.

6   "Life in America: Hazardous to Immigrants' Health?" *UCLA Public Health*, Autumn/Winter 2014.

7   Ashlee Cunsolo and Karen Landman observe, "By virtue of having a body, we are all vulnerable to loss." Cunsolo and Landman, *Mourning Nature: Hope at the Heart of Ecological Loss and Grief* (Chicago: McGill-Queen's University Press, 2017), 8.

8   Cunsolo and Landman, *Mourning Nature*, 3–4.

9   Holloway, "Your Children's Yellowstone."

10   Cunsolo and Landman, *Mourning Nature*, xiii, xv.

11   Cunsolo and Landman, *Mourning Nature*, 5.

12   Discussed in more detail below, it is important to name, right away, the fact that responsibility for ecological crises is not equally shared among all human communities. Patterns of consumption, transit, waste, technology

use, and energy use vary dramatically between developed and developing countries, and between the rich and poor even within the same countries.

13 Nancy Menning, "Environmental Mourning and the Religious Imagination," in Cunsolo and Landman, *Mourning Nature*, 39–40.

14 In the liturgical calendar of many Christian congregations, worshippers remember and lament the death of Jesus on Good Friday. When Jesus contemplated his own impending death in the Garden of Gethsemane, he threw himself to the earth, praying to God so fervently that the gospel of Luke describes his sweat "like great drops of blood falling down on the ground." (Luke 22:39-46. The other synoptic gospels describe the scene in similarly embodied ways. Jesus is described as so "distressed and agitated," so "deeply grieved," that he "threw himself on the ground and prayed." See Mark 14:33-35; Matt 26:36-39.) He was not alone, however: the disciples had accompanied him to this garden. He had asked them to stay awake while he prayed, but they failed. They had fallen asleep, perhaps an embodiment of their own grief or fear. It was difficult for the disciples to remain with Jesus in that garden, confronting the impending loss of their beloved friend and teacher. And in that same garden, one of them would even betray Jesus, bringing those who wanted to kill him to the very place where he was praying, weeping, sweating, and speaking with the disciples. Even those closest to Jesus thus were complicit in his suffering, and one of them in his death. The Good Friday service challenges participants to sit with Jesus' suffering and death and to enter into a posture of repentance for the ways that they individually and collectively forget and forsake the way of Jesus, even now. The Good Friday service at Wilderness Way Community in Portland, Oregon, has an unusual way of approaching this complicated liturgical space. Wilderness Way is a small community that, in lieu of familiar worship in a built sanctuary space, gathers weekly for a wide range of ecological and community-grounded practices, including spiritual autobiographical sharing, bible study, and hiking or other outdoor outings (followed, of course, by a potluck meal). In 2016, their evolving mission included an intention to "ground and cultivate 'wild' Christian disciples and fearless spiritual leaders, rooted in the natural world and the prophetic Christian tradition." Solveig Nilsen-Goodin, *What Is the Way of the Wilderness? An Introduction to the Wilderness Way Community* (Des Moines: Zion Publishing, 2016). Their Good Friday liturgy quite explicitly embodied their missional commitment to integrate Christian tradition and the natural world. There, on the banks of the Willamette River, the small worshipping community gathers for a reimagined Stations of the Cross walk, called "The River's Lament." Instead of, or alongside, the story of the arrest and crucifixion of Jesus, the liturgy tells (assuming the voice of the Willamette River) the story of the *river's* suffering and death. Told in the first person, the lament recounts the river's

story, celebrating the origins and beauty of the river and naming the ways in which it has been exploited, abused, and forsaken: "By the late 1920s, I was called an 'open sewer.' . . . In 2000, I was designated a Superfund site." One participant in the River's Lament, Mark Brocker, writes that he looked around and recognized his own complicity in the abuse of the Willamette River: "In that moment I grieved deeply what we had done." Brocker, *Coming Home to Earth* (Eugene, Ore.: Cascade Books, 2016), 65. In this Good Friday practice, the mourning attends explicitly to the ecological losses suffered by the Willamette River and to the responsibility of the mourners to offer their lives in honor of what has been lost. In this sense the work of mourning entails a transformation from the immediacy of the feeling of sadness and even guilt to the nurturing of a "pattern of life" that loves and cares for God's world. At the time of this writing (and since November 2017), the Wilderness Way had entered a time of discernment, substantially scaling back practices and commitments, retaining the monthly "walk in the woods" and potluck meal.

15   Cunsolo and Landman, *Mourning Nature*, 8.

16   Pope Francis, *Laudato Si'*, 142.

17   Pope Francis, *Laudato Si'*, 142–43.

18   Berry, "Native Hill," 31.

19   Although "Mary" freely shared this story in worship and later in more detail in an interview, she is here named with a pseudonym to preserve anonymity.

20   "A Brief Statement of Faith," in *Book of Confessions*, vol. 1, the Constitution of the Presbyterian Church (U.S.A.) (Louisville, Ky.: Presbyterian Church [U.S.A.] Office of the General Assembly, 2004).

21   Since the time of this writing, Rev. Goff has become pastor in a different congregation, Arlington Presbyterian Church in Arlington, Virginia.

22   Although the sanctuary has a traditional raised chancel, pulpit, and choir, that space sits empty. The sermon, sacraments, and liturgy happen on the floor in the midst of the gathered people.

23   Heb 12:1. This text is one often read and interpreted on All Saints' Day, as it was offered as a word of inspiration to early Christians experiencing persecution, encouraging them to be emboldened by the perseverance and faith of those who had died before them–the "great cloud of witnesses."

24   Rev. Goff greeted the people seated at the tables and explained what the congregation was about to do, since the worshippers were now entering a community space not ordinarily used as a worship space. Goff describes the garden as a primary gathering place for a feeding ministry of the church, called "Open Table":

> Open Table folks come and this is a place of respite. The bike messengers come and they hang out or people walking up here in the summer, it's super-hot. You sit under the shade. This is more than just raised beds. . . . We've

had (short-term mission work) groups who have come back and done work like, "Oh, this is so unexpected." I love that because that is a faith statement, "Oh, so unexpected." I love that this is unexpected space in this bigger urban space and that this is our ecosystem, so how do we connect? Nancy's obsessed with native plants, Derek's got his garlic and Violet's got the bees. We've got people who are cooking and folks come to eat. I love talking about the garden to open table folks. . . . [One guest said], "This is just so cute. This is so cute out here." Then I've had people tell me stories . . . : "Oh, my grandma used to have a garden." It gets this conversation going. It's a conversation piece. There's all of this relationality and I love that this garden is this space, particularly with the bees and hungry folks who are coming to eat.

From Goff's perspective, the garden belongs to the larger community, not just the members of the Church of the Pilgrims. It is a site of relationships, of collaboration, of rest, and of memory. She thus felt it important to greet the homeless neighbors who were seated at the tables as the congregation processed into the garden, acknowledge that the worshippers were entering their space, and invite them to participate in the liturgy. Many of them remained in the garden as the liturgy continued.

25   Ashley Goff, "From People of the Tower to People of the Porch: Liturgical Agrarianism at Church of the Pilgrims," *Liturgy* 32, no. 2 (2017): 7.

26   Don E. Saliers argues that full consideration of the religious affections requires drawing a distinction between *immediacy* of feeling, which is an important and powerful experience, and *depth* of emotion, which is established over time as human beings make connections between the depths of human experience and the symbols and rituals of Christian faith. Saliers, *The Soul in Paraphrase: Prayer and the Religious Affections* (New York: Seabury Press, 1980), 9.

27   Saliers, *Soul in Paraphrase*, 6.

28   Wendell Berry, *A Timbered Choir: The Sabbath Poems, 1979–1997* (Washington, D.C.: Counterpoint, 1998), 131.

29   Stephanie Paulsell, *Honoring the Body: Meditations on a Christian Practice* (San Francisco: Jossey-Bass, 2003), 5.

30   Stephanie Paulsell succinctly summarizes the tensions inherent in Pauline representations of the body as the tension between "being a body and having a body" (*Honoring the Body*, 16–21).

31   Williston Walker, *A History of the Christian Church*, 4th ed. (New York: Scribner, 1985), 39.

32   Nestorius, "First Letter to Celestine," in *Christology of the Later Fathers*, ed. Edward Rochie Hardy, Library of Christian Classics (Philadelphia: Westminster, 1954), 347.

33 Athanasius would argue precisely this point forcefully in the fourth century. Athanasius, "On the Incarnation of the Word," trans. Archibald Robertson, in Hardy, *Christology of the Later Fathers,* 70–71.

34 Paulsell, *Honoring the Body,* 31.

35 Jonathan Balcombe, *Second Nature: The Inner Lives of Animals* (New York: Palgrave MacMillan, 2010), 132.

36 Michael P. Kaschak et al., "Embodiment and Language Comprehension," in *The Routledge Handbook of Embodied Cognition,* ed. Lawrence Shapiro (New York: Routledge, 2014), 118–26.

37 Michelle Maiese, "Body and Emotion," in Shapiro, *Routledge Handbook,* 231–39.

38 While an ecological conversion calls for "recognition of our errors, sins, faults and failures, and leads to heartfelt repentance and desire to change," not all persons or communities or even cultures are equally culpable for ecological loss. Pope Francis, *Laudato Si',* 142. Indeed, the economic and technical development in many wealthy countries was pursued at the expense of basic environmental protections and human rights in poorer countries. Rural and agricultural communities have suffered environmental and economic losses as a result of unchecked development and agricultural transformations. Rather than ecological guilt, they are owed an "ecological debt." Their bodies have already paid the price for industrialization and environmental neglect. Pope Francis, *Laudato Si',* 36–37. Ecological mourning sometimes, then, requires of the mourner perhaps less confession of complicity in ecological degradation but more naming of wounds perpetuated within and upon a place and a community.

39 The town's name is pronounced "kuh-nee-tuh."

40 Kathleen Toner, "By Nourishing Plants, You're Nourishing Community," *CNN Heroes,* last modified March 21, 2016, accessed November 27, 2018, https://www.cnn.com/2015/09/24/us/cnn-heroes-joyner/index.html; Jeff Chu, "How a North Carolina Minister Sowed Seeds of Hope in a Food Desert," *Modern Farmer,* last modified October 19, 2017, accessed November 27, 2018, https://modernfarmer.com/2017/10/north-carolina-minister-sowed-seeds-hope-food-desert/.

41 Bridgette A. Lacy, "A Community Grows Its Way out of Poverty," *Faith and Leadership,* last modified October 6, 2015, accessed November 27, 2018, https://www.faithandleadership.com/community-grows-its-way-out-poverty. Joyner describes the region as a "food desert." *Rev. Richard Joyner and Tobias Hopkins, Conetoe Family Life Center,* Rural Advancement Foundation International, 2014, accessed November 27, 2018, https://vimeo.com/87299954. The language of "food desert" has been used by researchers in very important studies to describe areas with limited access to fresh healthy food (usually grocery stores) and often an elevated presence of fast food and

convenience stores. See Mari Gallagher, *Good Food: Examining the Impact of Food Deserts on Public Health in Chicago* (Chicago: Mari Gallagher Research & Consulting Group and LaSalle Bank, 2006). The language, however, is not universally appreciated, as it is employed by (often) a researcher external to the community who seemingly defines the community according to what it lacks. Still, the research is instructive in its analysis of the food available in a community. See Ayres, *Good Food*, 107–8. Furthermore, the language of "food desert" might support the mistaken impression that food access issues are an organic, if lamentable, occurrence, when in reality they result from histories of extraction, racism, and neglect. Activist Karen Washington prefers the term "food apartheid," because it raises the question: "What are some of the social inequalities that you see, and what are you doing to erase some of the injustices?" Anna Brones, "Karen Washington: It's Not a Food Desert, It's Food Apartheid," *Guernica*, last modified May 7, 2018, accessed November 29, 2018, https://www.guernicamag.com/karen-washington-its -not-a-food-desert-its-food-apartheid/.

42   Toner, "By Nourishing Plants."
43   Chu, "North Carolina Minister."
44   Chu, "North Carolina Minister."
45   *Rev. Richard Joyner and Tobias Hopkins.*
46   *Rev. Richard Joyner and Tobias Hopkins.*
47   Lacy, "Community Grows."
48   Agriculture in eastern North Carolina is vulnerable, generally speaking. For example, a catastrophic storm like 2018's Hurricane Florence not only devastates crop yields but also introduces environmental health crises by flooding local areas with water contaminated by animal waste from massive nearby livestock farms. Kendra Pierre-Louis, "Lagoons of Pig Waste Are Overflowing After Florence. Yes, That's as Nasty as It Sounds," *New York Times*, September 21, 2018, sec. Climate, accessed November 29, 2018, https://www.nytimes.com/2018/09/19/climate/florence-hog-farms.html.
49   "What We Do: Youth Development," Conetoe Family Life Center, accessed November 27, 2018, http://conetoelife.org/what-we-do/.
50   In this way they are coinvestigators with adults, to borrow language from Paulo Freire. They are the teachers as much as they are the learners. Freire, *Pedagogy of the Oppressed*, 68.
51   "Children's School," Wilderness Way Community, accessed November 29, 2018, http://www.wildernesswaypdx.org/childrens-school/.
52   Cherice Bock and Solveig Nilsen-Goodin, "Earth Day at Eloheh and the EcoReformation," *Watershed Discipleship*, July 6, 2017, accessed November 29, 2018, https://watersheddiscipleship.org/2017/07/06/earth-day-at -eloheh-and-the-ecoreformation/; "Plant-for-the-Planet," accessed November 29, 2018, http://plant-for-the-planet.org.

53 Nilsen-Goodin, *What Is the Way of the Wilderness?* 59.

54 Louv, *Last Child in the Woods*, 36.

55 Julie Dunlap and Stephen R. Kellert, "Introduction," in *Companions in Wonder: Adults and Children Exploring Nature Together* (Cambridge, Mass.: MIT Press, 2012), 8. And yet in many places in the United States, schools are cutting back recess time, computers and other devices occupy several hours of children's free time each day, and land privatization and fear of liability prompts communities to disallow children's free play in woods and ponds and trees. Louv, *Last Child in the Woods*, 237–44.

56 Louv, *Last Child in the Woods*, 93.

57 Lauret Savoy, *Trace: Memory, History, Race, and the American Landscape* (Berkeley, Calif.: Counterpoint, 2015), 5, 10, 12.

58 Louv, *Last Child in the Woods*, 94.

59 Carson, "Help Your Child," 46.

60 Carson, "Help Your Child," 46. Indeed, Carson's groundbreaking work in ecology was strengthened and to some degree founded upon these experiences of wonder and discovery that she shared with her young nephew, Roger, during his visits with her on the shore of Maine. Carson's perhaps better-known work, *Silent Spring*, interrupted her plans to develop a book-length manuscript on the "sense of wonder." Filled with urgency in response to research on the ecological and human devastation wrought by widespread pesticide use, Carson set aside the wonder project to write *Silent Spring*, a dystopia notably absent children and their wondering relationship with the outdoors. The writing and defending of *Silent Spring*, and a terminal cancer diagnosis, meant that Carson would never finish her beloved project on wonder. See Dunlap and Kellert, "Introduction," 1–4.

61 Carson, "Help Your Child," 25.

62 Chu, "North Carolina Minister" (emphasis in original). Importantly, when Richard Joyner received a "Local Food Hero" award in 2016 from Farm to Fork North Carolina, he was accompanied by two youths who have become leaders at the Family Life Center—Tobias Hopkins, who works in the gardens, and Marquon Pettaway, who works in the apiary.

63 Goto, *Grace of Playing*, 3. See also Jaco Hamman, "Playing," in *The Wiley-Blackwell Companion to Practical Theology*, ed. Bonnie J. Miller-McLemore (Malden, Mass.: Wiley-Blackwell, 2012), 48.

64 Goto, *Grace of Playing*, 19.

65 "What Is Sweaty Sheep?" *Team Sweaty Sheep: Re-creation through Recreation*, accessed November 29, 2018, http://sweatysheep.com/discover/what-is-sweaty-sheep/ (emphasis in original).

66 Gould, "Unenchanted Evening," 40; Dioum, "Paper Presented at the General Assembly."

CONCLUSION

1   For a beautiful treatment of the concept of responsible hope, see Ellen Ott
     Marshall, *Though the Fig Tree Does Not Blossom: Toward a Responsible Theol-
     ogy of Christian Hope* (Nashville: Abingdon, 2006).
2   Rasmussen, *Earth-Honoring Faith*, 223.
3   Larry Rasmussen calls these "anticipatory communities": "Anticipatory
     communities are home places where it is possible to reimagine worlds and
     reorder possibilities, places where new or renewed practices give focus to
     an ecological and postindustrial way of life. Such communities have the
     qualities of a haven, a set-apart and safe place yet a place open to creative risk.
     Here basic moral formation happens by conscious choice and not by default
     (simply conforming to the ethos and unwritten ethic of the surrounding
     culture). Here eco-social virtues are consciously cultivated and embodied
     in community practices" (*Earth-Honoring Faith*, 227).
4   Mary Oliver, "The Summer Day," in *New and Selected Poems* (Boston: Beacon,
     1992), 94.

WORKS CITED

Adler, Mortimer Jerome. *The Paideia Proposal: An Educational Manifesto*. 1st paperback ed. New York: Macmillan, 1982.

Aquinas, Thomas. *Summa Theologica*. Vol 3. Allen, Tex.: Christian Classics, Thomas More Publishing, 1981.

Aristotle. *Nicomachean Ethics*. Translated by Joe Sachs. Newburyport, Mass.: Focus Publishing, 2002.

Armstrong, Patricia. "Bloom's Taxonomy." *Vanderbilt University*. Last modified June 10, 2010. Accessed September 6, 2018. https://wp0.vanderbilt.edu/cft/guides -sub-pages/blooms-taxonomy/.

Astudillo, Neddy. "The Right to Love the Land." In *Earth and Word: Classic Sermons on Saving the Planet*, edited by David Rhoads, 1–7. New York: Continuum, 2007.

Athanasius. "On the Incarnation of the Word." Translated by Archibald Robertson. In *Christology of the Later Fathers*, edited by Edward Rochie Hardy, 55–110. Library of Christian Classics. Philadelphia: Westminster, 1954.

Ayres, Jennifer R. "Cultivating the 'Unquiet Heart': Ecology, Education, and Christian Faith." *Theology Today* 74, no. 1 (2017).

———. *Good Food: Grounded Practical Theology*. Waco, Tex.: Baylor University Press, 2013.

———. "Memories of Home: Theological Education, Place-Based Pedagogy, and Inhabitance." In *Grounding Education in the Environmental Humanities: Exploring Place-Based Pedagogies in the South*, edited by David Aftandilian and Lucas F. Johnston, 50–68. New York: Routledge, 2019.

———. *Waiting for a Glacier to Move: Practicing Social Witness*. Eugene, Ore.: Wipf and Stock, 2011.

Balcombe, Jonathan. *Second Nature: The Inner Lives of Animals*. New York: Palgrave MacMillan, 2010.

Bass, Dorothy C., and Craig Dykstra. "A Theological Understanding of Christian Practices." In *Practicing Theology: Beliefs and Practices in Christian Life*, edited by Dorothy Bass and Miroslav Volf, 13–32. Grand Rapids: Eerdmans, 2002.

Bauer, Walter Arndt William. *A Greek-English Lexicon of the New Testament and Other Early Christian Literature*. Chicago: University of Chicago Press, 1979.

Begley, Sharon. "Do We Really Need Nature?" *Mindful*, August 12, 2015. https://www.mindful.org/do-we-really-need-nature/.

Bellah, Robert N. *Habits of the Heart: Individualism and Commitment in American Life*. Berkeley: University of California Press, 1985.

Berry, Thomas. *The Great Work: Our Way into the Future*. New York: Random House, 1999.

Berry, Wendell. "It All Turns on Affection." Presented at the National Endowment for the Humanities Jefferson Lecture, Washington, D.C., April 23, 2012. https://www.neh.gov/about/awards/jefferson-lecture/wendell-e-berry-biography.

———. "A Native Hill." In *The Art of the Commonplace: The Agrarian Essays of Wendell Berry*, edited by Norman Wirzba, 3–31. Berkeley, Calif.: Counterpoint, 2002.

———. *A Timbered Choir: The Sabbath Poems, 1979–1997*. Washington, D.C.: Counterpoint, 1998.

Biodynamic Association. "Biodynamic Principles and Practices." Biodynamics. Accessed November 28, 2018. https://www.biodynamics.com/biodynamic-principles-and-practices.

Blanchard, Kathryn D., and Kevin J. O'Brien. *An Introduction to Christian Environmentalism*. Waco, Tex.: Baylor University Press, 2014.

Bock, Cherice, and Solveig Nilsen-Goodin. "Earth Day at Eloheh and the EcoReformation." *Watershed Discipleship*. July 6, 2017. Accessed November 29, 2018. https://watersheddiscipleship.org/2017/07/06/earth-day-at-eloheh-and-the-ecoreformation/.

Bosman, Julie. "Flint Water Crisis Inquiry Finds State Ignored Warning Signs." *New York Times*, January 19, 2018, sec. U.S. Accessed September 6, 2018. https://www.nytimes.com/2016/03/24/us/flint-water-crisis.html.

Bourdieu, Pierre Nice Richard. *The Logic of Practice*. Stanford, Calif.: Stanford University Press, 1992.

Bowers, C. A. *Educating for Eco-Justice and Community*. Athens: University of Georgia Press, 2001.

Brannen, Peter. "Earth Is Not in the Midst of a Sixth Mass Extinction." *Atlantic*. Last modified June 13, 2017. Accessed September 2, 2018. https://www.theatlantic.com/science/archive/2017/06/the-ends-of-the-world/529545/.

"A Brief Statement of Faith." In *Book of Confessions*. Vol. 1. The Constitution of the Presbyterian Church (U.S.A.). Louisville, Ky.: Presbyterian Church (U.S.A.) Office of the General Assembly, 2004.

Brocker, Mark. *Coming Home to Earth*. Eugene, Ore.: Cascade Books, 2016.

Brones, Anna. "Karen Washington: It's Not a Food Desert, It's Food Apartheid." *Guernica*. Last modified May 7, 2018. Accessed November 29, 2018. https://www.guernicamag.com/karen-washington-its-not-a-food-desert-its-food-apartheid/.

Brown, William P. *Wisdom's Wonder: Character, Creation, and Crisis in the Bible's Wisdom Literature*. Grand Rapids: Eerdmans, 2014.

Brueggemann, Walter. *The Land: Place as Gift, Promise, and Challenge in Biblical Faith*. 2nd ed. Minneapolis: Fortress, 2002.

———. *The Prophetic Imagination*. 2nd ed. Minneapolis: Fortress, 2001.

Buechner, Frederick. *Wishful Thinking: A Seeker's ABC*. Rev. and expanded. New York: HarperOne, 1993.

Burrus, Virginia. "Introduction: Theology and Eros after Nygren." In *Toward a Theology of Eros: Transfiguring Passion at the Limits of Discipline*, edited by Virginia Burrus and Catherine Keller, xiii–xx. New York: Fordham University Press, 2006.

Cacioppo, John, and Stephanie Cacioppo. "Loneliness Is a Modern Epidemic in Need of Treatment." *New Scientist*. Last modified December 30, 2014. Accessed September 5, 2018. https://www.newscientist.com/article/dn26739-loneliness-is-a-modern-epidemic-in-need-of-treatment/.

Calvin, John. *Institutes of the Christian Religion*. Translated by Ford Lewis Battles. Library of Christian Classics, 2 vols. Philadelphia: Westminster, 1960.

Carbine, Rosemary P. "Erotic Education: Elaborating a Feminist and Faith-Based Pedagogy for Experiential Learning in Religious Studies." *Teaching Theology & Religion* 13, no. 4 (2010): 320–38.

Carson, Rachel. "Help Your Child to Wonder." *Women's Home Companion*, July 1956.

Case-Winters, Anna. *Reconstructing a Christian Theology of Nature: Down to Earth*. Burlington, Vt.: Ashgate, 2007.

Chawla, Louise, Kelly Keena, Illène Pevec, and Emily Stanley. "Green Schoolyards as Havens from Stress and Resources for Resilience in Childhood and Adolescence." *Health & Place* 28 (2014): 1–13.

Chu, Jeff. "How a North Carolina Minister Sowed Seeds of Hope in a Food Desert." *Modern Farmer*. Last modified October 19, 2017. Accessed November 27, 2018. https://modernfarmer.com/2017/10/north-carolina-minister-sowed-seeds-hope-food-desert/.

Cobb, John B., Jr. *Sustainability: Economics, Ecology, and Justice*. Maryknoll, N.Y.: Orbis Books, 1992.

Code, Lorraine. *Ecological Thinking: The Politics of Epistemic Location*. New York: Oxford University Press, 2006.

"The Columbia River Watershed: Caring for Creation and the Common Good." January 8, 2001. Accessed September 26, 2018. http://www.inee.mu.edu/documents/30columbiariverwatershed_000.pdf.

Conetoe Family Life Center. "What We Do: Youth Development." Conetoe Life. Accessed November 27, 2018. http://conetoelife.org/what-we-do/.

Conradie, Ernst. *An Ecological Christian Anthropology: At Home on Earth?* Burlington, Vt.: Ashgate, 2005.

Cornelius, Janet Duitsman. *Slave Missions and the Black Church in the Antebellum South.* Columbia: University of South Carolina Press, 1999.

Cunsolo, Ashlee, and Karen Landman. *Mourning Nature: Hope at the Heart of Ecological Loss and Grief.* Chicago: McGill-Queen's University Press, 2017.

Cunsolo, Ashlee, and Neville R. Ellis. "Ecological Grief as a Mental Health Response to Climate Change-Related Loss." *Nature Climate Change* 8 (2018): 275–281. Accessed September 5, 2018. http://www.nature.com.proxy.library.emory.edu/articles/s41558-018-0092-2.

Damrosch, Barbara. "The Healing Powers of the Earth." *Washington Post,* April 23, 2015.

Davey, Monica, and Mitch Smith. "2 Former Flint Emergency Managers Charged over Tainted Water." *New York Times,* December 22, 2017, sec. U.S. Accessed September 6, 2018. https://www.nytimes.com/2016/12/20/us/flint-water-charges.html.

Davis, Lisa. "Pixie Sticks: Fairy Houses Are Popping Up in Backyards and along a New Permanent Trail." *Anniston Star.* (Anniston, Ala.), May 3, 2015. Accessed December 19, 2018. https://www.annistonstar.com/life/pixie-sticks-fairy-houses-are-popping-up-in-backyards-and/article_a7887de2-f070-11e4-bab0-6f725d2bb443.html.

Day, Nicholas. "The Rebirth of Recess." *Slate,* August 29, 2012. Accessed September 6, 2018. http://www.slate.com/articles/life/family/2012/08/recess_in_schools_research_shows_it_benefits_children_.html.

Dewey, John. *Democracy and Education: An Introduction to the Philosophy of Education.* New York: Free Press, 1966.

———. *Experience and Education.* New York: Touchstone, 1938.

Dillard, Annie. *Pilgrim at Tinker Creek.* 5th ed. New York: HarperCollins, 1988.

Drake, St. Clair, and Horace R. Cayton. *Black Metropolis: A Study of Negro Life in a Northern City.* New York: Harper and Row, 1962.

Dunlap, Julie, and Stephen R. Kellert. "Introduction." In *Companions in Wonder: Adults and Children Exploring Nature Together,* 1–24. Cambridge, Mass.: MIT Press, 2012.

Dykstra, Craig. *Growing in the Life of Faith: Education and Christian Practices.* 2nd ed. Louisville, Ky.: Westminster John Knox, 2005.

———. "Reconceiving Practice." In *Shifting Boundaries: Contextual Approaches to the Structure of Theological Education,* edited by Barbara G. Wheeler and Edward Farley, 35–90. Louisville, Ky.: Westminster John Knox, 1991.

Eisner, Elliott. "The Three Curricula That All Schools Teach." In *The Educational Imagination: On the Design and Evaluation of School Programs*, edited by Elliott Eisner, 87–107. Upper Saddle River, N.J.: Merrill Prentice Hall, 2002.

Evernden, Neil. *The Natural Alien*. Toronto: University of Toronto Press, 1985.

Farley, Edward. *Theologia: The Fragmentation and Unity of Theological Education*. Minneapolis: Augsburg Fortress, 1994.

Floyd, Richard A. *Down to Earth: Christian Hope and Climate Change*. Eugene, Ore.: Cascade Books, 2015.

Fowler, James W. *Becoming Adult, Becoming Christian: Adult Development and Christian Faith*. New York: Harper and Row, 1984.

———. *Weaving the New Creation: Stages of Faith and the Public Church*. Eugene, Ore.: Wipf and Stock, 1991.

Freedman, Samuel G. "A Chicago Church Sees Justice in Land's Bounty." *New York Times*, August 30, 2013.

Freire, Paulo. *Pedagogy of the Oppressed*. Translated by Myra Bergman Ramos. New York: Continuum, 1982.

Friedman, Lisa, and Glenn Thrush. "U.S. Report Says Humans Cause Climate Change, Contradicting Top Trump Officials." *New York Times*, November 3, 2017. Accessed September 2, 2018. https://www.nytimes.com/2017/11/03/climate/us-climate-report.html.

Gallagher, Mari. *Good Food: Examining the Impact of Food Deserts on Public Health in Chicago*. Chicago: Mari Gallagher Research & Consulting Group and LaSalle Bank, 2006.

Gardner, Howard E. "In a Nutshell." In *Multiple Intelligences: New Horizons*, 3–24. New York: Basic Books, 2006.

Gillis, Justin. "U.N. Climate Panel Endorses Ceiling on Global Emissions." *New York Times*, September 27, 2013.

Glave, Dianne D. *Rooted in the Earth: Reclaiming the African American Environmental Heritage*. Chicago: Lawrence Hill Books, 2010.

Goff, Ashley. "From People of the Tower to People of the Porch: Liturgical Agrarianism at Church of the Pilgrims." *Liturgy* 32, no. 2 (2017): 3–13.

Gorringe, T. J. *A Theology of the Built Environment: Justice, Empowerment, Redemption*. Cambridge: Cambridge University Press, 2002.

Goto, Courtney T. *The Grace of Playing: Pedagogies for Leaning into God's New Creation*. Horizons in Religious Education. Eugene, Ore.: Pickwick, 2016.

Gould, Stephen Jay. "Unenchanted Evening." In *Eight Little Piggies: Reflections in Natural History*, 23–40. New York: W. W. Norton, 1993.

Greene, Maxine. *Releasing the Imagination: Essays on Education, the Arts, and Social Change*. San Francisco: Jossey-Bass, 2000.

Gruenewald, David A. "The Best of Both Worlds: A Critical Pedagogy of Place." *Educational Researcher* 32, no. 4 (2003): 3–12.

Haag, Matthew. "64 Pounds of Trash Killed a Sperm Whale in Spain, Scientists Say." *New York Times*, April 13, 2018, sec. Science. Accessed September 6, 2018. https://www.nytimes.com/2018/04/12/science/sperm-whale-death-spain .html.

Hamman, Jaco. "Playing." In *The Wiley-Blackwell Companion to Practical Theology*, edited by Bonnie J. Miller-McLemore, 42–50. Malden, Mass.: Wiley-Blackwell, 2012.

Haraway, Donna. "Situated Knowledges: The Science Question in Feminism and the Privilege of Partial Perspective." *Feminist Studies* 14, no. 3 (1988): 575–99.

Harrington, Kit. "Magic, Wonder, Science and Exploration: The Educational Value of Fairy Villages." *Natural Start Alliance*. Last modified July 2015. Accessed December 19, 2018. https://naturalstart.org/feature-stories/magic-wonder -science-and-exploration-educational-value-fairy-villages.

Harris, Maria. *Teaching and Religious Imagination: An Essay in the Theology of Teaching*. San Francisco: Harper and Row, 1987.

Henry, Matthew. "Song of Solomon." In *Commentary on the Whole Bible Volume III (Job to Song of Solomon)*. Vol. 3. Christian Classics Ethereal Library, 1710.

Hiebert, Theodore. "The Human Vocation: Origins and Transformations in Christian Traditions." In *Christianity and Ecology*, edited by Dieter T. Hessel and Rosemary Radford Ruether, 135–54. Cambridge, Mass.: Harvard/CSWR, 2000.

———. *The Yahwist's Landscape*. New York: Oxford University Press, 1996.

Holloway, Margaret. "Your Children's Yellowstone Will Be Radically Different." *New York Times*, November 15, 2018. Accessed November 17, 2018. https://www.nytimes .com/interactive/2018/11/15/climate/yellowstone-global-warming.html.

Holmgren, David, and Richard Telford. "Permaculture Design Principles." Permaculture Principles. Accessed January 30, 2019. https://permacultureprinciples .com/principles/.

Holthaus, Eric. "Stop Scaring People about Climate Change. It Doesn't Work." *Grist*, July 11, 2017. Accessed September 5, 2018. https://grist.org/climate-energy/ stop-scaring-people-about-climate-change-it-doesnt-work/.

hooks, bell. *Belonging: A Culture of Place*. New York: Routledge, 2009.

Humphrey, Matthew. "Lived Theology in the Little Campbell Watershed." In *Rooted and Grounded: Essays on Land and Christian Discipleship*, edited by Ryan Dallas Harker and Janeen Bertsche Johnson, 112–23. Eugene, Ore.: Wipf and Stock, 2016.

"Hunt Highlights Plight of the Lonely." *BBC News*, October 18, 2013, sec. UK Politics. Accessed September 6, 2018. https://www.bbc.co.uk/news/uk-politics -24572231.

Hutchison, David. *A Natural History of Place in Education*. New York: Teachers College Press, 2004.

"If You Don't Know Where You Are, You Probably Don't Know Who You Are." *Quote Investigator*, September 29, 2017. Accessed September 24, 2018. https://quoteinvestigator.com/2017/09/29/where-who/.

Illinois State Museum. "Native Americans: American Indian Tribes of Illinois." Accessed December 21, 2018. http://www.museum.state.il.us/muslink/nat _amer/post/.

International Union for Conservation of Nature Commission on Education and Communication. "Love. Not Loss." IUCN. Last modified 2018. Accessed March 13, 2019. https://www.iucn.org/commissions/commission-education -and-communication/cec-resources/love-not-loss.

Jackson, Timothy P. *The Priority of Love: Christian Charity and Social Justice*. Princeton, N.J.: Princeton University Press, 2002.

Jackson, Wes. *Becoming Native to This Place*. Washington, D.C.: Counterpoint, 1996.

Jaeger, Werner. *Early Christianity and Greek Paideia*. Cambridge, Mass.: Belknap Press of Harvard University Press, 1965.

———. *Paideia: The Ideals of Greek Culture*. Vol. 1. New York: Oxford University Press, 1945.

Jones, Serene. "Graced Practices: Excellence and Freedom in the Christian Life." In *Practicing Theology: Beliefs and Practices in Christian Life*, edited by Dorothy Bass and Miroslav Volf, 51–77. Grand Rapids: Eerdmans, 2002.

Jordan, Mark D. "Flesh in the Confession: Alcibiades beside Augustine." In *Toward a Theology of Eros: Transfiguring Passion at the Limits of Discipline*, edited by Virginia Burrus and Catherine Keller, 23–37. New York: Fordham University Press, 2006.

Judson, Gillian. *A New Approach to Ecological Education: Engaging Students' Imaginations in Their World*. New York: Peter Lang, 2010.

Kaschak, Michael P., John L. Jones, Julie Carranza, and Melissa R. Fox. "Embodiment and Language Comprehension." In *The Routledge Handbook of Embodied Cognition*, edited by Lawrence Shapiro, 118–26. New York: Routledge, 2014.

Kaye, Anthony E. *Joining Places: Slave Neighborhoods in the Old South*. Chapel Hill: University of North Carolina Press, 2009.

Keller, Catherine. "Afterword: A Theology of Eros, after Transfiguring Passion." In *Toward a Theology of Eros: Transfiguring Passion at the Limits of Discipline*, edited by Virginia Burrus and Catherine Keller, 366–74. New York: Fordham University Press, 2006.

Lacy, Bridgette A. "A Community Grows Its Way out of Poverty." *Faith and Leadership*. Last modified October 6, 2015. Accessed November 27, 2018. https://www .faithandleadership.com/community-grows-its-way-out-poverty.

Leahy, Stephen. "Each U.S. Family Trashes 400 iPhones' Worth of E-Waste a Year." *National Geographic*. Last modified December 13, 2017. Accessed September 2, 2018. https://news.nationalgeographic.com/2017/12/e-waste-monitor-report -glut/.

Lee, Bernard J. "Practical Theology as Phronetic: A Working Paper from/for Those in Ministry Education." *Association of Practical Theology Occasional Papers* 1 (1997): 1–16.

Leopold, Aldo. "The Land Ethic." In *A Sand County Almanac and Other Writings on Ecology and Conservation*, 171–89. New York: Literary Classics of the United States, 2013.

———. "The Round River—A Parable." In *Round River: From the Journals of Aldo Leopold*, 158–65. New York: Oxford University Press, 1993.

Levad, Amy. *Restorative Justice: Theories and Practices of Moral Imagination.* Criminal Justice: Recent Scholarship. El Paso: LFB Scholarly Publishing, 2012.

"Life in America: Hazardous to Immigrants' Health?" *UCLA Public Health*, Autumn/ Winter 2014.

Link, William A. *North Carolina: Change and Tradition in a Southern State.* 2nd ed. Hoboken, N.J.: John Wiley and Sons, 2018.

Linzey, Andrew. *Creatures of the Same God: Explorations in Animal Theology.* Brooklyn,: Lantern Books, 2009.

———. "Is Christianity Irredeemably Speciesist?" In *Animals on the Agenda: Questions about Animals for Theology and Ethics*, edited by Andrew Linzey and Dorothy Yamamoto, xi–xx. Chicago: University of Illinois Press, 1998.

"The Lonely Society?" *Mental Health Foundation.* Last modified May 2, 2010. Accessed September 6, 2018. https://www.mentalhealth.org.uk/publications/ the-lonely-society.

Lorde, Audre. "Uses of the Erotic: The Erotic as Power." In *Sister Outsider: Essays and Speeches*, 53–59. Reprint ed. Berkeley, Calif.: Crossing Press, 2007.

Louv, Richard. *The Last Child in the Woods: Saving Our Children from Nature-Deficit Disorder.* Rev. and updated. Chapel Hill, N.C.: Algonquin Books of Chapel Hill, 2008.

MacIntyre, Alasdair C. *After Virtue: A Study in Moral Theory.* 2nd ed. London: Duckworth, 1984.

MacKendrick, Karmen. "Carthage Didn't Burn Hot Enough: Saint Augustine's Divine Seduction." In *Toward a Theology of Eros: Transfiguring Passion at the Limits of Discipline*, edited by Virginia Burrus and Catherine Keller, 205–19. New York: Fordham University Press, 2006.

Maiese, Michelle. "Body and Emotion." In *The Routledge Handbook of Embodied Cognition*, edited by Lawrence Shapiro, 231–39. New York: Routledge, 2014.

"Mailboxes, Mom and Pop Stands, and Markets: Local Foods Then and Now." *United States Department of Agriculture National Agricultural Library.* Accessed September 25, 2018. https://www.nal.usda.gov/exhibits/ipd/localfoods/exhibits/ show/food-locality/local-distance.

"A Man-Made World—The Anthropocene." *Economist.* Last modified May 26, 2011. Accessed September 2, 2018. https://www.economist.com/briefing/2011/05/ 26/a-man-made-world.

Marine Education Society of Australasia. "Habitats—The Great Barrier Reef." MESA. Accessed December 11, 2018. http://www.mesa.edu.au/habitat/gbr01.asp.

Martin, Miriam K. "Religious Education and a New Earth Consciousness: 'Let Us Play.'" *Theoforum* 41, no. 1 (2010): 93–112.

Mathews, Freya. *The Ecological Self*. London: Routledge, 1991.

May, Gerald G. *Will and Spirit: A Contemplative Psychology*. San Francisco: HarperOne, 1987.

McDermott, Gerald R. "Jonathan Edwards on the Affections and the Spirit." In *The Spirit, the Affections, and the Christian Tradition*, edited by Dale M. Coulter and Amos Yong, 279–92. Notre Dame, Ind.: University of Notre Dame Press, 2016.

McFague, Sallie. *The Body of God: An Ecological Theology*. Nashville: Augsburg Fortress, 1993.

———. *Super, Natural Christians: How We Should Love Nature*. Minneapolis: Augsburg Fortress, 1997.

Menning, Nancy. "Environmental Mourning and the Religious Imagination." In *Mourning Nature: Hope at the Heart of Ecological Loss and Grief*, 39–63. Chicago: McGill-Queen's University Press, 2017.

Merchant, Carolyn. "The Death of Nature." In *Environmental Philosophy: From Animal Rights to Radical Ecology*, edited by Michael E. Zimmerman, J. Baird Callicott, George Sessions, Karen J. Warren, and John Clark, 277–90. 2nd ed. Upper Saddle River, N.J.: Prentice Hall, 1998.

———. *The Death of Nature: Women, Ecology, and the Scientific Revolution*. 2nd ed. New York: HarperOne, 1990.

Moltmann, Jürgen. *God in Creation: A New Theology of Creation and the Spirit of God*. Minneapolis: Fortress, 1993.

———. *Theology of Hope: On the Ground and the Implications of a Christian Eschatology*. Translated by James W. Leitch. 5th ed. San Francisco: HarperSanFrancisco, 1967.

Moore, Mary Elizabeth. *Ministering with the Earth*. St. Louis: Chalice Press, 1998.

"Mortimer Adler's Reading List." *Thinking as Leverage*, October 5, 2012. Accessed September 6, 2018. https://thinkingasleverage.wordpress.com/book-lists/mortimer-adlers-reading-list/.

Motel, Seth. "Polls Show Most Americans Believe in Climate Change, but Give It Low Priority." *Pew Research Center*, September 23, 2014. Accessed September 2, 2018. http://www.pewresearch.org/fact-tank/2014/09/23/most-americans-believe-in-climate-change-but-give-it-low-priority/.

Murthy, Vivek. "Work and the Loneliness Epidemic." *Harvard Business Review*, September 26, 2017. Accessed September 6, 2018. https://hbr.org/2017/09/work-and-the-loneliness-epidemic.

Myers, Ched. "ChedMyers.Org." Accessed September 26, 2018. https://www.chedmyers.org/.

Myers, Linnet. "DIRT POOR." *Chicago Tribune*. February 28, 1999. Accessed September 20, 2018. http://www.chicagotribune.com/news/ct-xpm-1999-02 -28-9902280416-story.html.

Naess, Arne. "The Deep Ecological Movement: Some Philosophical Aspects." In *Environmental Philosophy: From Animal Rights to Radical Ecology*, edited by Michael E. Zimmerman, J. Baird Callicott, George Sessions, Karen J. Warren, and John Clark, 193–211. 2nd ed. Upper Saddle River, N.J.: Prentice Hall, 1998.

National Pollinator Garden Network. "Home." Million Pollinator Garden Challenge. Accessed December 11, 2018. http://millionpollinatorgardens.org/.

Niebuhr, Reinhold. *The Nature and Destiny of Man: A Christian Interpretation*. Library of Theological Ethics. Louisville, Ky.: Westminster John Knox, 1996.

Nilsen-Goodin, Solveig I., and Members of the Wilderness Way Community. *What Is the Way of the Wilderness? An Introduction to the Wilderness Way Community*. Des Moines: Zion Publishing, 2016.

North American Association for Environmental Education. "About EE and Why It Matters." NAAEE. Last modified May 19, 2015. Accessed September 1, 2018. https://naaee.org/about-us/about-ee-and-why-it-matters.

"North Carolina Election Results 2016." *New York Times*, August 1, 2017, sec. U.S. Accessed September 24, 2018. http://www.nytimes.com/elections/results/ north-carolina.

Nygren, Anders. *Agape and Eros*. Translated by Philip S. Watson. London: S.P.C.K., 1957.

Oliver, Mary. "Listening to the World: Mary Oliver." Interview by Krista Tippet. *On Being*. October 2015. https://onbeing.org/programs/mary-oliver-listening -to-the-world/.

———. "The Summer Day." In *New and Selected Poems*, 94. Boston: Beacon, 1992.

Orr, David W. "An Alternative to Bloom's Vision of Education." In *Ecological Literacy: Education and the Transition to a Postmodern World*, by David W. Orr, 97–108. SUNY Series in Constructive Postmodern Thought. Albany, N.Y.: SUNY Press, 1992.

———. "Ecological Literacy." In *Ecological Literacy, 85–95.*

———. *Ecological Literacy: Education and the Transition to a Postmodern World*, 97–108. SUNY Series in Constructive Postmodern Thought. Albany, N.Y.: SUNY Press, 1992.

———. "Epilogue." In *Ecological Literacy, 181–83.*

———. "Foreword." In *A Natural History of Place in Education*, by David Hutchison, ix–x. New York: Teachers College Press, 2004.

———. "Hope (in a Hotter Time)." In *Hope Is an Imperative, 324–32.*

———. *Hope Is an Imperative: The Essential David Orr*. Washington, D.C.: Island Press, 2011.

———. "Love." In *Hope Is an Imperative, 30–33.*

———. "Place and Pedagogy." In *Ecological Literacy, 125–31.*

———. "Place as Teacher." In *Hope Is an Imperative,* 213–28.

———. "Slow Knowledge." In *Hope Is an Imperative,* 13–20.

———. "What Is Education For?" In *Hope Is an Imperative,* 237–45.

Ostrow, Martin, and Terry Kay Rockefeller. *Renewal: Stories from America's Religious-Environmental Movement.* Cambridge, Mass.: Fine Cut Productions, 2007.

O'Sullivan, Edmund V., and Marilyn M. Taylor. "Glimpses of an Ecological Consciousness." In *Learning Toward an Ecological Consciousness: Selected Transformative Practices,* edited by Edmund V. O'Sullivan and Marilyn M. Taylor, 5–27. New York: Palgrave MacMillan, 2004.

Ott Marshall, Ellen. *Though the Fig Tree Does Not Blossom: Toward a Responsible Theology of Christian Hope.* Nashville: Abingdon, 2006.

Parkes, Colin Murray, and Holly G. Prigerson. *Bereavement: Studies of Grief in Adult Life.* 4th ed. New York: Routledge, 2010.

Parks, Sharon Daloz. *Big Questions, Worthy Dreams: Mentoring Emerging Adults in Their Search for Meaning, Purpose, and Faith.* Rev. ed. San Francisco: Jossey-Bass, 2011.

"Parroquia San José." September 2011. Accessed April 1, 2018. http://sanjosebeloit.blogspot.com/2011/09/parroquia-san-jose-saint-josephs-parish.html.

Paulsell, Stephanie. *Honoring the Body: Meditations on a Christian Practice.* San Francisco: Jossey-Bass, 2003.

Pazmiño, Robert W. *Foundational Issues in Christian Education: An Introduction in Evangelical Perspective.* 3rd ed. Grand Rapids: Baker Academic, 2008.

Perdue, Theda. *Native Carolinians: The Indians of North Carolina.* Raleigh: North Carolina Department of Cultural Resources, Division of Archives and History, 1985.

Peterson, John. "Glitter & Grease: I Don't Believe It." *Angelic Organics.* Accessed November 28, 2018. https://www.angelicorganics.com/ao/index.php?option=com_content&task=view&id=125&Itemid=324.

Pierre-Louis, Kendra. "Lagoons of Pig Waste Are Overflowing After Florence. Yes, That's as Nasty as It Sounds." *New York Times,* September 21, 2018, sec. Climate. Accessed November 29, 2018. https://www.nytimes.com/2018/09/19/climate/florence-hog-farms.html.

Pierson, Russ, and John Roe. "Marc Driscoll: Gas Guzzlers a Mark of Masculinity." *Sojourners,* October 18, 2016.

"Plant-for-the-Planet." Accessed November 29, 2018. http://plant-for-the-planet.org.

Plumwood, Val. "Nature, Self, and Gender: Feminism, Environmental Philosophy, and the Critique of Rationalism." In *Environmental Philosophy: From Animal Rights to Radical Ecology,* edited by Michael E. Zimmerman, J. Baird Callicott, George Sessions, Karen J. Warren, and John Clark, 291–314. 2nd ed. Upper Saddle River, N.J.: Prentice Hall, 1998.

Pope Francis. *Laudato Si': On Care for Our Common Home.* Huntington, Ind.: Our Sunday Visitor, 2015.

———. *Lumen Fidei.* New York: Crown Publishing Group, 2013.

Putnam, Robert D. *Bowling Alone: The Collapse and Revival of American Community.* New York: Simon & Schuster, 2000.

Rainie, Harrison, and Barry Wellman. *Networked: The New Social Operating System.* Cambridge, Mass.: MIT Press, 2012.

Randall, Ronne, and Nicola Evans. *Chicken Little.* New York: Parragon Books, 2015.

Rasmussen, Larry. *Earth-Honoring Faith: Religious Ethics in a New Key.* New York: Oxford University Press, 2012.

Rev. Richard Joyner and Tobias Hopkins, Conetoe Family Life Center. Rural Advancement Foundation International, 2014. Accessed November 27, 2018. https://vimeo.com/87299954.

Rich, Nathaniel. "Losing Earth: The Decade We Almost Stopped Climate Change." *New York Times,* August 1, 2018, sec. Magazine. Accessed September 5, 2018. https://www.nytimes.com/interactive/2018/08/01/magazine/climate-change-losing-earth.html.

Rivera, Mayra. "Ethical Desires: Toward a Theology of Relational Transcendence." In *Toward a Theology of Eros: Transfiguring Passion at the Limits of Discipline,* edited by Virginia Burrus and Catherine Keller, 255–70. New York: Fordham University Press, 2006.

Rosenfeld, Jordan. "Facing Down 'Environmental Grief.'" *Scientific American,* July 21, 2016.

Saliers, Don E. *The Soul in Paraphrase: Prayer and the Religious Affections.* New York: Seabury Press, 1980.

———. *Worship and Spirituality.* Akron, Ohio: OSL Publications, 1996.

Saville, Alphonso. "Where Are Our Brush Harbors Today??" *Patheos: Rhetoric, Race and Religion,* August 1, 2017. Accessed September 1, 2018. http://www.patheos.com/blogs/rhetoricraceandreligion/2017/08/brush-harbors-today.html.

Savoy, Lauret. *Trace: Memory, History, Race, and the American Landscape.* Berkeley, Calif.: Counterpoint, 2015.

Schmidt Roberts, Laura. "The Theological Place of Land: Watershed Discipleship as Re-placed Cultural Vision." In *Rooted and Grounded: Essays on Land and Christian Discipleship,* edited by Ryan Dallas Harker and Janeen Bertsche Johnson, 124–35. Eugene, Ore.: Wipf and Stock, 2016.

Sessions, George. "Deep Ecology: Introduction." In *Environmental Philosophy: From Animal Rights to Radical Ecology,* edited by Michael E. Zimmerman, J. Baird Callicott, George Sessions, Karen J. Warren, and John Clark, 165–82. 2nd ed. Upper Saddle River, N.J.: Prentice Hall, 1998.

Shulman, Lee S. "Making Differences: A Table of Learning." *Change* 34 (2002): 36–44.

Slotkin, Jason. "Behold the Fatberg: London's 130-Ton, 'Rock-Solid' Sewer Blockage."
    NPR.Org. Last modified September 12, 2017. Accessed September 2, 2018.
    https://www.npr.org/sections/thetwo-way/2017/09/12/550465000/behold
    -the-fatberg-london-s-130-ton-rock-solid-sewer-blockage.

Stegner, Wallace. "The Sense of Place." In *Where the Bluebird Sings to the Lemonade
    Springs: Living and Writing in the West,* 199–206. Reprint ed. New York: Modern
    Library, 2002.

Sutter, John. "Sixth Extinction: The Era of 'Biological Annihilation.'" *CNN.* Last
    modified July 11, 2017. Accessed September 2, 2018. https://www.cnn.com/
    2017/07/11/world/sutter-mass-extinction-ceballos-study/index.html.

Taggart Siegel. *The Real Dirt on Farmer John.* CAVU Pictures, 2005.

Taylor, Stuart. "A River Flows Through Us." Sermon, Elkin Presbyterian Church,
    Elkin, N.C., January 11, 2015. Accessed September 12, 2018. https://elkinpres
    .podbean.com/e/a-river-flows-through-us/.

———. "The River of Life." Sermon, Elkin Presbyterian Church, Elkin, N.C., April
    28, 2013. Accessed September 12, 2018. https://elkinpres.podbean.com/e/
    the-river-of-life/.

———. "St. Francis and the Canticle of Creation." Sermon, Elkin Presbyterian
    Church, Elkin, N.C., October 6, 2013. Accessed September 12, 2018. https://
    elkinpres.podbean.com/e/st-francis-and-the-canticle-of-creation/.

Themer, Robert. "Small Farms Grow in Pembroke." *Daily Journal.* Kankakee, Ill.,
    September 13, 2008.

Thurman, Howard. "The Sound of the Genuine: Baccalaureate Address." *Spelman
    Messenger,* Summer 1980.

Toner, Kathleen. "By Nourishing Plants, You're Nourishing Community." *CNN
    Heroes.* Last modified March 21, 2016. Accessed November 27, 2018. https://
    www.cnn.com/2015/09/24/us/cnn-heroes-joyner/index.html.

Tourism Partnership of Surry County. "Art & Soul of the Yadkin Valley." Accessed
    September 26, 2018. https://www.yadkinvalleync.com/.

Town of Elkin, N.C. "Town of Elkin, NC." Accessed September 26, 2018. http://
    www.elkinnc.org/.

Trinity United Church of Christ. "Urban Agricultural Center." Imani Village.
    Accessed September 18, 2018. https://www.imanivillage.com/urban
    -agricultural-center.

Turkle, Sherry. *Alone Together: Why We Expect More from Technology and Less from
    Each Other.* New York: Basic Books, 2012.

Turner, Victor W. *The Ritual Process: Structure and Anti-structure.* Chicago: University
    of Chicago Press, 1969.

United States Census Bureau. "QuickFacts: Flint City, Michigan." Accessed Septem-
    ber 6, 2018. https://www.census.gov/quickfacts/fact/table/flintcitymichigan/
    PST045217.

United States Environmental Protection Agency. "Ecoregions." Last modified November 16, 2015. Accessed September 18, 2018. https://www.epa.gov/eco -research/ecoregions.

———. "Healthy Watersheds Protection: Basic Information and Answers to Frequent Questions." Accessed September 26, 2018. https://www.epa.gov/hwp/basic -information-and-answers-frequent-questions.

———. "Level III and IV Ecoregions of the Continental United States." Last modified November 25, 2015. Accessed September 18, 2018. https://www.epa.gov/eco -research/level-iii-and-iv-ecoregions-continental-united-states.

Valenti, Joann M., and Gaugau Tavana. "Continuing Science Education for Environmental Journalists and Science Writers." *Science Communication* 27, no. 2 (2005): 300–310.

Van Meter, Timothy L. *Created in Delight: Youth, Church, and the Mending of the World*. Eugene, Ore.: Wipf and Stock, 2013.

"Visit the Yadkin Valley Region of North Carolina." Accessed September 24, 2018. http://visittheyadkinvalley.com/.

"Watershed Discipleship." Accessed September 26, 2018. https://watersheddiscipleship .org/.

"Watershed NOW." Accessed September 26, 2018. https://www.watershednownc .com/.

Weiss, Robert Stuart. *Loneliness: The Experience of Emotional and Social Isolation*. Cambridge, Mass.: MIT Press, 1974.

Westerhoff, John H., III. *Will Our Children Have Faith?* New York: Seabury Press, 1976.

Westervelt, Eric. "Trim Recess? Some Schools Hold On to Child's Play." *NPR.Org*. Last modified November 7, 2013. Accessed September 6, 2018. https://www .npr.org/2013/11/07/243713419/trim-recess-some-schools-hold-on-to-childs -play.

"What Is Sweaty Sheep?" *Team Sweaty Sheep: Re-creation through Recreation*. Accessed November 29, 2018. http://sweatysheep.com/discover/what-is-sweaty-sheep/.

Wiggins, Grant P., and Jay McTighe. *Understanding by Design*. Alexandria, Va.: Association for Superision and Curriculum Development, 2005.

Wilderness Way Community. Accessed November 30, 2018. http://www .wildernesswaypdx.org/.

———. "Children's School." Accessed November 29, 2018. http://www .wildernesswaypdx.org/childrens-school/.

Wilkerson, Isabel. "The Long-Lasting Legacy of the Great Migration." *Smithsonian*, September 2016. Accessed September 18, 2018. https://www.smithsonianmag .com/history/long-lasting-legacy-great-migration-180960118/.

———. *The Warmth of Other Suns: The Epic Story of America's Great Migration*. Reprint ed. New York: Vintage, 2011.

Wilson, Edward O. *Biophilia*. Cambridge, Mass.: Harvard University Press, 1984.

Windle, Phyllis. "The Ecology of Grief." *BioScience* 42, no. 5 (1992): 363–66.

Wisconsin First Nations. "Map." Accessed December 21, 2018. https://wisconsinfirstnations.org/map/.

Wong, Alia. "So Many Tests, So Little Information." *Atlantic.* Last modified October 28, 2015. Accessed September 6, 2018. https://www.theatlantic.com/education/archive/2015/10/testing-testing/412735/.

Wright, Richard. *12 Million Black Voices.* Reprint ed. New York: Basic Books, 2002.

Yadkin Riverkeeper. "About." Accessed September 26, 2018. http://www.yadkinriverkeeper.org/about.

———. "Yadkin Riverkeeper Protects the Yadkin Pee Dee River Basin." Accessed September 26, 2018. http://www.yadkinriverkeeper.org/.

Zirschky, Andrew. *Beyond the Screen: Youth Ministry for the Connected but Alone Generation.* Nashville: Youth Ministry Partners and Abingdon Press, 2015.

Zolli, Andrew. "Learning to Bounce Back." *New York Times,* October 18, 2016.

INDEX

adolescents (/children/ youth): at Conetoe Family Life Center, 120–24, 128; beauty and, 123 (*see also* beauty); context and, 43; ecological grief and, 23; as ecological learners, 41, 70, 80, 120, 146n6, 171n50; as ecological leaders, 119, 120–21, 122–23, 171n50, 172n62; Francis of Assisi as, 85–86; networked, 150n29; recess and, 159n40 (*see also* recess); segregation of, 153n57; Sunday schools and, 57; *see also* children

adults: as ecological learners, 23, 41, 43, 70, 75, 80, 123; as ecological mentors, 75, 83, 122

aesthetics: *see* beauty

affections: and dispositions, 9, 21, 24, 28–29, 37, 76–77, 80–81; and emotions, 5, 7–8, 24, 49, 76, 79, 80, 169n26; ecological, 7, 9, 24, 37, 76, 79–80, 105, 115, 118, 129, 150n32; formation of, 3, 5, 21–24, 37, 49, 72, 79–80, 118, 129, 150n32; inhabitance and, 3, 5, 6, 7, 9, 17, 22–28, 32, 37, 80, 87–90, 118, 129, 161nn6, 18; ordering of, 7; virtues and, 22–24, 76–77,

79–81; wisdom and, 17, 21–22, 24, 49, 72, 76–77, 80–81, 115

agape, 27–31, 131–42n41; Aquinas on, 27–28; child named, 111–12; eros and, 30, 143n48; features of, 141n41; Jackson on, 141n41; Nygren on, 142nn45, 47, 48, 143n49

agriculture: Angelic Organics and, 106–7, 121; in Conetoe, 118–24; creation and, 13, 134n20; destructive policies of, 33–34, 131n4, 170n38 (*see also* sin); global warming and, 44; place and, 93–94; policy, 3; questions of, 81–82; "radical" in, 14; suffering and, 152n50; San Jose Parish and, 99–100; Trinity United Church of Christ and, 95–96, 103 (*see also* Imani Village); urban, 96–97, 169n24 (*see also* Church of the Pilgrims; Imani Village); vulnerability of, 170n38, 171n48; virtues and, 20–21; wisdom and, 21

alienation, 129; from creation, 14; ecological, 4, 110, 129; education for, 23; home and, 7, 12; isolation and, 55; nature-deficit disorder and,

18, 21, 30, 41, 47, 77, 78, 127; ecological, 51; educational, 61, 73–74, 79–80 (*see also paideia*); engaging, 77; human, 9, 17, 77 (*see also* inhabitance; play); imagination and, 52; practices of, 79–84, 125, 128 (*see also* inhabitance); recess and, 78, 83 (*see also* recreation; recess); wonder and, 46–47, 54

critical consciousness, 94, 156n77

critical literacy, 62

critical pedagogy, 62, 94, 157n6, 163n40; *see also* Freire, Paulo

critical pedagogy of place, 94, 163n40; *see also* Elkin Presbyterian Church; San Jose Parish; Trinity United Church of Christ

death, 110, 111, 112, 115; bodily, 116; earth and, 110–11, 114, 118; ecological, 32–35, 110, 114 (*see also* compost); fear of, 140n26; God's death, 116; inhabitance and, 4, 5, 82, 106–8, 130 (*see also* Angelic Organics; San Jose Parish); of Jesus, 167n14; life and, 110–14, 124 (*see also* Conetoe Missionary Baptist Church); Mount Washington and, 31–32; of place, 134n17 (*see also* Appalachia; Berry, Wendell; Flint, Michigan; Oliver, Mary); prodigal son and, 18; renewal and, 18, 22, 110, 130; wonder and, 31

degradation, environmental, 4, 33, 40, 170n38

despair: antidotes to, 24, 126, 130; ecological, 123, 129; inhabitance and, 128, 130; resilience to, 128; *see also* affections, ecological

Dewey, John: experiential learning and, 75; moral formation and, 156n76

Dillard, Annie, commitment to place and, 134

dirt: gardening in, 114; goodness of, 20, 23; in sanctuary, 113; soil and, 138n1; *see also* compost

dirty faith, 19–20

dirty virtue, 19–20

displacement, 29, 100, 165n63; *see also* place, displacement

dispositions: and habits/*habitus*, 21, 138n7; of inhabitance, 20, 21, 55, 66–68, 76, 80, 101, 121, 124, 127; virtue ethics and, 21, 41, 66, 80, 138n7

dispositions, ecological, 24–37, 40–42, 67–68, 80, 121

dualism, 36

ecological education: and the affections, 5, 22, 46, 49, 76, 79, 80, 105–29, 150n32; as long-term project, 32, 66; contrasted with environmental education, 3, 20–22, 32, 40, 42, 44–48, 51, 74, 76, 79, 89–91, 96, 99, 102–3, 117, 146n6

ecological faith: definition of, 9–10, 21–22, 37, 39–41, 56–57, 79–81, 82, 85, 86, 88, 94, 108, 126; telos of, 4, 8, 19–20, 24, 39

ecological self, 29–30, 34, 39–41, 50–62, 75, 77, 108, 118, 130, 151nn36, 43

ecology: as null curriculum, 45; etymological roots of, 9, 17

economic justice and the environment, 4, 9, 65, 97; connections between, 65, 152n50; tensions between, 99

economic systems, 34, 37, 45, 81, 94, 97, 119, 131n4, 160n50

ecoregions, 97, 164n45

ecosystems: anthropocene and, 127–28; changes to, 79; definitions of, 4, 55, 67; ecoregions and, 164n45; eros and, 31; as habitats, 2–3; human damage to, 44, 109, 131n4, 147n11; inhabitants and, 50; relating to, 14, 23, 50, 67, 81; protecting, 49; sin and damage to, 33; study of (definition), 9; as work of human life, 12

ecozoic age, 139n16, 150n33

Edible Schoolyard, 151n45

education: as transformation, 6, 23, 39–42, 46, 60–63; formal instruction, 57, 153, 57; technical, 4, 44–46, 60, 74, 79; theoretical, 43, 60, 151n36,